Religion in
the City of Angels

Studies in
American History and Culture, No. 2

Other Titles in This Series

Religion in
the City of Angels

American Protestant Culture and Urbanization,
Los Angeles, 1850-1930

by
Gregory H. Singleton

RESEARCH PRESS

Library of Congress Cataloging in Publication Data

Singleton, Gregory H   1940-
    Religion in the City of Angels.

    (Studies in American history and culture ; no. 2)
    Bibliography: p.
    Includes index.
    1. Los Angeles—Church history. 2. Protestant
churches—California—Los Angeles—History. 3. Los
Angeles—History. I. Title. II. Series.

BR560.L67S58   280'.4'0979494   78-27391
ISBN 0-8357-0974-4
ISBN 0-8357-0975-2 pbk.

CONTENTS

CONTENTS

TABLES

CONTENTS

APPENDIX TABLES

CONTENTS

INTRODUCTION

As Americans moved west in the nineteenth century, they established communities and built cities. The new settlements, although distinctive and innovative, included the more salient features of eastern culture. The imprint of Anglo-American tradition was on the physical design of western towns, the organization of municipal government, local institutions, and socio-economic structures. The traces were immediately visible in those settlements established on the prairies where none existed before. In the towns which were the sites of communities originally founded by another culture whose adherents still occupied the land, elements of the conquerors' way of life became discernable soon after the migration of Americans to the newly acquired territories.

Protestantism was among the most important of these elements and was integrally related to others. Religious organizations provided familiar institutions of social cohesion and control in an unfamiliar environment, and the Protestant ethos was an ingredient in the desire of leading citizens in western towns to stimulate population and economic growth so that their new homes could proudly be called cities. The story of the American migration to Los Angeles and the subsequent rapid growth of that agrarian village into an industrial and commercial metropolis is a striking example of the transplantation of a cluster of values and organizational forms during the continental expansion of the United States.

The complete story, for Los Angeles in particular and American culture in general, contains a development that is difficult to outline. It involves the complexities of urbanization and the effects of that process on the status of religious organizations in American cities. Protestant Angelenos at the turn of the century were aware that their churches in urban areas to the east had fallen on evil days, but they were in full control of their city and there appeared to be no threat from immigrants and Catholics, the assumed causes of ills from Boston to Chicago. They willed and worked for urban growth in the City of the Angels. The process itself, rather than alien peoples and religions, soon yielded a situation for Protestant organizations in Los Angeles similar to that in Eastern cities.

This study is an attempt to correlate and integrate the insights and suggestions of two distinct bodies of literature in American historiography and apply them to my research into the development of one city. Urban history and religious history, both in subject matter and major interpretive traditions, seem to have little in common. As a social historian interested in the varieties of functions of religious organizations in an urban milieu, I have found it impossible to discuss the changing roles of these organizations in the City of Angels apart from the process of urbanization. I have also found it impossible to analyze the development of the city without reference to the function of Protestant churches. The literature on the development of many American cities has convinced me that Los Angeles is by no means unique in this regard.

The vast sociological material on urban religions has been helpful in stimulating thought about the general problems raised by this study and in interpreting the data on the twentieth century specifically. For the dynamics of development over an eighty year period, however, I have developed a set of operating assumptions and conceptual categories from my own research and the two historiographical traditions I hope to blend. A complete catalogue of these assumptions and categories, and the many qualifications they require, would result in an encyclopedic compilation of theoretical considerations on the historical sociology of urban religion which would constitute an individual volume. As a social historian I have no desire to offer a pale imitation of Wittgenstein (even less of Diderot). Nevertheless, some mention must be made of the broader themes and problems which are implicit in this study.

Urbanization. Discussion of and disagreement over this term constitutes a major portion of contemporary urban scholarship. Beyond the subtleties of the arguments there are two major interpretive trends. One defines urbanization in a regional or national context as the growth in the proportion of the total population in urban settlements, social structures, and styles of life. The other is addressed primarily to specific localities and outlines the development of specialized, interdependent, and complex social organization.[1] Implicit in both of these definitions are increases in social and economic diversity. In the development of Los Angeles between 1850 and 1930 all of these elements are important to an understanding of the changing social structure of the city and the place of religious organizations in that structure. The most simple index of the dynamics of urbanization for a single locality is the increase in population and differential assessments of the degree of social diversity. The format provided in Table 1 will be used throughout the study to present this information for Los Angeles over time and in comparison with other cities. The indices of diversity used are religion, ethnicity, and economic activity.

In American historiography, the process of urbanization is usually understood in the context of social and economic nationalization and corporatization. There is much value in this notion, and the pages that follow tend to reaffirm this general proposition, but all too often, the case is stated in exaggerated form. *Gemeinschaft* and *gesellschaft* are useful concepts to the Americanist as well as to the Europeanist, but the tendency to interpret the American experience between Appomattox and Versailles as a cosmic restructuring of society and values, propelling a nation of village-dwellers into a complex urban and industrial civilization over a brief period of a few decades simply is not commensurate with what we know about American society before 1865 and after 1919.[2] In a fortunate exception to this general interpretive trend—a study of Springfield, Massachusetts, in the nineteenth century—it is argued that the nature, function, and quality of social relationships, and how they change over time, is at least as important to our understanding of urbanization as the strength of "localism" and "nationalism" at given times.[3] In the case of Los Angeles, local Protestant traditions were implanted by *national* organizations. When early Angelenos became localistic around the turn of the century, they did so as a deliberate policy, but were sensitive enough to the large corporate society to define their own civic culture and hopes for the future in the context of the larger society. The patterns that led to a peripheral status for religious organizations in the City of the Angels were discernable *before* the emergence of the area as a major national metropolis.

The patterns are related to the activities of the Protestant community during the time that it was central to civic life. Not only is the Los Angeles experience contrary to the "village to nation" interpretation, but it is also one which indicates that urbanization as a process cannot be understood apart from the interdependence of key elements in the local social structure. Urbanization does not "happen to" an area, but is the result of complex trends, both local and national. In Los Angeles, no element was more crucial to urban growth than the influence of a half-dozen Protestant denominations, and no element was affected more by the process—or as adversely. The urbanization of Los Angeles was directly related to the expression of nineteenth-century American Protestantism called *voluntarism*. The structural changes in the early twentieth century, and the effects of those changes on religious organizations, can, in part, be defined as *secularization*. These two concepts are essential to understanding the Los Angeles experience between 1850 and 1930 and they may well be important in understanding the social implications of urbanization in American history generally.

TABLE 1

COMPARISON OF SELECTED CITIES BY SIZE AND DIVERSITY
(1900)

| | | DIVERSITY INDEX | | |
	size	ethnic	religious	economic
New York	3,437,000	.67	.66	.69
Chicago	1,699,000	.61	.59	.62
Philadelphia	1,204,000	.58	.63	.65
Boston	561,000	.64	.59	.68
San Francisco	343,000	.53	.65	.62
Los Angeles	102,000	.46	.28	.47

NOTE: The diversity index has a range from 1 to 0. An index of 0 indicates absolute homogeneity. An index of 1 is a practical impossibility, but the larger the value approaching 1, the greater the diversity. See Appendix VI for data source and derivation of the index.

Voluntarism. There is a sobering lesson in the history of consciousness to be learned from the fact that the rhetoric of American Protestantism prior to the 1890's is often deceptive to twentieth-century ears. More recently than one would care to believe, for example, Roger Williams' biblical notions of religious liberty have been cited as the origin of a decidedly secular doctrine of the separation of church and state.[4] Voluntarism was a common nineteenth-century term that has suffered from over-precision by a few scholars and vague misinterpretation at the hands of a larger number. Historians of religion define the concept narrowly (albeit correctly) as a peculiarly American development in ecclesiology, involving the founding of denominational and interdenominational charitable, educational, and reform organizations, dating from the 1820's.[5] Voluntarism has been loosely defined by others to include a wide variety of political and social associations as well as Protestant agencies.[6] For this second group of scholars, the root word of voluntarism—voluntary—is an operating assumption commensurate with the development of social democracy. Indeed, it is not unusual to find voluntarism included as one of the

xvi

specifications of Jacksonian Democracy. Chapter 1 contains a brief sketch of the origins and institutional forms of voluntarism. Here I am concerned with specifying the concept in such a way that its social implications beyond ecclesiology can be clearly seen without diluting its nineteenth-century meaning by improperly including under its rubric any and all groups formed by mutual consent.

The term was first used by Lyman Beecher in the late 1810's to describe the basis of financial support for disestablished churches. The system of lay denominational and interdenominational organizations he suggested was not posited as a free market of religious agencies and ideologies, but as a method of perpetuating the status of a handful of "evangelical" denominations in the absence of official state support. Voluntarism in its origins referred to the contributions of capital and energy from the laity necessary to perpetuate religious hegemony by a few denominations. Will Herberg's *Protestant—Catholic—Jew* argument may be well suited to the twentieth century, and the basic outlines of a contemporary "common religion" may find its origin in an adaptation of voluntarism, but the nineteenth-century advocates of the concept were definitely *not* spokesmen for an unlimited ecumenicism.[7]

Beecher's rhetoric and the organizational realities of the voluntaristic organizations in the nineteenth century indicate that the spirit of ecumenicity extended only to denominations derived from the British Reformation experience (except for the Dutch Reformed Church in New York and New Jersey). Furthermore, the voluntary system was most prominent (almost exclusive to) northern commercial towns and agrarian villages which shared a rather common social structure. Voluntarism, then, is limited to specific religious communities in the North-East and extensions of that society into the West. Baptists in the North and Mid-West were very much involved in the system. Baptists in the South were not. Mormons, whose roots were in the northeastern development of the British Reformation tradition, adopted a social system and an ideology which placed them outside the voluntaristic community.[8]

In the form and scope of organization, the voluntary associations drew upon the collective experience of their denominations. Charitable, educational, and reform agencies affiliated with various denominations were common enough in the eighteenth century. Voluntarism simply extended lay involvement to a greater number of church members. Even this was not entirely a new development. The widening of lay participation can be seen at least as early as the War of 1812. In scope, voluntaristic activity was both local and national. The various organizations were concerned with maintaining community cohesion built around religious institutions, but most of them developed national lay bureaucracies for coordination and cooperation. Most of the organizations were also interested in the extension of their socio-religious system to newly settled areas in the West. In this sense, the voluntary associations—especially those of an interdenominational nature—merged and transcended the localism of the Congregationalists and Baptists and the nationalism of the Presbyterians, Methodists, and Episcopalians.[9]

The "elitist" and social control functions of the voluntary associations in the nineteenth century are by now historiographical commonplace and have been stated by other scholars *ad nauseum*.[10] Suffice it to say that this is an important element in my specification of the term. The internal functions of the system for the voluntaristic community will be more precisely analyzed in the following chapters, but a few generalizations can be stated here. First, the various associations and their constituent denominations defined an economically and ethnically homogeneous community. In those areas where the system was indigenous, the membership of the constituent denominations was composed of economic elites, moderately affluent farmers, merchants, artisans, professionals, and a few upwardly mobile laborers. This was true of individual parishes of different denominations, in spite of the assumption on the part of some scholars that Episcopalians equalled wealth and Baptists were the lesser sorts. Increasingly in the nineteenth century, the Anglo-Saxon background of the denominations and their members was invoked by the voluntary associations. Until the 1870's, continental Protestant groups, such as the Lutherans, were systematically excluded from associational activity, and the rhetoric of voluntary organizations made it quite clear that their common Anglo-Saxon heritage was essential to understanding *American* Protestantism. It is no accident that such rhetoric was articulated at the time of increasing non-British (and non-Protestant) immigration.[11]

The voluntaristic denominations also defined the participants in local social and political activities. In this sense, until the time of the Civil War, and in some communities beyond then, the voluntaristic community did not comprise a *faction* in the socio-political structure so much as it was the prerequisite for entrance into that structure. This was true of commercial cities as well as agrarian villages. Associated with the "community of interest" function of voluntarism suggested here was a more literal geographical and familial definition of community. Voluntaristic Protestants tended to live in cohesive neighborhoods, entended through generations, and their children tended to marry their own kin. The sense of geographical community was also national, and extended westward following the territorial expansion of the United

States. The purpose of the American Home Missionary Society, among other voluntary associations, was not to recruit new converts from among the immigrants or Indian populations, but to supply ministers and basic religious organizations for the Anglo-Saxon Protestant migrants.[12]

It is incorrect, therefore, to think of the voluntaristic churches as "denominations." As a group, through their associational activities, and given the status of their individual members in the society at large, the American, or voluntary, Protestant denominations functioned as *a church* according to the Weber-Troeltsch typology. They assumed they were—and to a large extent they in fact were—coextensive with their society. Indeed, they were obsessed with their identification as *American* Protestant denominations, in contradistinction to *immigrant* forms of religion and native *sects*, which had abandoned the British Reformation tradition and defined themselves as apart from or in opposition to society.[13]

It should not be assumed that the church-like stance of the American Protestant denominations was universally adopted by the membership. In the 1830's a prominent Congregational minister accused his fellow churchmen of what he called *Protestant Jesuitism*; and in the late 1850's a group of dissident members of voluntaristic churches met in New York to call into question the hegemony exercised by their denominations in the United States. These are important for their exceptionality. Harmony did not always exist between or within constituent denominations, but the instances of doctrinal amelioration and institutional cooperation far exceed the moments of antagonism. Furthermore, it must be remembered that the most bitter and lasting schisms occurred between the northern and southern forces in the major denominations—one might almost say between the voluntaristic and non-voluntaristic factions. Occasionally a schism would occur in which a minority faction, believing the dominant British-origin denominations to be *too* church-like and too concerned with the matters of this world, would withdraw into a deliberate sect-like organization. Such a group was the Disciples of Christ, which, typical of this category of denominations, re-entered into full associationalism and social contact with other British-origin Protestants shortly after mid-century.[14]

All of these qualifications notwithstanding, the voluntaristic denominations defined the American "establishment" throughout most of the nineteenth century every bit as much as did the official Church of England, which, incidentally, suffered at least as much internal dissidence and disaffection as the American Protestant hegemony. In spite of the contemporary connotations of the term, voluntarism is best understood as America's equivalent of a state church, with all of the social, political, and economic implications of that designation. Beyond that, and of greater importance, it was an expression of the Anglo-Saxon American's deepest sense of local community and national civilization.

"Secularization." The term is placed in quotes here because there is less certainty about its meaning than in the case of the previous two concepts. There is common agreement that urbanization has something to do with the growth of cities, and voluntarism meant something to its adherents. "Secularization," however, is not the result of any particular movement, nor does it relate to a measurable (perhaps not even definable) process. The most successful approach to the subject had defined the term as a trend toward more rational life styles. Studies of child-rearing manuals demonstrate a decline in religious assumptions about nurture; campus ministries since the early 1900's report a continuing decline of interest in traditional religious categories to at least 1950; and studies of theological students indicate a growing disdain for orthodoxy.[15] The history of American literature tends to support this general ambience of "secularization." In the late nineteenth century, writers as diverse a Theodore Dreiser and Mark Twain explored the implications of a mechanistic universe. Half a century before, Nathaniel Hawthorne and Herman Melville had delved into the dark depths of the Calvinist cosmology. Henry Adams gave personal testimony to his awareness of a profound change in the basis of Western culture as he stood before the chasm of "The Dynamo and the Virgin."[16]

There are a number of problems with this definition of secularization, not the least of which is the lack of adequate specification of terms such as "religious" and "rational." The data are too impressionistic, and the most convincing evidence—that from literature—is simply unrepresentative. Furthermore, even if we were to grant a degree of legitimacy to the general thrust of the interpretation, there are two impressive counterinterpretations to contend with. Martin Marty and Peter Berger have argued that since the turn of the century there has been a radical rephrasing of religious commitment that has taken many forms, including deinstitutionalized Christianity which may be mistaken for secularism.[17] Somewhat reversing the focus of attention, William Clebsch has suggested that there are many religious elements in the functions of secular culture with increase as the general society incorporates areas of responsibility once held by religion. Conrad Cherry has shown the obverse of this situation by analyzing the quasi-religious nature of national holidays.[18] As a corollary Will Herberg, Duncan Howlett, and other have postulated a common American faith, devoid of doctrinal nuances.[19] If we adopt a measurable definition of secularization, such as the proportion of the population as members of religious organizations over time, then we are likely to find that the last century has been a period of religious growth rather than "secularization."[20]

Yet, to consider American social development between 1850 and 1930 without concluding that "secularization" was part of the process if counterintuitive to the extent that I was unable to set the undefined category aside as I conducted my research and formulated my argument.[21]   It was not until the project neared completion that I realized that my intuition was working so strongly against my scholarly and analytical instincts because I had accepted quite fully and unquestioningly the assumption of some of the Protestants I studied that they had been the victims of secularization. In retrospect, I am thankful for the tenacity of my intuition, not because it was correct, but because I finally discovered an imperative and valid scholarly reason for retaining this conceptual category. Secularization (now removed from quotes) is important to understanding the relationship between American Protestantism and urbanization, both generally and in Los Angeles particularly, because that is how may of the voluntaristic faithful interpreted their own experience. Furthermore, the way in which they defined the process has a direct relationship to urbanization and voluntarism, as I have specified the term.

"We live in the age of great cities," wrote Samuel Loomis in 1887. "Each successive year finds a stronger and more irresistable current sweeping toward the centre of life."[22] Loomis was concerned that the voluntary Protestant denominations were ignoring the implications of this rapid growth. William T. Stead, in 1894, urged the church to change the city from a den of iniquity to a true commonwealth of Christian faith where men could live in brotherhood and harmony.[23] Although the city was considered a cluster of social problems by American Protestants, it also seemed to pose serious threats for the voluntary system, and by implication, American culture. As early as 1872, Charles Loring Brace warned that a move to the city weakened religious ties among old-stock Americans, leaving the cities as repositories of great Roman Catholic strength.[24] Stimulated by Brace's argument, urban Protestant institutions conducted religious surveys in New York, Boston, Cleveland, and Chicago, and concluded that only Roman Catholicism and Judaism, representing large immigrant populations, were able to work effectively in the city.[25] Furthermore, new groups, such as Christian Science, which had a tendency to further divide Protestant strength, began to emerge in large cities.[26]

By the turn of the century, anxiety was the general mood of Protestantism in America. Walter Rauschenbusch was distressed that traditional Protestant institutions were incapable of ministering to the needs of the new industrial order.[27] William Blackstone preached the Gospel of individual redemption, regarding urban culture as beyond the hope of communal salvation.[28] Josiah Strong, only slightly more optimistic, wrote in 1905, "We must save the city if we would save the nation." He urged his fellow Protestants to change the city before it became the arena of non-Protestant and secular leadership.[29] Protestants in Los Angeles looked on with a little pity and a good deal of smugness. Two decades later, some would utter similar lamentations in a vain effort to cast out the demons of secularization. Most, both in the East at the turn of the century and in Los Angeles in the 1920's, accepted the new social order—some with quiet resignation, other with enthusiasm.

It is no coincidence that the numbers and membership of voluntary associations began to decline at the same time that secularization was invoked by Protestant spokesmen as the cause of ills. It *was* secularization in the sense that society—especially urban society—had grown too complex and compartmentalized for the voluntaristic system. The American Protestants had more to do with this development than any other group in the nation, however. The very organizations which supported the system contained the embryonic seeds of a complex, compartmentalized, bureaucratized, corporate social structure. It was the voluntaristic Protestants who provided the capital on which the emerging new industrial empire was built. It was also the voluntaristic Protestants who supplied, through their sons, the managerial and professional corps for maintaining the new corporate society. The voluntary associations died not so much from assault as from neglect. The direction of the dynamics of American society shifted from the voluntary association to the expertise of the new middle class. If the sons of voluntaristic fathers abandoned intensive associational church life, they did perpetuate Anglo-Saxon dominance in American society. The fact that a choice was made can be counted as evidence for secularization.[30]

In a broader sense, however, it is not at all clear that secularization is a viable concept for American society taken as a whole. Emile Durkheim and others after him have argued that a common religion emerges from the competing forms in an integrated society.[31] The hints of a "national faith" since the turn of the century show definite traces of nineteenth-century voluntarism. The essence of the older "established" church has been to a certain extent maintained, even though the constituent organizations of the twentieth-century "established" church have gone far beyond the British-origin denominations to include non-theistic humanism and faith-healers. Commensurate with this has been the decline of social, political, and economic barriers which at one time posed difficult problems for Americans outside the voluntary system. For Americans beyond the Protestant core, secularization must seem a strange term for the extension of religious equity and social participation.

But I have addressed myself in this study to the American Protestant churches and all of the arguments used above tend to reinforce the concept of secularization from that perspective. Not only was the handful of denominations which had been the "established" church forced to share that distinction with an increasingly heterogenous group of religious bodies, but in the twentieth century, religion was no longer central to community life in most places in the nation. Being part of the "established" church was not particularly self-defining nor efficacious. By the first decade of this century, Catholics, Jews, and others may have seen very dimly the beginning of an integrated society and the glimmerings of a common American faith. Voluntaristic Protestants, on the other hand, saw very clearly the rapid decline of the cohesion of *their* America and the beginnings of a secular age. It was in this context that Los Angeles received over a score of citations as a model Protestant city from admiring churches to the east between 1900 and 1920.

Los Angeles can hardly be claimed as a "representative" example of the interrelationships of the three major conceptual categories discussed above. Indeed, given the city's unique reputation as a haven for exotic cults, it would appear to be the least likely site for such a study. The unfortunate reputation of the city need not detain us long. Simply stated, Los Angeles as the "kook capital of the world" has been asserted many times, but I have seen nothing offered in the way of proof. To the extent that it is true during the latter part of my study (a very slight extent), it is understandable only in relation to the former period of voluntaristic control. Chapter 6 contains a detailed discussion of this problem.

Yet the question remains, why Los Angeles? First, because no major city in twentieth-century America has been as little studied or understood. The few scholarly works that do exist, although intelligent and thorough, overlook the Protestant experience so crucial to understanding the early American period of the City of the Angels.

They have separated urban growth from the community ethos and organizational form of the people who stimulated the process of urbanization.[32]

This is hardly the most compelling reason. My major interest is not specifically in Los Angeles, but in the complexities of urbanization as a process, voluntarism as a form of social cohesion and organization, and secularization as a blending and extension of the former two concepts. For this purpose, Los Angeles' uniqueness is useful. The American town was "founded" by voluntaristic Protestants during the last years of that system in the East. It was the last Anglo-American settlement of any consequence to be built around Protestant assumptions about the nature of community which had persisted from colonial times. The eastern voluntary agencies which aided in the Protestant settlement of the City of the Angels were doomed, but the system thrived in the Southern California community until the 1920's. The factors which cloud the intricate relationships between voluntarism, urbanization, and secularization (immigration, machine politics, industrialization) are largely absent from Los Angeles. The process which must be extracted from a complex web of social relationships in other cities is more readily visible. The self-consciousness with which Los Angeles Protestants sought to maintain their unique status among American cities and yet become an economically successful metropolis brings many of the important features into sharp relief.

This self-consciousness also resulted in the preservation of a number of important sources such as church directories and records. It is no accident that these materials exist in plentiful supply for six denominations in Los Angeles; Congregationalist, Presbyterian, Methodist, Protestant Episcopal, Baptist, and Disciples of Christ. These were the only denominations in Los Angeles from the voluntary tradition. Quite predictably, they defined the membership of the Los Angeles Federation of Churches until well into the 1920's; and their constituents defined the social, economic, and political "establishment" in the city until the 1920's. In Chapters 2-4, the reason for my concentration of these six denominations, as well as my treating them as one unit, is made clear, and additional statistical justification is presented in Appendix II. It should be clear by this point, however, that there is a logic in the choice of denominations studied.

The documentation for this study ranges from manuscript collections to interviews with senior citizens who have shared their past in the City of the Angels with me, from notes of sermons taken by anonymous and forgotten seminary students to church directories, and from mimeographed agency reports with only internal clues as to the date of publication to marriage licenses. In order to make the following chapters manageable, I have consigned a considerable portion of the description of analysis of sources and methods to appendices.

The chapters are arranged in chronological sequence, but this study is intended as an analytical rather than narrative treatment. Chapter 1 establishes the social basis of Catholic and predominantly Mexican California in the 1850's and 1860's in order to demonstrate the basic incompatability between the early voluntaristic Protestants and a culture significantly different from their own. Chapter 2 traces the establishment of a social structure which facilitated the migration of American Protestants and the establishment of the rudiments of the voluntary system, outlined in Chapter 3. Chapter 4 is an analysis of the social reality of the voluntaristic Protestants during their period of greatest control, 1890-1920. Chapter 5 explores the various ways in which the Protestant social reality stimulated the process of urbanization which created a new, nonvoluntaristic social base. The varieties of responses and reactions to the new social realities during the 1920's are analysed in Chapter 6. The Epilogue suggests the significance of this material for an understanding of the relationship between Protestantism and American society over time. Throughout, I have assumed that the social structure itself was as important an element in change as were external "causes."

NOTES

[1] For useful summaries of these interpretations, see David Popence, "On the Meaning of "urban" in Urban Studies," *Urban Affairs Quarterly*, I (September, 1965), 17-33, and John Friedman, "Two Concepts of Urbanization: A Comment," *Ibid.*, I (June, 1966), 78-84. I have also relied heavily on Richard L. Meier, *A Communications Theory of Urban Growth* (Cambridge, Massachusetts, 1962) and Alan R. Pred, *The Spatial Dynamics of U. S. Urban-Industrial Growth, 1800-1914: Interpretive and Theoretical Essays* (Cambridge, Massachusetts, 1966).

[2] The *gemeinschaft* to *gesellschaft* argument is found in its most exaggerated form in Robert Wiebe, *The Search for Order: 1877-1920* (New York, 1967). An example of a more subtle statement of the theme is James Weinstein, *The Corporate Ideal in the Liberal State: 1900-1918* (Boston, 1968). The literature to support my assertion (that what we know about our society prior to the 1860's and during the twentieth century negates the Wiebe, Weinstein, *et al.*, argument *on this point*) is vast. For a sampling of recent research, see the essays by Clyde Griffen, Herbert Gutman, Stephen Thernstrom, Stuart Blumin, Leo Schnore, and Peter Knights in *Nineteenth-Century Cities: Essays in the New Urban History* (New Haven, 1969). Kenneth B. Lockridge, "Social Change and the Meaning of the American Revolution," *Journal of Social History*, VI (Summer, 1973), 403-439 contains some intriguing suggestions which would place the beginnings of the "transformation" of American society—or some of the more important aspects of it—back to at least the early eighteenth century

[3] Michael H. Frisch, *Town Into City: Springfield, Massachusetts, and the Meaning of Community, 1840-1880* (Cambridge, Massachusetts, 1972), esp. pp. 1-6 and 238-250.

[4] A balanced criticism of the historiography on Williams and the separation of church and state is Edmund S. Morgan, *Roger Williams: The Church and the State* (New York, 1967).

[5] See Robert T. Handy, *A Christian America: Protestant Hopes and Historical Realities* (New York, 1971), *passim*; Winthrop Hudson, *The Great Tradition of the American Churches* (New York, 1953), pp. 63-136; Sidney E. Mead, *The Lively Experiment: The Shaping of Christianity in America* (New York, 1963), pp. 103-33; a recent summary of the definition of the term as it is used among church historians is in Sidney E. Ahlstrom, *A Religious History of the American People* (New Haven, 1972), pp. 382-383. For an excellent exception to the general insularity of histories of religion on this point, see Martin E. Marty, *Righteous Empire: The Protestant Experience in America* (New York, 1970), pp. 35-56 and 89-99.

[6] This interpretation of voluntarism is found throughout the following works: Alice Felt Tyler, *Freedom's Ferment: Phases of American Social History to 1860* (Minneapolis, 1944); Arthur M. Scholsinger, "Biography of a Nation of Joiners," in *Paths to the Present* (Boston, 1949) and *The American as Reformer* (Cambridge, Massachusetts, 1950). These are only representative. It would require a number of pages to do justice to the variety of scholars who have used the vague definition of voluntarism

throughout their works. An excellent summary of this meaning of the term is in Rowland Berthoff, *An Unsettled People: Social Order and Disorder in American History* (New York, 1971), pp. 254-274.

Beyond the misuse of the term, some social historians have ignored the concept completely when addressing themselves to nineteenth-century Protestantism. For a criticism of this tendency, see Gregory H. Singleton, "Essay Review: 'Mere Middle-Class Institutions:' Urban Protestantism in Nineteenth-Century America," *Journal of Social History*, VI (Summer, 1973), 489-504.

[7] *Autobiography, Correpondence, Etc., of Layman Beecher, D. D.*, ed. Charles Beecher (New York, 1871), I, 344-452; Winthrop Hudson, *The Great Tradition of the American Churches*, pp. 63-79. This definition of voluntarism was standard by mid-century; see Robert Baird, *Religion in America: or an Account of the Origin, Relation to the State, and Present Condition of the Evangelical Churches in the United States. With Notices of the Unevangelical Denominations* (New York, 4th ed., 1856), pp. 265ff.

The discussion of voluntarism in this and the following paragraphs is based on material I have presented in more detailed form earlier: "The Dynamics of 'WASP' Culture: From Ethnic Cohesion to the 'Organization Man,'" American Historical Association, New Orleans, Louisiana, December 28, 1972; "The Changing Function of Protestant Organizations in American Society; 1790-1890," Organization of American Historians, Chicago, Illinois, April 13, 1973. The data and interpretations of these papers have been summarized in my "Protestant Voluntary Organizations and the Making of Victorian American," *American Quarterly* (December, 1975), reprinted in Daniel Walker Howe (ed.), *Victorian America* (Philadelphia, 1976). For documentation, the reader may obtain copies of the unpublished papers from the Documentation Project of the International Affairs Library at Columbia University. The following notes for this section, therefore, will be somewhat abbreviated.

[8] See Mead, pp. 16-37; H. Richard Niebuhr, *The Social Sources of Denominationalism* (New York, 1929); and Bertram Wyatt Brown, "The Anti-Mission Movement in the Jacksonian South and West: A Study in Regional Folk Culture," *Journal of Southern History*, XXXVI (November, 1970), 501-529.

[9] See Handy, *passim*, Mead, *passim*, and William Gribbin, *The Churches Militant: The War of 1812 and American Religion* (New Haven, 1973).

[10] See, e.g., John R. Bodo, *The Protestant Clergy and Public Issues, 1812-1848* (New York, 1954); Charles Foster, *An Errand of Mercy: The Evangelical United Front, 1790-1837* (Chapel Hill, 1960); Charles C. Cole, Jr., *The Social Ideas of the Northern Evangelists, 1820-1860* (New York, 1954); Clifford S. Griffin, *Their Brothers' Keepers: Moral Stewardship in the United States, 1800-1865* (New Brunswick, 1960); and W. David Lewis, "The Reformer as Conservative: Protestant Counter-Subversion in the Early Republic," in *The Development of an American Culture* (Englewood Cliffs, 1970); eds. Stanley Coben and Lorman Ratner. A recent critical review of this interpretation is Lois W. Banner, "Religious Benevolence as Social Control: A Critique of an Interpretation," *Journal of American History*, LX (June, 1973), 23-41.

11These generalizations are based on an analysis of my research cited in Note 7. Also see Marty, pp. 14-23; Charles H. Anderson, *White Protestant Americans: From National Origins to Religious Group* (Englewood Cliffs, 1970), pp. 13-32. Appendix II contains a detailed discussion of the social and economic homogeneity of the voluntary denominations; also see Bruce E. Steiner, "New England Anglicanism: A Genteel Faith?" *William and Mary Quarterly*, XXVII (January, 1970), 122-35.

12On this last point, see the "Introduction" to each of the following collections of documents edited by William Warren Sweet: *Religion on the American Frontier: A Collection of Source Material:* Vol. I: *The Baptists, 1763-1830* (New York, 1931); Vol. II: *The Presbyterians, 1783-1840* (Chicago, 1936); Vol. III: *The Congregationalists, 1783-1840* (Chicago, 1939); *The Methodists, 1783-1840* (Chicago, 1946). Also see Colin Brummitt Goodyknoontz, *Home Missions on the American Frontier* (Caldwell, Idaho, 1939); T. Scott Miyakawa, *Protestants and Pioneers: Individualism and Conformity on the American Frontier* (Chicago, 1964); and Ben Merchant Vorpahl, "Presbyterians and the Frontier Hypothesis: Tradition and Modification in the American Garden," *Journal of Presbyterian History*, XLV (September, 1967), 180-92.

13The typology I am using is the generalized Weberian construct sophisticated by Ernst Troeltsch in *The Social Teaching of the Christian Churches*, trans. Olive Wyo (New York, 1931; German edition, 1911). For my purposes in this study, I have modified the Weber-Troeltsch typology along the lines found in the following works: Betty R. Scharf, *The Sociological Study of Religion* (London, 1970), Ch. 5; D. A. Martin, "The Denomination," *British Journal of Sociology*, XII (Fall, 1962), 583-596; Samuel C. Pearson, Jr. "From Church to Denomination: American Congregationalism in the 19th Century," *Church History*, XXXXVIII (March, 1969), 67-76; and the entire issue of *Journal for the Scientific Study of Religion*, VI (Spring, 1967), which is devoted to a discussion of "Church-Sect Reappraised."

14Calvin Colton, *Protestant Jesuitism: By a Protestant* (New York, 1836); the proceedings of the 1850's meeting of the short-lived group, the Young Men's Christian Union, were reported in *The Religious Aspects of the Age, With a Glance at the Church of the Present and the Church of the Future, Being Addresses Delivered at the Anniversary of the Young Men's Christian Union of New York, on the 13th and 14th Days of May, 1858* (New York, 1858). An example of interdenominational squabbles is found in Earl R. McCormac, "An Ecumenical Failure: The Development of Congregational Missions and Its Influence Upon Presbyterians," *Journal of Presbyterian History*, XLIV (Dec., 1966), 266-85. On the Disciples of Christ, which began as a sect, but was one of the voluntaristic denominations by the time of the Protestant migration to Los Angeles, see Note 73 in Chapter 3. The most sophisticated analyses of the general "sect to denomination" development in nineteenth-century America are Ruth B. Bordin, "The Sect to Denomination Process in America: The Freewill Baptist Experience," *Church History*, XXXIV (March, 1965), 77-94, and Carl Oblinger, *Strange Abberation: The Holiness Movement in Illinois* (Evanston, 1973).

15See Huston Smith, "Secularization and the Sacred: The Contemporary Scene," in *The Religious Situation: 1968* (Boston, 1968), pp. 583-600; Peter Berger, "A Sociological View of the Secularization of Theology," *Journal for the Scientific Study of Religion*, VI (Spring, 1967), 3-16; Daniel Lerner, *The Passing of Traditional Society* (New York,

1958), esp. pp. 47-52; Larry Shiner, "The Concept of Secularization in Empirical Research," *Journal for the Scientific Study of Religion,* VI (Fall, 1967), 207-220; Gabriel le Bras, "Dechristianisation: mot fallacieux," *Social Compass,* X (1963), 448-451; Bernard E. Meland, *The Secularization of Modern Cultures* (New York, 1966); and E. L. Mascall, *The Secularization of Christianity* (London, 1965). The specific examples cited here are taken from Forrest J. Berghorn and Geoffrey H. Stuse, "Are American Values Changing? The Problem of Inner-or-Other Direction," *American Quarterly,* XVIII (Spring, 1966), 52-62; and "Trends in Beliefs and Concerns," mimeograph report of the United Campus Ministry, October 13, 1957.

A useful survey of the literature is Richard K. Fenn, "The Secularization of Values: An Analytical Framework for the Study of Secularization," *Journal for the Scientific Study of Religion,* VII (Spring, 1969), 112-124.

[16] See Sholom J. Kahn, "Mark Twain's Last Years," *Studi Americani,* II (June, 1965), 47-59; Harry Levin, *The Power of Blackness: Hawthorne, Poe, Melville* (New York, 1958); *The Education of Henry Adams* (Boston, 1918), Ch. XXV.

[17] Martin E. Marty, Stuart E. Rosenberg, and Andrew M. Greeley, *What Do We Believe?* (New York, 1968), pp. 3-49; Peter Berger, *The Noise of Solemn Assemblies* (Garden City, New York, 1961). Also see Harvey Cox, *The Secular City: Secularization and Urbanization in Theological Perspective* (New York, 1965).

[18] William A. Clebsch, *From Sacred to Profane America: The Role of Religion in American History* (New York, 1968); Conrad Cherry, "Two American Sacred Ceremonies: Their Implications for the Study of Religion in America," *American Quarterly,* XXI (Winter, 1969), 739-754.

[19] Will Herberg, *Protestant—Catholic—Jew* (Garden City, New York, 1954) and "There is a Religious Revival," *Review of Religious Research,* I (Fall, 1959), 49-50; Duncan Howlett, *The Fourth American Faith* (New York, 1954).

[20] See Glen M. Vernon, "Measuring Religion: Two Methods Compared," *Review of Religious Research,* III (Spring, 1962), 159-165; Benson Y. Landis, "A Guide to the Literature on Statistics of Religious Affiliation with References to Related Social Studies," *Journal of the American Statistical Association,* LIV (June, 1959), 335-357; William Peterson, "Religious Statistics in the United States," *Journal for the Scientific Study of Religion,* I (April, 1962), 165-173.

[21] I am not alone in this inability to drop the category in spite of the lack of a satisfactory specification. See Arthur Schlesinger, "A Critical Period in American Religion, 1875-1900," *Massachusetts Historical Society Proceedings,* LXIV (June, 1932), 523-547, which appeared one year later as Chapter X ("The Changing Church") in *The Rise of the City,* New York, 1933); Aaron Ignatius Abell, *The Urban Impact on American Protestantism, 1865-1900* (Cambridge, 1943); Henry F. May, *Protestant Churches and Industrial America* (New York, 1949; rev. ed. 1967); the "Introduction" to Robert D. Cross (ed.), *The Church and the City: 1865-1910* (Indianapolis, 1967); David Reimers, "Protestantism's Response to Social Change: 1880-1930," in *The Age of Industrialism: Essays in Social Structure and Cultural Values,* ed. Frederic Jaher (New York, 1968).

For an excellent attempt to go beyond this dilemma, see Paul A. Carter, *Spiritual Crisis of the Gilded Age* (DeKalb, Illinois, 1971).

[22]Samuel L. Loomis, *Modern Cities and Their Religious Problems* (New York, 1887), pp. 18-19.

[23]William T. Stead, *If Christ Came to Chicago!* (Chicago, 1894).

[24]Charles L. Brace, *The Dangerous Classes of New York* (New York, 1872).

[25]See B. J. McQuaid, "The Decay of Protestantism," *North American Review*, CXXXVI (1883), 135-152; H. F. Perry, "The Workingman's Alienation from the Church," *American Journal of Sociology* (1898-1899), 622; C. A. Briggs, "The Alienation of Church and People," *Forum* (1893-1894), 375-377; O. F. Adams, "Aristocratic Drift of American Protestantism," *North American Review* (1886), 194-199; and T. B. Wakeman,"Our Unchurches Millions," *Arena* (1890), 604-613.

Also see, Nathan I. Huggins, *Protestants Against Poverty: Boston's Charities, 1870-1900* (Westport, Conn., 1971) and the second section of Carroll Smith Rosenberg, *Religion and the Rise of the American City: The New York City Mission Movement, 1812-1870* (Ithaca, 1971).

[26]For insight into these peripheral groups, see Donald B. Meyer, *The Positive Thinkers: The American Quest for Health, Wealth and Personal Power from Mary Baker Eddy to Norman Vincent Peale* (Garden City, New York, 1965); A. Leland Jamison, "Religions on the Christian Perimeter," in *The Shaping of American Religion*, eds. James Ward Smith and A. Leland Jamison ("Religion in American Life;" Princeton, New Jersey, 1961), pp. 162-231; and Raymond J. Cunningham, "The Impact of Christian Science on the American Churches, 1880-1910," *American Historical Review*, LXXII (April, 1967), 885-905.

[27]Walter Rauschenbusch, *Christianity and the Social Crisis* (New York, 1907).

[28]William E. Blackstone, *Jesus Is Coming* (New York, 1903).

[29]Josiah Strong, *The Challenge of the City* (New York, 1907), pp. 9-10.

[30]This is based on my unpublished material cited in Note 7 above, as is much of the following two paragraphs.

[31]For general theoretical consideration in developing this line of argument, I have depended most heavily on Emile Durkheim, *The Elementary Forms of The Religious Life*, trans. Joseph W. Swain (Glencoe, 1974); Max Weber, *The Sociology of Religion*, trans. Ephraim Fischoff (Boston, 1963); and Anthony F. C. Wallace, *Religion: An Anthropological View* (New York, 1966). A handful of studies by French sociologists of religion have been very useful: e.g., Gabriel le Bras, *Etudes de sociologie religieuse* (Paris, 1955); Emile Pin, *Practique religieuse et classes sociales* (Paris, 1956); and F. A. Isambert, *Christianisme et classe ouviere* (Tournai, 1961). For the American Context, I have drawn most heavily on Niebuhr, *op. cit.;* Liston Pope, *Millhands and Preachers:*

A Study of Gastonia (New Haven, 1942); E. Digby Baltzell, *The Protestant Establishment: Aristocracy and Caste in America* (New York, 1964); Gerhard Lenski, *The Religious Factor* (Garden City, New York, 1961); and N. J. Demerath, III, *Social Class in American Protestantism* (Chicago, 1965).

[32]For historians, the two most important works are Louis B. Perry and Richard S. Perry, *A History of the Los Angeles Labor Lovement: 1911-1941* (Berkeley, 1963) and Robert M. Fogelson, *The Fragmented Metropolis: Los Angeles, 1850-1930* (Cambridge, 1967). A useful re-evaluation of the historical materials and literature is Stephan Thernstrom, "The Growth of Los Angeles in Historical Perspective: Myth and Reality," (mimeograph report: Institute of Government and Public Affairs, University of California, Los Angeles, 1970).

CHAPTER 1

PROTESTANT BEGINNINGS IN LOS ANGELES

I

The Reverend Walter Colton, Congregational minister and chaplain assigned to the U.S.S. *Congress*, saw a great future for Southern California after his brief visit to Los Angeles in March, 1847. Americans who had migrated to California, he predicted, would be strongly attracted to the area, "when the phrensey of the mines has passed." The location of the pueblo "in the bosom of a broad fertile plain" was pleasing to him; and, in a biblical mood, Colton rhapsodized, "To these plains the more quiet emigrants will ere long gather, and convert their drills into pruning-hooks, and we shall have wines, figs, dates, almonds, olives, and raisins from California."[1] This idyllic vision of the pueblo was shared by the Right Reverend William Ingraham Kip, newly consecrated Episcopal Bishop of California, when he visited Los Angeles in October of 1855. "As we approached the town there was a marked change from the treeless sterility of the plains. We found ourselves winding through the midst of vineyards and gardens, and on all sides saw workmen engaged in the manufacture of wine."[2] His encounter with the American residents convinced him that Los Angeles was a fertile field for religious endeavor.[3]

Other clerical visitors shared this optimism about the spiritual and secular future of Los Angeles. By the early 1850's Presbyterian, Methodist, Baptist and Episcopalian Home Mission agencies, making decisions based on reports from ministers who had traveled through the area, marked the village as a desirable site for religious expansion.[4] All four of these denominations were less interested in the conversion of the indigenous Mexican Catholic population than in the establishment of familiar religious institutions for the increasing number of *gringos*. "It is our duty to keep the message of salvation alive for our countrymen in a land where the gospel has been imperfectly preached," declared the *Missionary Herald* in 1854.[5]

Everyone involved in religious expansion in the newly admitted state of California was enthusiastic about the possibilities for Protestantism in Los Angeles, except the ministers who were sent to labor in that vineyard. The first of these, the Reverend James W. Brier, a Methodist, arrived in the village by oxcart in 1852, filled with a desire to "preach the resurrected Christ" and establish a Sunday School for the religious instruction of the children of American migrants.[6]   Three months later he left, unable to adjust to the "spiritual hardness of heart" he found in Los Angeles.[7]   Brier's reaction and rapid departure may be explained by his perfectionist theology and his first encounter with a society that did not share his Mid-Western Protestant assumptions. His theology led him to expect men to be good, and his prior ministerial experience—three months as pastor of an Illinois congregation—led him to believe that the goodness of man was expressed in a uniquely American way.

The Reverend James Woods came to Los Angeles with a different set of assumptions and wider experience. Born in Massachusetts and raised as a stern Calvinist, Woods followed his father's profession and became a Presbyterian minister. After serving as pastor to a number of eastern congregations for over a decade, he was appointed to California by the Board of Home Missions of the Presbyterian Church in 1848. Woods organized congregations in the San Francisco and Stockton areas and moved his missionary field to Los Angeles in October of 1854. On March 18, 1855, he organized a congregation of twelve members.[8] Although he was inclined to see the limitations rather than the possibilities of the human condition, and is greater experience in singing the Lord's song in a strange land than his Methodist contemporary notwithstanding, Woods shared Brier's disdain for the spiritual state of Los Angeles. Religious bureaucrats may have seen a community of Anglo-American Protestants in the future, but Woods saw a village composed primarily "of the low drunken Mexican or Indian class."[9] It was difficult, even for one to whom the innate depravity of man was a given assumption, to adjust to a settlement where eleven deaths were recorded within a two week period—"only one of them a natural death."[10]   Woods left Los Angeles in September, 1855, for Sonoma County, and his original impression of Los Angeles remained unchanged: "The name of this city is in Spanish the city of the Angels, but with much truth might it be called the city of demons."[11]

II

In the early days of California statehood, Los Angeles was a community of neither seraphim nor devils, but a rather interesting village of native Mexicans and Indians, "Mexicanized" *gringos*, and newly arrived Americans and Europeans. A recent historian of the city has characterized the pueblo in 1850 as a simple agrarian community with nothing to foreshadow its rise as a metropolis over the next eighty years. While the physical characteristics of the area—no natural harbor, geographic isolation created by the surrounding mountains—seem to have been a contra-indication for urban growth, Los Angeles society was more diverse and complicated in 1850 than its population of 1,610 would indicate at first glance. Certainly the structure of the pueblo was more complex than the frontier areas in the Mid-West, and the organization of the local agrarian economy had at least as much in common with industrial society as it did with traditional single-family farming.[12]

The social and economic structure of the village had been developing for seven decades. *El Pueblo de Nuestra Senora la Reina de Los Angeles* was founded under the Spanish Governor Felipe de Neve on September 4, 1781. It had earlier been thought that the various missions on *El Camino Real* would be converted to towns with the Indian population as citizens. The failure of the mission system to "Iberianize" the natives ended these plans, and the royal government sought new sites for mission soldiers who had served their tour of duty to settle with their families. One of these was located on a plain eight miles west of San Gabriel Mission and east of the Porciuncula River.[13] Eleven farmers and their families settled the area, laid out a plaza, and divided the land into *solares* for buildings and *suertes* for farming.[14] The pueblo grew fairly steadily from a population of forty-six in 1781 to approximately 800 in the 1830's. In the following twenty years, the population doubled. The greatest period of increase followed Mexican Independence from Spain in 1821. Successful farming and ranching in the area, the secularization of the missions, and the policy of the new Mexican government to encourage individual application for the newly released land stimulated settlement in Los Angeles.[15]

A few of the migrants to the area were Americans who had taken Mexican citizenship in order to qualify for land grants. Often, these men married into prominent Mexican families. Don Juan Bandini, a wealthy *ranchero*, gained three American-born sons-in-law during the Mexican period: Charles Johnson, J. Cave Couts, and Abel Stearns. All became Catholic and were considered "Mexicanized" by later *gringo* migrants. Stearns became the most prominent of Bandini's sons-in-law. Born in Massachusetts in 1798, he was orphaned by the age of twelve and went to sea. In 1827, Stearns left his maritime exploits and began work as a clerk in Mexico, where he formed lasting relationships with two British merchants. Prompted by his friends' enthusiasm for commercial expansion in Southern California, he went to Los Angeles as a storekeeper.[16]

Stearns was at first disappointed with his life in the pueblo. He had some difficulty adjusting to the "false pride, laziness, ingratitude" of the native population.[17]The local trade, far from being an extension of the sophisticated commerce he had known in Mexico City, was conducted primarily on the barter system. He soon discovered a new economic world in which he could operate with greater prestige and profit: the life of a *ranchero*. At about the same time that Stearns acquired his land, he also gained entry to the social world of the large land owners through marriage to Bandini's daughter, Maria Arcadia, twenty-six years younger than himself. Stearns was obviously sensitive to the possible interpretations of his motives. "Desiring to avoid the ridicule which the difference in ages might arouse among thoughtless young people, she being fourteen years of age and I forty," Stearns petitioned the Prefect of California to dispense with the three proclamations required by law in order to hold the wedding as soon as possible.[18] The two were married in May, 1841, and Stearns became an increasingly important land owner.

Stearns adjusted rather easily to the life styles of the upper-class California Mexicans, and adopted the title Don Abel Stearns in signing documents. This appears to have been a common practice among American-born land owners. Stephan Foster became Don Estevan Foster and John and Francis Temple became Dons Juan and Francisco. Both Temples had taken Mexican wives, and Juan married a woman twenty years his junior.[19] Some early *gringos*, such as Thomas Oliver Larkin, became successful merchants without becoming Mexicans citizens, converting to Catholicism, or marrying local wealth.[20]

By the time California was admitted as a state in 1850, Los Angeles had become an important agricultural center. Although relatively isolated, the pueblo had established trade with areas to the north and south.[21] This commerce was organized by merchants whose offices were all located near the plaza. They served the entire county, which was the social unit rather than the town. A cursory glance at aggregate population statistics suggests that the county was a rather homogenous community. A clear majority, eighty-five percent, had been born in Old Mexico and three-quarters of these were born in California. About ten percent were born in the United States, with twenty-eight states of nativity represented. Another five percent came from fifteen European nations (almost half from the British Isles), seven Latin American countries, China, and Canada.

Given this homogeneity in nativity, the ethnic concentration in the area was to be expected. Less than ten percent of the residents in the county were listed as Oriental, Indian, or Negro. The actual number of non-Caucasians may have been even smaller. Seven of the fifteen Negroes in the county carried Spanish names and were listed as members of households with the same family name. The census agent may have interpreted darker complexion as a racial distinction.[22] This was not uncommon among newly arrived *gringos.*[23] The same problem may have been a factor in the classification of Indians. The distinction that was to become so important in later Los Angeles history was not made in the 1850 census. Both Mexicans and *gringos* are listed as Caucasians. Nativity, however, serves as a fair indicator of the relative size of each of these two groups.

The ethnic division of the county was closely associated with the occupational structure. Sixty-nine percent of the total work force was involved in farming or ranching.

TABLE 2

NATIVITY OF RESIDENTS OF LOS ANGELES COUNTY
1850

Mexico	85.3%
United States	9.6
North-East	(1.2)
Mid-Atlantic	(2.0)
Mid-West	(2.0)
South	(4.2)
"On the Road"	(0.2)
Europe	4.2
South America	.6
Asia	.1
Canada	.2

Source: *Census of the City and County of Los Angeles, California, for the Year 1850* (Los Angeles, 1929).

TABLE 3

RACIAL DISTRIBUTION IN LOS ANGELES
1850

Caucasian	90.1%
Chinese	.1
Indian	9.4
Negro	.4

Source: *Census for the City and County of Los Angeles, California for the Year 1850* (Los Angeles, 1929).

The vast majority of these were laborers on large farms or huge ranches. Over ninety-five percent of these laborers were Mexican or Indian.[24] Over eighty percent of the small farmers were native Mexicans, and most owners of the larger estates were either prominent members of Old Mexican families or "Mexicanized" *gringos.*[25]

TABLE 4

OCCUPATIONAL DISTRIBUTION IN LOS ANGELES
1850

Agriculture[a]	12.6%
Ranching	5.7
Laborer[b]	57.6
Other	24.1

Source: *Census for the City and County of Los Angeles, California for the Year 1850* (Los Angeles, 1929).

a.   Includes vinegrowers.

b.   650 total, of whom 623 were ranch laborers.

A little less than one-quarter of the total labor force was not involved in direct agricultural activities, and all but seven of these were Americans or Europeans. Fifty of these were merchants or traders.

There were a number of professionals in the county: lawyers, physicians, and teachers. A variety of local service occupations, such as bakers, cabinet-makers, coopers, saddlers, and tailors, made up the bulk of the non-agricultural trades. A few of the occupations listed in the 1850 census have no clear application to known economic activities in the county: brewers, distillers, hatters, watch-makers, and one shipmaster.[26] It is possible that the men so classified, all from states to the east or foreign-born, were not employed at the time but had listed the occupation held at the last place of residence. If so, it is not unreasonable to assume that some of the recent migrants to Los Angeles came from areas with fairly sophisticated social and economic structures. Clearly, their sense of community and the options for the future would be different from the native Californians.

Given this ethnic-occupational division, it would seem that native Californians controlled the economy of the land and recently arrived *gringos* controlled trade and ancillary functions. Certainly, the vast majority of land owners were Mexican, but a disproportionate share was owned by Americans and Europeans. No native Californian owned a plot of land valued at more than $25,000. The five ranchers of New England nativity owned estates with an average valuation of $27,400.

TABLE 5

LAND OWNERSHIP BY NATIVITY AND VALUE
LOS ANGELES: 1850

NATIVITY	NUMBER OF OWNERS	TOTAL VALUE	AVERAGE
Mexico	226 (82.7%)	$735,000 (55.5%)	$3,252
United States	19 (7.0%)	266,000 (20.1%)	14,000
Other	28 (10.3%)	324,000 (24.4%)	11,714

Source: *Census of the City and County of Los Angeles, California for the Year 1850* (Los Angeles, 1929).

There is no way to correlate manuscript census data with the residential structure of the pueblo, but there appears to have been little ethnic segregation. That which did exist was probably a function of the peculiarities of the town and county settlement. *Gringo* migrants tended to locate in the pueblo rather than the surrounding countryside. While approximately fifteen percent of the population of the entire county were Americans and foreign-born, one quarter of the townsmen came from these backgrounds.   The various boarding houses in the town were almost exclusively the residences of single men from states to the east or Europe. The Inn run by Lewis Granger is typical. Of the thirty-three boarders, seven were New Yorkers, four were from Kentucky, two each were natives of Ohio, Missouri, Pennsylvania, Scotland, and Ireland, and one boarder was born in each of the following: Louisiana, Illinois, Connecticut, North Carolina, Maine, Maryland, Tennessee, and England. Only one native Californian, Jose Domingo, was a resident of Granger's Inn.[27] The occupations of the residents of the Inn offer a fair sampling of the non-agricultural work of the town: four laborers, two clerks, and one tinner, shoemaker, blacksmith, baker, lawyer, hatter, lumberman, printer, and miner. These Inns served as a social and political center for this group of *gringo* professionals and artisans. During the first three decades of the American period of Los Angeles, political petitions had their origins, and at times their only support, from such boarding houses.[28] On a few occasions, the boarders would combine forces with "Mexicanized" *gringos* and prominent Mexicans, but the constant thrust of political action was decidedly from the town *gringos*.[29]

In the countryside, the largest groups of dwellings for single men were the dormitories for farm and ranch laborers, who were almost all native Mexicans or Indians. In contrast to the boarding house residents, who comprised about ten percent of the town's population, these agrarian workers made up over forty percent of the population of the rural areas of the county and eighteen percent of the total county. This situation created a significant difference between the town and the countryside. There were one hundred males to every eighty females in the rural areas. About forty percent of the adult population (over the age of 15) of the ranch and farm dwellers and slightly over sixty percent of the villagers were married.[30]

With the exception of the boarding houses and dormitories, residential segregation appears to have been absent from Los Angeles at mid-century. If the order of households reported in the 1850 census is any indication of neighborhood integrity, *gringos* and Mexicans lived in close proximity to each other in the pueblo. Furthermore, twenty-three percent of the married Yankees and Europeans had Mexican wives. Usually, the couple lived near the female's family.[31]

The importance of the *gringo* population in the commerce of the pueblo, the concentration of the largest plots of land in the hands of Americans and Europeans, and the degree of intermarriage lend validity to the claim of an early Los Angeleno that his community in the 1850's was a "semi-*gringo*" village.[32] The corollary of this observation, of course, is that many of the *gringos* were "semi-Mexican." Ethnicity, however, tended to be a minor factor in the social life of the city. Harris

Newmark, for example, was a German-Jew who migrated to Los Angeles in 1853 as a merchant and was made welcome in the most respectable Mexican and American households. He was pleasantly surprised that the major distinction made by the local residents was between "respectable" and "evil" elements.[33]   Only one year earlier, Abel Stearns held a Washington's Birthday Ball to which he invited many native Californians and excluded *gringo* gamblers and drunks, whom he considered socially unacceptable.[34]

In the early 1850's, national holidays had a "semi-Mexican" and cosmopolitan flavor. The Fourth of July, for example, was celebrated as a *fiesta*, and patriotic songs of the United States, Mexico, and European nations were played.[35]   Similarly, local offices were distributed among *gringos* and Mexicans. Los Angeles retained the traditional offices of First and Second *Alcalde* for one year after statehood. During the American period Stephan Foster and Jose del Camen Lugo held those positions, succeeded by Abel Stearns and Juan Sepulveda.[36]

The good relations between the various ethnic groups in Los Angeles should not be interpreted as evidence of an idyllic calm community. The pueblo earned its reputation as a rough and violent frontier community. It was considered necessary to carry side-arms for protection, and the sight of men going about their daily business, with six-shooters strapped to their waists shocked eastern visitors.[37]   Justice was notoriously ineffective, and occasionally the citizenry would take the law into its own hands. In July, 1852, Abel Stearns organized a vigilance committee to try and hang Doroteo, a cattle thief who had murdered two Yankee buyers. Lewis Granger's boarding house became the nucleus of the group, but Stearns included a number of Mexican residents to make the hanging a community rather than a *gringo* act.[38]   For the most part, murder between "undesirable" elements, whether Mexican or *gringo*, was ignored as an effective "pest control."[39]   Although violence was ever present, most Los Angelenos simply went about their daily lives in shops, stores, and fields, with the regular flow of life occasionally interrupted by a *fiesta*, large wedding, lynching, or theatrical performance, such as the 1851 production of *Richard III* at the "Rough and Ready Theatre."[40] Harris Newmark recalled that Los Angeles in the 1850's was "free and easy. . .permitting people in the ordinary affairs of life to do practically as they pleased. . .there were few if any restrictions."[41]   Into this village Protestant ministers, who were singularly unsuited to a "free and easy" environment, were sent by ecclesiastical bureaucrats who assumed that American culture could be implanted in new territory as easily as the American flag.

III

The religious traditions that confronted each other in Los Angeles were not so much Catholic and Protestant as they were casual and intensive. Most residents of the pueblo were decidedly Catholic, but few were actively so. Perhaps because being a member of the Roman Church was so integrally a part of being Spanish-American, the religious intensity of evangelical Protestantism was never in evidence in pre-*gringo* Los Angeles. Although a parish had been established as early as 1784, the Franciscan fathers could not persuade villagers to build a church until 1814. Only the promise of a constant supply of brandy during the construction convinced the local residents to undertake the project.[42] The population of the area increased more than eight times over the next five decades, but it was not felt necessary to construct an additional church building until 1869.[43]

The Catholics of the area, both lay and cleric, were neither threatened by nor hostile to other forms of religion. For the most part they ignored them. Los Angelenos got an early taste of Protestantism in a rather bizarre form. William Money, Scottish immigrant, self-proclaimed physician, astrologer, historian, and theologian, migrated to the pueblo in 1840, from Sonoma County.[44] He immediately founded the Reformed New Testament Church with himself as "Bishop, Deacon, and Defender of the Faith of Jesus Christ."[45] Money wrote a good number of anti-Catholic tracts and recruited a membership of two dozen native *Californios.*[46] Until his death in 1880, Money was left unharassed and neglected by the Catholic church and most of the townspeople. He was undoubtedly regarded as a crank, but the similar treatment afforded later ministers from more conventional denominations suggests a common unconcern with religious enthusiasm.

It is interesting that Money was able to attract only the native Mexican population and no *gringos.*[47] This can be explained, in part, by the availability of more traditional forms of Protestant worship and practice in the years following statehood. For ten years previously, however, Money represented the only form of Protestantism in the area. Some of the American migrants, of course, became Catholic, and a few were Jewish.[48] For the rest, there seems to be two likely possibilities. Some may have migrated to California with no—or very weak—religious affiliation and no desire to form any ecclesiastical attachments. Others may have been like Samuel Clemens who, when he discovered that Virginia City was no place for a Presbyterian, did not remain one for very long.[49] The facts that early Protestant activity in Los Angeles was stimulated by outside agencies rather than requests from the pueblo, and that any interest in this activity was not demonstrated until the late 1850's, tend to support these assumptions.[50]

In contrast to this rather casual religious tradition, the ministers assigned to Los Angeles came from a rather unique experience of religious revitalization.   Indeed, the agencies that sent them were creatures of a general reorientation in early nineteenth-century American Protestantism.   Coincident with the disestablishment of churches in New England, and similar changes in the relation between church and state in other areas in the early years of the Republic, various denominational and interdenominational agencies were established to promote and continue interest in Protestant Christianity.   It was from a desire to perpetuate the traditional function of Anglo-American Protestantism in the community rather than an attempt to formulate another set of goals that led to this new direction.   There is great consistency in Lyman Beecher's role in defending a close alliance of church and state and his subsequent writings and activities on behalf of voluntarism.   Following the May, 1818, victory of the Fusion Party in Connecticut, which insured the end of state support for the churches, the New England cleric "suffered what no tongue can tell."[51]   Rather than turn despair into defeat, Beecher interpreted that new order of things as an opportunity for   churches to continue their cohesive role in communities through persuasion rather than coercion.   In place of the organic support once offered by the state, he suggested closer cooperation between various denominational   agencies,   the   establishment   of   ancillary interdenominational organizations, and a "systematization" of the various groups into a loose confederation of evangelical Christianity.[52]

The organizations that existed before the conscious beginnings of voluntarism were, for the most part, missionary societies.   The term "missionary" conjures images of isolated clergy working in foreign lands or   among   aborigine   populations.   Certainly,   there   were   early organizations which fit the stereotype.   The New York Missionary Society, usually cited as the first American effort in proselytic activity, was founded in 1796 as a local cooperative agency of the Presbyterian, Baptist, and Dutch Reformed Churches to evangelize the Indians.[53]   In 1810, an association of students at Andover Theological Seminary formed the nucleus of the American Board of Commissioners for Foreign Missions.[54]   By   mid-century,   American   churches   were   spending approximately $600,000 per year on foreign missions.[55]   An indication of the relative importance attached to this sort of external missionary emphasis, however, is the $9,000,000 spent annually by these same churches   on   home   missions   and   related   activities   in   the   1830's.[56]

The normal pattern of pre-Civil War proselytic activity in America was set by the Missionary Society of Connecticut, founded in 1798 by Congregationalists to establish churches for migrants to frontier areas.[57] Societies in Massachusetts and New Hampshire were established at the turn of the century and followed the practices of the Connecticut organization.[58]   By the early 1820's, Baptist Domestic Missionary Societies appeared in all New England and Mid-Atlantic states, and the Presbyterian, Methodist, and Episcopalian denominations established national committees on missionary activity which were concerned almost exclusively with domestic programs, especially on the frontier.[59]   It was the Home Mission societies that Lyman Beecher saw as the pivotal organizations of the voluntary system.   As the nation expanded and Americans left their stable communities for the frontier, Protestant Christianity could extend over space carrying the message of salvation and establishing the religious basis of community cohesion.[60]   Ancillary organizations, such as the American Bible Society and the American Education Society, could be used to revitalize Protestantism at both the individual and community level.

The community interest so evident in Beecher's writings was to be expected.   He was a New Englander with a strong sense of the integrity of religion and society at the local level.   The preoccupation with community was not peculiar to Beecher or New England Protestants, however.   It was always implicit, and often explicit, in the writings and activities of the various associations.[61]   The fact that very little support for this general movement came from the South, the area of least village and town settlement, is indicative.[62]   Certainly, missionary practice on the frontier gives evidence of the importance of community to these Protestant societies.   Religious organization often became the basis for the building of local institutions.[63]   A sense of community based on Protestant faith and practice was usually assumed to be the *sine qua non* for civilization.   An 1829 report of the American Home Missionary Society noted that the center of American population was rapidly moving "beyond the Allegheny."   Leave the future leader of the nation without the gospel, the report warned, and he will become a "ruffian giant."[64]

The various ancillary organizations founded during the 1820's, such as the American Sunday School Union and the American Tract Society, gave their energies to the revival of religious interest in more established communities as well as to their supportive role in the missionary enterprise.[65]   These agencies gave rise to a new group of organizations concerned with the quality of moral life in America, such as the American Temperance Society, founded in 1825.[66]   The proliferation of these associations gives evidence of a strong desire among American Protestants to intensify and expand their religious experience.

One observer in the early nineteenth century remarked that, "matters have come to such a pass that a peaceable man can hardly venture to eat or drink, to go to bed or get up, to correct his children or kiss his wife," without the benevolent guidance of at least one—probably more—church related societies.[67]

Just as the voluntary system gave from to American Protestantism, the cooperative activity of the various agencies gave an institutional definition for the denominational constituency that came to be identified with normative American religious practice. The American Tract Society, founded in 1825, established a publishing committee composed of representatives from the Baptist, Congregationalist, Dutch Reformed, Protestant Episcopal, and Presbyterian churches.[68] Specific denominational names would change over time. The Methodists soon began to rely less on their own national structures and entered the field of cooperative action.[69] Old denominations, such as the Dutch Reformed, became either numerically insignificant or absorbed in larger organizations.[70] New denominations, such as the Disciples of Christ, would be formed from the splinterings and consolidations of older bodies.[71] The one common element in constituent denominations of the voluntary system was their organizational and ideological roots in English and Western-European Reformed traditions. Neither the Lutheran family of churches, nor the Unitarian derivations from Congregationalism, nor the new enthusiastic religious movements were well represented—often not represented at all—on the boards of the various agencies.[72]

This spirit of cooperation minimized conflict and competition in the mission field. In 1826, for example, the Standing Committee on Missions of the Presbyterian Church formed a coalition with the Congregationalists and established the American Home Mission Society.[73] There were many examples of aid given by one denomination to specific missionary activities of others, and cooperation was most in evidence in the building of new schools for the training of ministers in or near their own communities.[74] These interrelated developments produced a missionary theology intended to move men to personal and communal renewal, but it assumed that those who heard the message shared a common view of a young, expanding, homogeneous America, and that revitalization included the intensification of vaguely shared values and assumptions about community life. It was an approach well suited to the Old Northwest and the Great Plains with populations of migrant Easterners. It was to prove less successful in areas with different social structures, such as Los Angeles in the 1850's.

IV

With the opening of the Far West, publications such as the *Home Missionary* urged immediate action on the part of Protestant expansion. Later publications were to assume that traditional church members would migrate into the area and be the foundation for new communities. The *Home Missionary* in 1849, however, suggested that the West Coast could be made Protestant territory only by importing Christians, as well as Christian institutions. The anonymous editorial writer noted with displeasure the native Mexican population and the recent American migrants who fled to California solely for private gain.[75] The lack of community spirit associated with the boom times of the Gold Rush and the dominance of the Roman Catholic Church, which was a perceived threat in its incipient form in the East, were certainly contraindications for Protestant success in California.[76]

If the present conditions did not seem favorable, the past history of evangelical activity in the area was less so. Jedediah "Bible Toter" Smith, a Methodist missionary, arrived at San Gabriel in November, 1826, the first Protestant minister to leave a record of his presence since the Reverend Francis Fletcher conducted an Anglican service for the crew of the *Golden Hinde* in what is now Marin County. It is not clear why Smith went to California, but he found nothing to keep him there and returned within a few weeks.[77] Congregationalist minister Jonathan Green was sent by the American Board of Commissioners for Foreign Missions to San Francisco in 1829, to explore the possibility of establishing a "New England Colony" along the coast. His report was firmly negative.[78] Until California became a part of the United States, Protestant clerical activity in the Mexican territory was limited to military and naval chaplains and a few ministers sent by foreign mission agencies. The chaplains, whose contact was limited almost entirely to American personnel and who may have been conditioned to think of ultimate territorial expansion, were rather enthusiastic about the religious possibilities for the future.[79] The missionaries were less enthusiastic. Most of these clergymen were recalled from work in the Hawaiian Islands, and the reassignment often seems to have been a form of punishment. At least nine of the two dozen clergy sent by the American Board before 1850 had various complaints lodged against them in their Pacific missionary field ranging from exploitation of local labor to the paternity of native children.[80]

Many of the early Protestant clergy in California left the ministry and took up more secular occupations. At least five of those sent by missionary societies were last seen rushing to fields of gold in the inland mountains.[81] Some adopted more conventional occupations and became prominent in local society. The Reverend Thaddeus M. Leavenworth, Episcopalian and U. S. Army chaplain, arrived in San Franciso with his regiment in April, 1847.   He was approached by a few townspeople requesting that he stay in the area and establish a church when his commission expired. Leavenworth did stay in San Francisco, but he left the ministry, opened a drug store, and was elected *alcalde* of San Francisco in August of the same year.[82]

Some of the later arrivals, however, began the establishment of Protestant churches in California. Timothy Dwight Hunt, a Presbyterian missionary, arrived in San Francisco from Honolulu in October, 1848 (with no scandal attached to his departure). A small group of Protestants convinced him to stay in that city as their chaplain at a salary of $2,500 per year. Hunt organized the first Protestant congregation in the area and joined the Congregational Association in 1852, there being no Presbyterian organization in the state at that time.[83]

The Baptist Church began to think of California as a viable field for religious expansion in 1849 when, in response to a request from eight American citizens in San Francisco, a church was constructed and supplied with a minister.[84] Most of this activity centered around the Bay Area. By the time California joined the Union, there were twelve active Protestant ministers in California: six in San Francisco, three in Sacramento, and one each in Benicia, Monterey, and San Jose. All had been sent by an organization that shared the assumptions of the voluntary system, and all were from denominations that were part of the American Protestant establishment: five Presbyterians, three Episcopalians, two Methodists, one Baptist, and one Congregationalist.[85]

When California became a state, missionary organizations took an immediate interest in sending clergymen, establishing churches, and building local institutions. The 1849 editorial of *Home Missionary* was considered both pessimistic and impractical.   It was assumed that Americans would migrate of their own accord and a conscious attempt to "colonize" the new state was unnecessary. Presbyterian, Congregational, and Baptist organizations, as well as the Home Missionary Society, gathered the impressions of ministers who had traveled through California from published works and personal correspondence.   Areas that seemed likely candidates for future American migration were given exclusive consideration.[6]   In no case was a desire expressed to Protestantize—or Americanize—the Mexican Catholics. "If American communities are to be built," claimed a report of the American Home Missionary Society in 1850, "the gospel must be there to guide the builders."[87] The existing human landscape was not considered a factor.

Los Angeles was one of the areas marked for future expansion. Whether the religious bureaucrats who made this decision should be considered visionaries or simply men who made a lucky guess, the human landscape was very much a factor, and the promise of a Protestant community was not realized immediately. In many ways, the choice was a strange one. Unlike San Francisco, where Protestant residents made requests for ministers, there is no evidence that any Los Angelenos shared a similar desire prior to the sending of missionaries.[88] Indeed, these early agents of Protestantism were met with indifference.

James W. Brier had dismissed Los Angeles with one sentence. James Woods was a longer resident of the area and left a more extensive record of his missionary frustration. He found few of the Americans who were supposed to have migrated, and turned his thoughts, though not his actions, to the native population. Witnessing an execution of a Mexican criminal, Woods wished that he could speak Spanish "to direct him to that saviour who pitied and pardoned the thief on the cross." Ignoring the fact that a Catholic priest attended the proceedings, he assumed that the condemned man "in all probability had never heard of the plan of salvation and knew nothing of a saviour's mercy."[89] Woods' attitude toward Catholicism became an obsession. After attending a local burial service, he concluded, "Surely this is but a grade above paganism."[90] He made a few attempts to establish some rapport with the Catholic clergy, but returned to his room and wrote in despair, "Idolatry, idolatry, idolatry."[91] He dismissed the Mexican population as "all Catholics and without the knowledge of God."[92]

Woods was able to spend so much of his energy in frustrated disgust with the Catholic population because the American population seemed uninterested in his presence. He believed the *gringo* population to be about one thousand (certainly an overestimate), and complained that his largest congregation contained approximately thirty women, girls, and boys, "and yet it was considered a large congregation."[93] Usually his group consisted of no more than a dozen souls. The population of committed Christians, Woods estimated, was even smaller. "There is comparatively no interest felt here upon the subject of religion—it is like the valley of dry bones. . .I cannot hear of more than four or five who profess religion."[94] His disgust with Catholicism was equalled by his revulsion for his fellow countrymen. "I hear every few minutes the voices and conversation of Americans, betting, cursing, and blaspheming as they stand leaning against my window blind. This is a nominally Christian town, but in reality heathen."[95]

It was no surprise that Woods left his Los Angeles assignment in 1855. The Presbyterian Board of Home Missions, however, was not certain that the pueblo should be abandoned and sent the Reverend T. N. Davis to replace him.[96] Davis came to Los Angeles with a great deal of enthusiasm after having served in newly established churches in Iowa. After he had held his new position for less than a year, Davis echoed the sentiments of his predecessor. "There is a torrent of vice and immorality which obliterates all traces of the Christian Sabbath," he complained.[97] He could no longer countenance living in a town "where society is disorganized, religion scoffed at, where violence runs riot, and even life itself is unsafe."[98]

Neither the Presbyterian Board nor the American Home Missionary Society seemed especially interested in Los Angeles following the experiences of their early attempts. It was not until 1859, at the request of five citizens of the village, that the Presbyterians sent another missionary, William Boardman.[99] Cooperating with the American Home Missionary Society, Boardman sought to establish an interdenominational congregation serving the adherents of American Protestantism. On May 4, 1859, seventeen *gringos* drew up the Constitution of the First Protestant Society of Los Angeles. Noting the "absence of a regularly organized Protestant church," these recent migrants wished to secure "for ourselves and others in our city the privileges of divine worship according to the Protestant order."[100] There was an implied assumption in the establishment of the society that organizations in the East would not continue to support missionary activity in an area once thought to be so promising and proving to be so unsuccessful. Plans were laid to collect money which could be used in the future to found congregations of denominations participating in the voluntary system.[101] This assumed that future migrants would share the desire of the Protestant Society to extend religious activity in Los Angeles and that financial support would be enlarged by this migration. The voluntary system had been accustomed to rather rapid realization of goals in its westward expansion. By 1862, only three years after the founding of the First Protestant Society of Los Angeles, the interest of the Presbyterian Board and the American Home Mission Society was exhausted. The projected desires of subsequent migrants did not materialize, and Boardman was withdrawn from his Los Angeles position.[102]

Between the decline of the support of voluntaristic agencies and the late 1860's the attempts to extend Protestantism into Los Angeles were carried on by two denominations: the Methodist and Protestant Episcopal Churches. After the disastrous early effort of James Brier, the Methodist Board of Home Missions sent the Reverend Adam Bland, a missionary with wider experience, to replace his neophyte brother.[103] In a negotiation that would have greater symbolic importance to future Los Angeles Protestants, Bland leased the abandoned El Dorado Saloon as a Methodist chapel and day school for girls.[104] The chapel was sparsely attended, the girls' school remained an unfulfilled dream, and the Reverend Bland left the City of the Angels exclaiming that its people were "the worst I have ever met."[105] The Methodist Board sent Elijah Merchant to replace Bland. Methodist services were continued until Merchant's resignation in 1858.[106] The local laity were among the most enthusiastic supporters of the First Protestant Society of Los Angeles, and continued Methodist worship in the absence of clergy for seven years. In 1866, Adam Bland returned to Los Angeles at the request of the Methodist Board.[107] He was given assurance that the community was more tame and that a much larger congregation would greet his arrival. Both claims were a bit extravagant, but conditions had improved enough to give permanence to Bland's new pastorate in Los Angeles.[108]

The Protestant Episcopal Church continued its early interest in the pueblo through modest activities between 1855 and 1864. The Right Reverend William Ingraham Kip, originally sent to California as a missionary in 1853, and rapidly consecrated as missionary Bishop to the state, was encouraged by the interest of a few Los Angelenos during his visit in early October of 1855. Their remarks to Kip may contain a hint of the problem of earlier Presbyterian and Methodist attempts in the village. These Protestant migrants wanted to establish a church, he reported, but not one of the more evangelical denominations. "They wanted something which did not preach Nebraska or Kansas, slavery or anti-slavery, and that was not identified with any of the *isms* of the day."[109] These were the issues that many of the recent migrants had left behind them. They were also among the issues that were of great importance to voluntaristic organizations and representatives. The missionaries sent to California did not intend to minister to a new society, but to bring American culture, with its many political and sectional tensions, to the new land.

Kip, who in his own ecclesiastical structure was both a bureaucrat and a missionary, considered the role and potentialities of Protestantism in the Far West in a different context then organizational officers in the East and functionaries in the field. Mildly criticizing his fellow churchmen "residing all their lives in a settled state of society," Kip questioned the assumptions of the interdenominational agencies and his own church. Those who held responsibility for missionary activity, he charged, "have no idea of the difficulty of forming a congregation from a population who have not heard the gospel preached for years, who are living under no religious restraints, and among whom the religious element is yet to be created."[110] Quoting a fellow prelate from earlier days, however, Kip concluded his observations on Los Angeles with a couplet that indicates a spirit more akin to Brier, Woods, and Bland than the good Bishop was willing to admit in his own words: "Every prospect pleases, and only man is vile."[111]

By 1857, an Episcopal parish, St. Luke's, was established with a local physician, Matthew Carter, authorized as lay reader. Within a year, the church was dissolved for lack of attendance.[112] The Bishop continued his interest, however, and kept an open offer to send a priest as soon as enough villagers would petition for the organization of a parish. By 1864, Kip grew tired of waiting and sent the Reverend Elias Birdsall as missionary to Los Angeles.[113] He found a willing, though not enthusiastic, group of attendants at Sunday services, and a permanent parish was established in 1869. Birdsall was able to purchase the unfinished structure begun by the First Protestant Society of Los Angeles, and the parish church of St. Athanasius was soon completed.[114] Birdsall was reassigned to other missionary activity in 1870, and was replaced by J. B. Gray as parish priest.[115] By 1871, St. Athanasius Church had forty communicant members, a weekly attendance of about one hundred, and a Sunday School.[116]

The experience of the Protestant Episcopal Church in Los Angeles was unique only in the continued interest and support of the Bishop. The pattern of failure in the 1850's and moderate success in the 1860's was common to all Protestant denominations. Bland's reorganized parish became a permanent congregation, and a second Methodist Church was established in 1875.[117] The American Home Mission Society became interested in Los Angeles after these limited gains, and sent the Reverend A. Porter in 1866, who organized the First Congregational Church a year later. Porter was replaced in 1868, by a permanent minister, I. W. Atherton.[118] By 1871, the church had forty members and one hundred Sunday School attendants.[119]

During the 1860's and 1870's the activity of the Protestant denominations in Los Angeles were limited to establishing and maintaining congregations. They were not involved in the moral crusades of their brethren in Norther California. The community salvation efforts of voluntaristic Protestants began very early in San Francisco. Denominations joined in that city as early as 1849 to combat the sin of excessive drinking.[120] The Baptist *Pacific Banner* gave this work second priority only to the saving of souls..[121] The Sons of Temperance were organized in San Francisco in 1850, and had over five hundred members by 1854.[122] An 1855 referendum for restrictive liquor laws was defeated by fifty-five percent of the populace in the state. In Los Angeles the measure was rejected by a vote of 606 to 75.[123] Voluntaristic organizations continued in the Bay Area, but the newly formed congregations in Los Angeles could ill afford to divide their energies. The Bay city was an important community in the broader national society and continued to receive support from organizations in the East.[1244] The pueblo remained insignificant in a national context and the bursting of earlier enthusiastic illusions about Protestant growth in the area led to a decline in support. The simple continuance of the incipient Protestant community in the Catholic town demanded all of the energy of religious organizers and isolated Los Angeles Protestants from the actions on behalf of community betterment that were so important in the north.

Certainly, Protestant beginnings in Los Angeles were less than auspicious. Two related questions are raised by this meager genesis. Why did Protestant ministers find more to recommend Los Angeles in the 1860's and 1870's than in the 1850's, and why did the Protestant population expand in size and influence between 1880 and 1900 to become the pride of evangelical Christianity? A partial answer to the first question can be found in the nature of migration to the town. In 1850, few families from older states could be found in Los Angeles. Most Americans were single men or had taken Mexican wives.[125] By 1870, a greater percentage of family units began migrating to Los Angeles. Of the two congregations for which records remain in the 1870's, most of the communicants were members of families who had recently moved to Los Angeles from the Mid-West, and most entered the congregation not as new converts, but by letters of transfer.[126] This was precisely the pattern for the establishment of congregations in newly acquired territory envisioned by voluntaristic missionary societies. What they could not predict were the changes occurring in Los Angeles society between 1850 and 1880 which would render the Catholic population powerless and create the opportunity for Protestant civic leadership. These changes help explain both the early moderate success following initial failure and later accomplishments that were to surpass the aspirations of even the most enthusiastic bureaucrats in the early 1850's.

NOTES

[1]Walter Colton, *Three Years in California* (New York, 1850), p. 355.

[2]William Ingraham Kip, *The Early Days of My Episcopate* (New York, 1892), p. 83.

[3]*Ibid.*, pp. 85-92.

[4]Presbyterian Board of Home Missions, *Report* (Philadelphia, 1851), pp. 123-124; *Twenty-First Annual Report of the Missionary Society of the Methodist Episcopal Church* (New York, 1850), pp. 97-112; Associated Baptist Mission Boards, *Report* (New York, 1853), pp. 23-39; *Report of the Diocese of New York* (New York, 1852), pp. 76-77.

[5]*Missionary Herald* (September, 1854), p. 156.

[6]Diary of James W. Brier, Henry E. Huntington Library, San Marino, California.

[7]*Ibid.*

[8]Marco R. Newmark, "The Story of Religion in Los Angeles, 1781-1900, "*Historical Society of Southern California Quarterly*, XXVIII (March, 1946), p. 38. Hereafter, this journal and its predecessors will be cited as HSSCQ.

[9]James Woods, Diary, Henry E. Huntington Library, San Marino, California.

[10]*Ibid.*

[11]*Ibid.*

[12]Fogelson, p. 1. For the configuration of the more traditional, and somewhat less complex, structure of American agrarian communities see James C. Malin, *The Grassland of North America* (Lawrence, 1950); Merle Curti, *The Making of an American Community* (Stanford, 1959); Mildred Throne, "A Population Study of an Iowa County in 1850," *Iowa Journal of History*, LVII (1959), pp. 305-330; William L. Bowers, "Crawford Township, 1850-1870," *Ibid.*, LVIII (1960); pp. 1-30; Allan G. Bogue, *From Prairie to Corn Belt* (Chicago, 1963); and Rodney O. Davis, "Prairie Emporium: Clarence, Iowa, 1860-1880, A Study of Population Trends," *Mid-America: An Historical Review*, LVI (April, 1969), pp. 130-139. The pattern is not unlike that defined for Colonial New England in Kenneth Lockridge, *A New England Town the First Hundred Years* (New York, 1969). A provocative, if highly impressionistic, argument is made for the "recapitulation" of the New England town through time and space in Page Smith, *As a City upon a Hill* (New York 1966), pp. 53-77. Although the argument here will not agree with Smith's exaggerated claims, it seems likely that a common form of social organization was rather persistent and necessary to the continuation of Protestant culture. For an interesting contrast to the essentially Mexican social organization of the cattle culture in Los Angeles, see Robert Dykstra, *The Cattle Towns* (New York, 1967).

[13]Fogelson, pp. 5-12.

[14]Hubert Howe Bancroft, *California Pastoral, 1769-1848* (San Francisco, 1868), pp. 317-419.

[15]Fogelson, pp. 15-17.

[16]Robert Glass Cleland, *The Cattle on a Thousand Hills: Southern California, 1850-1880* (San Marino, California, 1941), pp. 184-185; Leonard Pitt, *The Decline of the Californios: A Social History of the Spanish-Speaking Californians, 1846-1890* (Berkeley and Los Angeles, 1966), p. 107. I have depended heavily on these two works in the preparation of this chapter.

[17]Pitt, p. 113.

[18]Stearns Marriage Papers, Stearns Manuscripts, Henry E. Huntington Library, San Marino, California.

[19]Pitt, p. 124.

[20]*Ibid.*, pp. 18-19.

[21]Remi A. Nadeau, *City Makers* (Garden City, New York, 1948), pp. 31-43.

[22]*Census of the City and County of Los Angeles, California, for the Year 1850* (Los Angeles, 1929), p. 37.

[23]See Count Leonetto Cipriani, *California and Overland Diaries, 1853-1871*, trans. and ed. Ernest Falbo (San Francisco, 1962), p. 76.

[24]All of those listed as "servants" are also listed as Indians.

[25]Only two owners of land valued at more than $10,000 could not be definitely identified as a member of one of these two groups, and there is no evidence to suggest that they might not have been.

[26]The applicability of trades was determined from tax records of the late Mexican period and descriptions of Los Angeles around 1850.

[27]*Census. . .Los Angeles. . .1850*, pp. 44-45.

[28]Determined from a survey of petitions received by the state legislature recorded in the *Journal* of the California State Senate and Assembly, 1850-1880.

[29]See letters from Stearns to Granger dated July 17, 1853; February 23, 1854; and October 2, 1854: Stearns MSS.

[30]*Census. . .Los Angeles. . .1850*, passim.

[31]Determined from an approximated reconstruction based on *Ibid.*

[32]Horace Bell, *Reminiscences of a Ranger, or, Early Times in Southern California* (Santa Barbara, California, 1881), p. 31. Also see Pitt, Chapter VII, upon which this discussion relies heavily.

[33]Harris Newmark, *Sixty Years in Southern California* (New York, 1916), pp. 184-185.

[34]Cleland, p. 94; Pitt, p. 126.

[35]Bell, pp. 126-127; Newmark, p. 157; Pitt, p. 126.

[36]Pitt, p. 132.

[37]Woods, Diary.

[38]Los Angeles *Star*, July 24 and 31, 1852; Newmark, *passim*; Pitt, pp. 156-157.

[39]Horace Bell, *On the Old West Coast: Being Further Reminiscences of a Ranger* (New York, 1930), pp. 164-180. Stearns, Bandini, Pico, and Foster discussed the problem in these terms in their correspondence in the Stearns MSS.

[40]Los Angeles *Star*, July 19, 1851.

[41]Harris Newmark, p. 29.

[42]Marco Newmark, p. 43; and Gilman M. Ostrander, *The Prohibition Movement in California, 1848-1933* ("University of California Publications in History;" Berkeley and Los Angeles, 1957), p. 67.

[43]Marco Newmark, pp. 35-38.

[44]William B. Rice, *William Money, a Southern California Savant* (Los Angeles, 1943), *passim*.

[45]An unsympathetic account of the founding of the church was published in the Los Angeles *Star*, October 22, 1853.

[46]The first of his vitriolic essays, *Reform of the New Testament Church* (Los Angeles, 1854), has the dubious distinction of being the first book published in Los Angeles: Pitt, pp. 222-223.

[47]The ability of Money, a peripheral Protestant, to attract only the Mexican population may bear close comparison with similar tendencies in the recruiting patterns of Pentacostalists in the 1960's: see Bryan R. Wilson, *Sects and Society* (Berkeley and Los Angeles, 1961), pp. 66-92.

[48]Max Vorspan and Lloyd P. Gartner, *History of the Jews in Los Angeles* (San Marino, California, 1970), pp. 5-6, claim that eight residents of Los Angeles in 1850 were "recognizably Jewish."

[49]Mark Twain, *Roughing It* (New York, 1872), p. 215.

[50]Not until 1867 did a Los Angeleno communicate with the American Home Missionary Society.

[51]*Autobiography, Correspondence, etc., of Lyman Beecher, D.D.,* ed. Charles Beecher (New York, 1871), I, p. 344.

[52]*Autobiography. . .Beecher,* I, pp. 452-453. In the discussion of voluntarism, I have drawn heavily upon Sidney Mead, *The Lively Experiment* (New York, 1963); Winthrop Hudson, *The Great Tradition of the American Churches* (New York, 1953), pp. 27-41 and 63-109; William A. Clebsch, *From Sacred to Profane America: The Role of Religion in American History* (New York, 1968); Ernest Lee Tuveson, *Redeemer Nation* (Chicago, 1968); and Marty, pp. 35-99.

[53]Oliver Wendell Elsbree, *The Rise of the Missionary Spirit in America, 1790-1815* (Williamsport, Pa., 1928), p. 34.

[54]William E. Strong, *The Story of the American Board* (Boston, 1910), pp. 24-35.

[55]*Ibid.,* p. 174.

[56]*American Home Missionary Society Report, 1834,* p. 43.

[57]Goodykoontz, p. 106.

[58]Elsbree, pp. 69-81.

[59]See Charles L. White, *A Century of Faith: Centenary Volume Published for the American Baptist Home Mission Society* (Philadelphia, 1932); Hermann Nelson Morse, *From Frontier to Frontier; an Interpretation of 150 Years of Presbyterian National Missions* (Philadelphia, 1952); Wade Crawford Barclay, *History of Methodist Missions* (3 vols; New York, 1949-1957); and Julia C. Emery, *A Century of Endeavor, 1821-1921, A Record of the Domestic and Foreign Missionary Society of the Protestant Episcopal Church in the United States of America* (New York, 1921).

[60]*Autobiography, Correspondence. . .Beecher,* I, pp. 368-392 and II, pp. 31-78.

[61]The most important source of this literature is the monthly *Home Missionary* (1829-1899).

[62]The American Home Missionary Society reports through 1860 indicate that no more than six percent of their contributions came from the South.

[63]See Miyakawa; Sweet, *Religion on the Frontier;* Goodykoontz; White; Morse; Barclay; and Emery.

[64]*American Home Missionary Society Report, 1829,* p. 37. See also Lyman Beecher, *A Plea for the West* (New York, 1835).

[65]Hudson, pp. 64-111.

[66] *Ibid.*, p. 73.

[67] Quoted in Stow Persons, *American Minds (New York, 1958), p. 160.*

[68] Hudson, p. 115.

[69] Barclay, II, p. 176.

[70] James R. Schoner, "Institutional Flux in American Protestantism" (Unpublished doctoral dissertation, Union Theological Seminary, New York, 1957).

[71] *Ibid.* For the chronicle of one of the more fascinating Protestant groups, and its various realignments with other denominations, see R. P. Duclos, *Histoire du Protestantisme Francais au Canada et aux Etats-Unis* (Lausanne 1913).

[72] This is a point that is basic to an understanding of American Protestantism and the voluntary system. It has been hinted at any number of times by Niebuhr, Mead, and others, but the importance of the point seems not to have gained general acceptance. Charles H. Anderson, *White Protestant Americans: From National Origins to Religious Group* (Englewood Cliffs, New Jersey, 1970), for example, does not seems to realize that members of Finnish Lutheran bodies and Hungarian Reformed denominations are rather distinct from American Protestantism.

[73] Hudson, p. 153.

[74] Charles I. Foster, *An Errand of Mercy: The Evangelical United Front* (Chapel Hill, 1954) and Donald C. Tewksbury, *The Founding of American Colleges and Universities Before the Civil War* (New York, 1932).

[75] *Home Missionary* (June, 1849), p. 236.

[76] For eastern Protestant impressions see issues of *Home Missionary* and *Missionary Herald* in 1849 and 1850. For the anti-Catholic bias that formed a part of Protestant interest in California, see Ray Allen Billington, *The Protestant Crusade, 1800-1860* (New York, 1938).

[77] Hubert Howe Bancroft, *History of California* (San Francisco, 1884-1890), III, p. 153; W. J. Ghent, *The Early Far West* (New York, 1931), p. 216.

[78] *Missionary Herald* (November, 1830), pp. 43-57. *Ibid.* (December, 1830), pp. 173-197.

[79] See Colton, *passim*; *Spirit of Missions* (October, 1847), p. 338; *Twenty-Third Annual Report of the Missionary Society of the Methodist Episcopal Church* (New York, 1852), p. 104.

[80] *Annual Report of the American Board of Commissioners for Foreign Missions, 1836-1850, passim.*

[81] John H. Brown, *Reminiscenses and Incidents of the Early Days in San Francisco* (San Francisco, 1886), p. 34; *Overland Monthly*, X, 2nd series (October, 1887), pp. 361-378.

[82]Bancroft, *History of California*, V, p. 513; Brown, p. 67; *California Star*, May 8, 1847.

[83]Timothy Dwight Hunt, "Diary," Library of San Francisco Theological Seminary, San Anselmo, California.

[84]*The Pacific*, March 6, 1856.

[85]Clifford M. Drury, "A Chronology of Protestant Beginnings in California" (Pamphlet published by the Centennial Committee of the Northern California-Western Nevada Council of Churches, no date), pp. 8-10.

[86]See, e. g., *American Home Missionary Society Report, 1850*, p. 84.

[87]*American Home Missionary Society Report, 1850*, p. 137.

[88]*Supra*, pp. 40-42.

[89]Woods, "Diary," November 12, 1854.

[90]*Ibid.*, January 24, 1855.

[91]*Ibid.*, December 24, 1854.

[92]*Ibid.*, (no date, but in 1854).

[93]*Ibid.*, December 10, 1854.

[94]*Ibid.*, November 12, 1854.

[95]*Ibid.*, (no date, but in 1855).

[96]Marco Newmark, p. 43; Presbyterian Board of Home Missions, *Report* (Philadelphia, 1855), pp. 73-102.

[97]Los Angeles *Star*, August 16, 1856.

[98]*Ibid.*

[99]Presbyterian Board of Home Missions, *Report* (Philadelphia, 1859), p. 143.

[100]Constitution of the First Protestant Society of Los Angeles, May 4, 1859," (Henry E. Huntington Library, San Marino, California).

[101]Los Angeles *Star*, May 16, 1859; July 8, 1859; August 21, 1859.

[102]Marco Newmark, p. 44.

[103] *Twenty-Fourth Annual Report of the Missionary Society of the Methodist Episcopal Church* (New York, 1853), p. 252; Martin Rist, "Methodism Goes West," in *The History of American Methodism*, eds. Emory Stevens Bucke, *et al.* (New York, 1964), pp. 420-468.

[104] Los Angeles *Star*, September 18, 1853; Bell, *On the Old West Coast*, pp. 146-147.

[105] Rist, p. 457.

[106] Marco Newmark, p. 52.

[107] *Thirty-Seventh Annual Report of the Missionary Society of the Methodist Episcopal Church* (New York, 1866), p. 239.

[108] At least, this was Bland's estimation in his re-inaugural sermon as reported in the Los Angeles *Star*, March 5, 1866.

[109] Kip, p. 84.

[110] *Ibid.*, p. 85.

[111] *Ibid.*

[112] Marco Newmark, p. 45.

[113] *Ibid.*, pp. 231-243.

[114] Marco Newmark, p. 45; Los Angeles *Star*, February 17, 1866.

[115] Protestant Episcopal Convention, Diocese of California, *Proceedings* (1870), p. 28.

[116] *Los Angeles City Directory, 1871*, p. 27.

[117] Marco Newmark, p. 38.

[118] *American Home Missionary Society, Report, 1866*, p. 107; *Ibid., 1868*, p. 73.

[119] *Los Angeles City Directory, 1871*, p. 26.

[120] Ostrander, pp. 6-7.

[121] *Pacific Banner*, December 11, 1852.

[122] *California Christian Advocate*, October 10, 1851; May 13, 1852; Ostrander, p. 9.

[123] Sacramento *Union*, October 3, 1855.

[124] See, e.g., *Report of the American Tract Society* (1850-1870), portions on the Far West.

125Based on a tabulation from *Census. . .Los Angeles. . .1850.*

126."Records of the First Congregational Church of Los Angeles, to 1900," and "Records of St. Athanasius Protestant Episcopal Church of Los Angeles, to 1900," Henry E. Huntington Library, San Marino, California.

CHAPTER 2

FROM MEXICAN PUEBLO TO AMERICAN TOWN

I

Between 1850 and 1880, Los Angeles expanded from a village with a population of 1,610 to a large town of 11,183. The county increased in roughly the same proportion. Although much smaller than San Francisco during the three decades, the rate of growth of the Southern California town was greater, and it was the most prominent urban area in the region. San Diego was still a village in 1880, with a population of only 2,637.[1] The changes in the social basic of Los Angeles culture were no less striking than the surface indications.

In the mid-nineteenth century, cattle equaled wealth in Los Angeles. The twenty most affluent citizens were all ranchers, and all ranch owners were in the top twenty percent of the community ranked according to wealth. Thirty years later, merchants and farmers, especially owners of orchards, had replaced the ranchers as the dominant economic faction in the community. Furthermore, wealth tended to be concentrated in the town, rather than distributed rather randomly through the country, as it had been in 1850. Prime ranch land had been widely dispersed, but the large orchards of the 1800's were located in or close to the town.[2] Farm land increased from about 2,000 acres in 1850, to over 300,000 acres in 1880, a rate far greater than the growth of population.[3] Almost half of the farm land in the latter year was located on the sites of former ranches.[4]

TABLE 6

POPULATION GROWTH AND SOCIAL CHANGE
IN LOS ANGELES, 1850-1880

| | Size | Diversity Index | | |
		Ethnic	Religious	Economic
1850	1,610	.27	.00	.13
1860	4,385	.31	.14	.17
1870	5,728	.34	.19	.16
1880	11,183	.43	.22	.21

Source: See Appendix VI.

The change in the basis of the local agrarian economy was caused by the vagaries of the cattle market, a devastating drought, and a series of misadventures.   Following California statehood, some ranch owners in Los Angeles were forced to spend large sums of money to secure titles to land that had been either unprocessed under Mexican law in 1850, or had been questionable before that time.   Abel Stearns, for example, sent Don Juan Temple as his confidential agent to Mexico in 1856 to secure a compromise for a few hundred acres of disputed land. The mission was a success, but the venture cost Stearns $10,000 above the cost of the land.[5]

TABLE 7

OCCUPATION OF LOS ANGELES RESIDENTS
IN TOP TWENTY PERCENT RANKED ACCORDING TO WEALTH:
1850-1880 (IN PERCENTAGES)

	Rancher	Farmer	Merchant	Professional
1850	87.3	2.8	7.6	3.3
1860	85.9	2.6	9.1	3.4
1870	51.2	17.5	28.4	3.9
1880	17.3	32.9	41.6	8.2

Source: *Census of. . .Los Angeles. . .1850.*   U.S. Bureau of the Census, Manuscript Census Returns, Los Angeles County, 1860; *Ibid.,* 1870, U.S. Bureau of the Census, Tenth Census, 1880, Enumerator's Rollbook, Los Angeles County.

Stearns was better equipped to sustain this expense than most of his fellow *rancheros,* and he often lent his friends the money to secure title. Unfamiliarity with American credit practices, however, caused many of these land owners to build up large debts.   Stearns underwrote a mortgage on Los Coyotes Rancho, owned by Pio Pico, to offset the cost of title negotiation.   Pico was unable to pay the note, and Stearns purchased the land at value plus interest.   By 1862, Pico was able to repay his friend the principal of $19,500, but still owed almost the same amount in interest.[6]

During the 1850's, the expense incurred by the *rancheros* in securing their titles left them ill-prepared to face the depression in the cattle market in 1860-1861. The overproduction of the Los Angeles beef supply, in an attempt to increase capital gains to pay off debts, led to a buyer's market which did not abate until 1864.[7] Over 15,000 cattle were slaughtered in the summer of 1861 in order to make a marginal profit off the hide and tallow trade.[8] The ranchers' debts, of course, increased.

The market decline was closely followed by a natural disaster. In the fall, winter, and spring of 1863-1864, Southern California suffered a serious drought. How many cattle died or were slaughtered for the minimal gains from ancillary trade is not known. The effect of the drought can be seen, however, in the census data on agriculture. There were 70,000 head of cattle reported in Los Angeles County in 1860, but by 1870, only 20,000 head remained in the area's herds.[9] After the "Great Drought" of the 1860's, most *rancheros* faced financial ruin. The most powerful of these, Abel Stearns, retained physical possession of his land, but the title was held by creditors.[10] In an attempt to secure new loans to pay off old ones, in August of 1871, Stearns went to San Francisco, a city he despised and whose wealth he considered vaguely related to the poverty in his own community. At the age of seventy-three Abel Stearns died in an exclusive hotel in the most affluent city in the state.[11] He left behind a family and a community with no apparent economic future. Whether his attempts to revitalize the *ranchos* would have been successful is questionable, but it was certain that no one else could have done so. In his absence, the minor droughts of 1872 and 1876-1877 killed an economy and life style that was already dying.[12]

Los Angeles may have become a ghost town or a poor Mexican village if the incipient *gringo* merchant class had lacked visions of grandeur and had not been insistent on the necessity of a railroad in the town. Small trade to San Francisco and San Diego had been conducted throughout the nineteenth century, and the cattle market enlarged the operation. With the decline of the *rancheros,* Los Angeles no longer had a major product which could be moved on the hoof. A rather limited trade with Inyo in dry goods, produce, and a few local manufactures, begun in 1869, convinced local businessmen that a wider and more extensive trade was possible. The major rival for a line from the new Southern Pacific was San Diego. Although the more southerly community was much smaller, it had a harbor. Through a great effort on the part of Harris Newmark and John G. Downey, both local merchants, and with the support of constant petitions originating from Granger's Inn, the 1871 bill authorized the building of the south branch of the Southern Pacific "by way of Los Angeles."[14] It soon became apparent to Los Angelenos that the corporation was inclined to interpret the law as a requirement that the line only run at some point through the county. A Committee of Thirty, all *gringos* headed by Newmark and Downey, began negotiations to persuade the Southern Pacific to bring the railroad through the town proper.   After some bitter disputes the corporation forced the town to support some of the construction, and the Board of Supervisors proposed a $610,000 bond issue which was grudgingly passed.[15]   Suffering from the collapsing cattle empire, Los Angelenos could not really afford the cost of the railroad, but they could afford the lack of the branch line even less.

The railroad made the town more attractive to merchants and migrants interested in more extensive farming.   Agriculture, other than the cattle and vine industries (which had also been adversely affected by the drought) consisted primarily of subsistence farming during the days of the *rancheros*.   The cattle industry controlled the city and the county, and it was not until the early 1870's that the taxation placed on farm land, approximately four times the amount on range land, was reduced.[16] A few early *gringos* had begun trade farming before land was made available through the subdivision of the ranches.   Less than 100,000 eggs were produced in Los Angeles in 1860, primarily for home consumption. By 1869, an egg trade with Inyo and other surrounding villages resulted in 100,000,000 eggs in that year.[17]   With the availability of more land and the favorable soil conditions, orchard farming became a part of the economy of Los Angeles.   In 1867 there were approximately 9,000 orange trees in the county.   An additional 23,000 had been planted by 1871.[18]   The new farming interest was made up almost entirely of *gringos*.

TABLE 8

NATIVITY OF FARMERS IN LOS ANGELES, 1850-1880 (IN PERCENTAGES)

	Mexico[a]	New England	Mid-Atlantic	Mid-West	South	Other[b]
1850	82.7	3.4	.8	3.6	6.4	3.1
1860	80.5	3.9	.7	4.2	6.8	3.9
1870	52.1	11.3	8.9	9.4	14.2	4.1
1880	14.7	20.8	16.3	17.9	26.3	4.0

Source: Same as Table 7.

a.   Including California.

b.   Primarily Europe.

The increase in the population was primarily the result of *gringo* migration.   Although a significant portion of the population of the county continued to be of Mexican origin, the town became increasingly American. Not all of the *gringo* migrants, of course, were farmers. The proportion of the total work force of skilled workmen, merchants, and professionals in the 1870's far exceeded that of the small pueblo in 1850. By 1880, local merchants and manufacturers established shops and stores of considerable size, hiring as many as thirty people.

TABLE 9

NATIVITY OF LOS ANGELES RESIDENTS
1850-1880 (IN PERCENTAGES)

	1850	1860	1870	1880
Mexico	85.3	77.6	49.5	25.6
U.S.—of Mexican Parentage	----	2.1	12.6	19.4
United States	9.6	11.7	26.3	38.7
Other	5.1	8.6	11.6	16.3

Source: Same as Table 7.

For the Centennial celebration of the signing of the Declaration of Independence, it was the glories of local produce and products that became the theme of the parade down Main Street. It was a traditional Fourth of July, shorn of the cosmopolitan feature of the *fiestas* hosted by Abel Stearns in earlier years. It was a true American holiday which linked the past glories of the Republic with the future promise of Los Angeles. Wagons from local firms, gaily decorated and festooned with bunting, displayed the economic diversity of the town.   Breweries, laundries, windmill manufacturers, furniture makers, agricultural interests, a coffee factory, and the Los Angeles Sewing Machine Company took part in the procession.[20] Page and Gravel Black smith Shop placed a large picture of George Washington welding the links of the chain in the Union on top of their van.

TABLE 10

OCCUPATIONAL STRUCTURE OF LOS ANGELES IN 1875
(IN PERCENTAGES)

Labor[a]	41.6
Agriculture[b]	13.3
Merchants	28.6
Professional[c]	16.5

Source: *Los Angeles City Directory*, 1875.

a.   Further division is impossible and may not be applicable.   None are Agricultural.

b.   87.4% Farmers.

c.   Includes 28 teachers and 22 Clergymen; 62.1% Physicians and Attorneys.

Each side of the wagon carried the legend: "He who encourages home industry is a public benefactor.   Mechanics—the foundation of civilization and progress.   The American Mechanic—the strength of the Union, the symbol of patriotism and the bone and sinew of the nation."[21] Then Reinert's cooperage display bore the legend, "Show us a leak in the Union and we will tighten it," and the Trapp Fruit Company proclaimed their motto, "Home Produce," emblazoned on the American Eagle.[22]

Banking institutions to finance and coordinate the new economic base of Los Angeles society had been absent in the town until the 1870's. The financial disasters brought by the drought sharply reduced the flow of credit from San Francisco. On August 1, 1873, the situation had become so serious that the local merchants, headed by Charles Nordhoff recently from New York, and William E. Hughes of Wheeling, West Virginia, joined together in order to generate enough capital to revive the economy. Hughes had been active in the Chamber of Commerce in his home town, and the emergency organization became the nucleus of a more permanent association under his prodding.[23] The first act of the Los Angeles Chamber of Commerce was to support the efforts of William Workman and Francis Temple to establish a bank in and for Los Angeles.[24] The two men were long-time residents of the area and found themselves unable to refuse loans requested by friends. In the panic of 1875, the Workman and Temple Bank had overextended its capital supply. A gallant attempt was made to regain solvency through a personal loan from E. J. "Lucky" Baldwin, whose orchards were the most successful enterprise in the county in the 1870's.[25] The Bank failed in a few weeks. Los Angelenos again were forced to look to San Francisco. Until economic independence from the Bay City was achieved in the late 1880's, the creation of local banks, which would be solvent and which would not be branches of San Francisco institutions, remained a constant desire of the Chamber of Commerce and the wider community of merchants.[26]

II

The desire for autonomy and a disdain for the northern California city were also prevalent in Los Angeles during the days of the *rancheros*, and the steps taken to achieve this desire led to developments which facilitated the dramatic shift from the Catholic ranch culture to one of Protestant merchants and farmers. As early as 1849, Abel Stearns expressed discontent with the denomination of the north in the Mexican state legislature. The northern counties, especially San Francisco, he charged ,were "teetotally and universally against anything Spanish."[27] In early 1851, Lewis Granger wrote a letter to the editor of the *Daily Alta California* charging the paper with "puerile effusions in matters concerning this part of California."[28] By November, Granger became convinced that no good would come to Southern California through the new American state. With three other *gringos* and three *Californios*, all owners of large ranches, he drafted a "Declaration to Divide the State of California." "Whatever of good the experiment of a State government may have otherwise led to California," the Declaration claimed, "for us of the Southern Counties it has proved only a splendid failure."[29] Heavy taxation, the bypassing of commerce, and neglect of the region's needs in legislation were the stated grievances. The Declaration called for separation of the state, "friendly and peaceful but still complete, leaving the North and South to fulfill their grand destinies under systems of laws suited to each."[30]

The Declaration was a hyperbolic statement of sentiments in Los Angeles, and there was no general support for such a drastic proposal. More realistically, a group of prominent Los Angelenos led by Stearns negotiated with John A. Lewis, a former Boston reporter then with the *Daily Alta California*, to establish a newspaper to promote local interests.[31] Lewis was uninterested, but suggested John McElroy, also a northern California journalist, and under his editorship, the first edition of the Los Angeles *Star* appeared on May 17, 1851.[32] Stating the complaints that were later to be written in the Declaration, the premier editiorial of the *Star* urged, "Let there be immediate action, and Southern California will no longer be a mere 'hewer of wood' and 'drawer of water' to the North."[33]

Throughout the 1850's and 1860's, two themes dominated the pages of the Los Angeles newspaper: the need for a southern route of the Pacific railroad system and mild boosterism. In both cases the *gringo*-dominated press combined an interest in the development of Southern California with a set of assumptions that were almost as foreign to the culture of Los Angeles as were those of the first missionaries in the area. The need for a railroad was perceived as a necessity to bring the village more fully into the life of the state and nation and to balance the cattle empire with commercial activity.[34]

In promoting a more stable and less violent life for Los Angeles, the *Star* concentrated on those elements of the community that were of least interest to the majority of the population, whether *ranchero* or laborer. The newspaper noted with exultation the Reverend Adam Bland's attempt to found a Sunday School.[35] When the Reverend T.M. Davis became the second Presbyterian minister to leave Los Angeles in disgust, the *Star* lamented the "truly deplorable state of society." The village then had no Protestant church or minister, and it was a "case of destitution. . .without precedent in the state."[36] By the mid-1860's it was noted that "Protestants who die here, if they are not Masons, have to take their chances of having any religious ceremonies at their graves and so far as getting married, their only show is to employ a Judge or J.P."[37] These words appealed to only a minority of Los Angelenos, but the *Star* was tolerated because it fulfilled its basic function: to serve the interests of Southern California. Having to depend on Yankee journalists, the community had to accept the fact that Yankee assumptions would form a part of the news coverage.

The *Star* gave voice to a small faction of Los Angeles society which facilitated and supported basic changes in the structure of the life of the community. In the early 1850's, local government was an accurate reflection of the deferential nature of the culture. the *alcalde* system had been a method of giving official recognition to the prominent *rancheros* who held charismatic leadership.[38] In late 1850, a city government with a single mayor and a common council was adopted and a charter was drafted which made the town officials government functionaries rather than social leaders.[39] The community was still led by men such as Stearns, Bandini, Foster, and Pico, however. The new government had been achieved and continued to be maintained because the electoral system was both foreign and superfluous to the larger deferential community. All of the pleading of local officials, and all of the editorials of the *Star* could not halt the periodic committees of vigilance.[40] They were led, after all, not by ruffians but by the grand *rancheros*. It was not until the Chinese Massacre of 1871 that vigilantism came to an end in Los Angeles. Following an assault by a gang of Chinese on a local merchant in a disagreement over a debt, Los Angeles *gringos* formed a vigilance committee, and for the better part of an hour a battle ensued in which the vigilantes were victorious. Some elements of Los Angeles society, including the incipient Protestant community, considered the Chinese Massacre a sign of increasing violence in the town. Under Methodist leadership, the Law and Order Society was immediately formed for the purpose of securing professional law enforcement.[41]

Until the 1870's local offices were held by a collection of nondescript *gringos*. After that time merchants began to dominate the mayoral positions and the Common Council. Many of these men were involved in the Chamber of Commerce, and the town government was able to give active and effective support to the attempts to revise the economy of the area. With the increase of *gringo* migration, a greater proportion of the population participated in local elections. Various forms of association among the *gringos* gave evidence of the alternative structure of social organization which was incipient in the first two decades of the American period of Los Angeles history. Jews were an extremely small minority in the early years, but there may have been a *minyan* for services as early as 1851.[42] It was not until 1862 that a congregation was firmly established, however. In that year a fund-raising affair was held to collect funds for building a temple, and many non-Jewish *gringos* took an active part.[43] It was a social activity not unlike those experienced by migrants in their former communities to the east. Indeed, the affair may have been purely social for many of the Jewish participants. I. W. Hellman, president of the congregation in 1871, lamented, "I am sorry to see that the Jewish young men, who certainly should be the first to join kindred institutions, have so far not done it."[44]

There were many other forms of social organizations available to *gringos*, Jewish and Protestant, by the 1870's. Beginning in the early 1850's, newly arrived Americans formed local clubs and affiliates of national fraternal associations; a Masonic lodge was established in 1854, and an Odd Fellows unit was founded in the next year. The purely local clubs, such as the Mechanics Institute, the Young Men's Social Assembly, and the Harmony Club, all formed in 1857, were boarding house organizations whose constituents were young, single, and newly arrived. The fraternal social association was the norm among the *gringo* population until the 1870's. The last of these, the Los Angeles Social Club, was established in 1871. Ethnic divisions at this time were still of little importance. Commenting on the founding of the Club five decades later, Harris Newmark recalled an "early era of sympathy, tolerance, and good feeling, when the individual was appreciated at his true worth and before the advent of men whose bigotry has sown intolerance and discord."[46]

The societies founded during the 1870's and 1880's were more purposive. Some were economic organizations of new interests in the community, such as the Chamber of Commerce and the Southern California Farmer's Club, established in 1872, which became part of the Grange in 1874.[47] A few were professional associations, the most prominent of which were the Los Angeles County Medical Association (1870) and the Los Angeles Bar Association (1878).[48] Most were clubs for special interests. Among these were the Los Angeles Musical Association (1871), the Southern California Horticultural Society (1877), and the Owl Dramatic Club (1880).[49] A few were benevolent institutions, similar to the voluntaristic associations such as the Ladies' Benevolence Society and the Los Angeles Free Dispensary, both formed in 1877.[50]

The interest of the town government in civic betterment now had organized support. As early as 1867, a group of citizens formed a local corporation to establish reservoirs, but it was not until 1871 that more extensive (and expensive) projects were undertaken.[51] In September of that year, Fire Engine Company Number 1 was organized, and in three years four other companies had been established.[52] In 1872, a citizens' committee was appointed to raise funds by subscription and a plan a municipal library.[53] The work of the Los Angeles Free Dispensary was augmented in 1878 by the Los Angeles County Hospital and Almshouse.[54] In all cases, the citizens appointed to direct these civic organizations were recently arrived *gringos* primarily from states in the North-East and Mid-West.

Accompanying the Americanization of Los Angeles society and institutions was the beginning of residential segregation. The town had a higher percentage of the *gringo* population than the county as a whole and far greater than had been the case in the 1950's. Those Mexicans who lived in the town were concentrated primarily in the Santa Ana and San Jose Districts by the 1870's. The number of marriages between *gringos* and Mexicans declined sharply. Most of the influential and active merchants were recent arrivals in the town and had brought wives and families with them. They either located near settled *gringos* or began new residential areas themselves.

The residential segregation of the town was more than equalled by occupational differentiation. Few Mexicans are to be found among the merchant class, and the wealthiest farmers were all *gringos.* The most serious problem for the Mexican population, however, was unemployment. If the droughts had been disastrous for the large *rancheros,* they had been completely debilitating for the lesser sorts. Most of these who had owned land lost it, and those who had been part of the large labor force of the cattle empire were jobless and without the skills necessary for entry into the new and unfamiliar social order.[55] It was the Mexican population that made the greatest use of the new Almshouse.[56] Their culture had been replaced, the leaders of their society to whom deference was due were gone, and they had to turn to charitable associations they did not understand supported by a participatory society they could not enter.

III

Although Protestantism was undoubtedly an important element in the early organization of social life in the Old Northwest, it may be a mistake to assume that religion was a casual factor. In Los Angeles, those elements of American culture of which Protestantism was a part preceded the involvement of churches in community life to any significant degree. Rather than a new settlement peopled by fellow Americans with a common cultural background, early missionaries encountered, a "foreign" and indifferent population. Rather than either adapt to the established order or engage in prolonged evangelistic work to change it, the missionaries and the societies that sent them withdrew until Los Angeles had a configuration more conformable to the familiar pattern of American community life. American Protestantism was then prepared to establish churches for worship and the guidance of the moral, spiritual, and social life of the town.

By 1880, there were eleven Protestant churches in Los Angeles, all but two associated with the American Protestantism of the voluntary system. Of the nine, only two had been established before 1870, and the oldest was founded in 1865.[57] The First Presbyterian Church claimed 1855 as its organizing date, but there is nothing but denominational affiliation to link Wood's early congregation with the church founded in 1874.[58] In many ways, these churches entered into the community not as a missionary endeavors, but as one of many organized activities of the new social order. The Los Angeles *Star* in previous decades had placed the blame for lack of Protestant activity on the inhospitable nature of the community. In the 1870's, however, the newspaper became impatient with the indolence of the Protestants. Commenting on the newly completed Synagogue in 1873, a *Star* editorial declared that it was "indeed a handsome building." Turning to the Protestant churches, the newspaper exclaimed, "Their halls are rented affairs with benches! Look at the Episcopal nondescript affair! Do all these fine looking men and noble ladies—all our business people—feel no contrition, no sense of shame, as they walk up to these pitiful shanties?"[59]

Protestants responded to the challenge by hosting various fund-raising affairs which were supported by the community. Wood frame church buildings, similar to Mid-Western ecclesiastical architecture, which in turn were similar to New England meeting houses, began to appear in the late 1870's[60] These churches had not yet gained the central position of moral and spiritual leadership which they desired. Throughout the decade, the complaint of the first rector of St. Athanasuis Episcopal Church was repeated: "In our day people do not wish to be reminded to their faults. A minister to be popular in this place must be possessed of great eloquence, extensive learning, a handsome face, fine form, excellent teeth, small feet and hands, and possessed of no religion whatever." [61] The churches were being attended, however, and they would soon become something more in the community than one of the many associations and an alternative form of entertainment.

The rather rapid rise of the American Protestant churches in the life of the community in the subsequent two decades may have been facilitated by the establishment of denominational associations in the area. The Los Angeles churches quickly made contact with other congregations in Southern California. As early as 1853, entire congregations from the Mid-West began to establish communities around Los Angeles, and many of the newer small settlements in the county were Protestant colonies. El Monte was settled by a group of Illinois Baptists.[62] In 1869, a congregation of Iowa Methodists purchased part of the San Pedro Rancho and founded Compton as a dry community.[63] Another dry settlement was established by western Pennsylvania Presbyterians in 1871 as the colony of Westminster.[64] Promotional hand bills for the settlement announced that citizens of any Christian faith were welcome, but all settlers would be required to help build the Presbyterian church. To this was added the stipulation, "We want good, moral, church-going, Sabbath observing people."[65] The largest of these colonies was Pasadena, founded by Methodists and Presbyterians from Indiana in 1873. The town was, of course, dry.[66]

In 1870, Los Angeles was made a District of the California Conference of the Methodist Church, and six years later the Southern California Conference was organized with two districts, twenty-seven churches, twenty-three clergy, and 1,257 members. The Methodist Church, South, also had established a Southern California Conference by this time with 996 members.[67] The sister denominations cooperated with each other, and ministers frequently exchanged pulpits.[68] The Los Angeles Baptist Association was established in 1869 at the El Monte church.[69] A Baptist church had not yet been established in the town of

Los Angeles. The association had no real powers, but it did direct the founding of new congregations.[70] The Presbyterian and Congregational churches also formed local organizations. The Episcopal Church was still under the auspices of missionary boards, but plans were well underway by 1880 to establish a local diocese.

By 1880, Los Angeles had become an American community and the Protestant churches, with a greater sense of stability and familiarity with the new social order, were ready to assume a larger role in the life of the town. There was little doubt that it was to be a voluntaristic community. For many settlements in the Old Northwest, an important event in the solidification of the voluntary system had been the founding of a denominational college for the training of local clergy. On September 5, 1881, Southern California Protestants announced their new function in Los Angeles as guardians of the public ethos by laying the corner stone of the first building of the University of Southern California. Which Bishop I. W. Wiley of the Southern California Conference presiding, local Methodist worthies told their auditors and each other that the institution was like a seed that would become a giant Sequoia to provide academic and moral instruction of the youth, ministers for local churches, and intellectual guidance for the community.[71] Although a number of Protestant ministers had been interested in higher education in the area during the 1870's, the specific plan for the University of Southern California had been developed by two Methodists, one layman, and one cleric. Robert Maclay Widney, the Ohio-born local judge who had presided over the Law and Order Society of Los Angeles, who was instrumental in the founding of the Chamber of Commerce, and who was a organizer of the Los Angeles Bar Association, began thinking of a church-related school in the early 1870's. In 1875, the Reverend John R. Tansey, an elder associated with the Conference office had similar inclinations, and the two men had little difficulty convincing either the Conference or their fellow citizens to support the project. Three wealthy Los Angelenos, all former merchants involved in local real estate and banking, donated over 300 acres of land for the location of the campus and the continuing support of the University.[72]

The Articles of Foundation insured that the University would remain under Methodist control, and strongly recommended that first priority be given to Methodist ministers in filling the faculty.[73] The first instructional officers met these specifications. The Reverend Marion McKinley Bovard, native of Alpha, Indiana, was appointed President and elected to the Chair of Moral, Intellectual, and Natural Sciences. His brother, the Reverend Freeman D. Bovard, held the first Chair of Ancient Languages and Mathematics.[74] Precisely how the University was to guide the community remained unclear, but the academic and moral training of the young was provided through a fairly broad curriculum and a set of rules regulating most hours of the day and a wide variety of activities. Daily chapel services were compulsory.[75] The rules prohibited a catalogue of the more objectionable sins, including tobacco and liquor. In order to protect the student from harm, and keep him from mischievous activities, the University did not tolerate absence from dormitory rooms at night "except to attend the sick."[76]

The founding of the University of Southern California had importance for Los Angelenos in general and Protestants in particular. All local newspapers announced in rather exaggerated exclamations that the town had arrived. "Los Angeles now rivals Berkeley as a center of education. It will soon rival San Francisco as a center of commerce."[77] The University was not seen as a sectarian achievement by most citizens, but as another example of the growth of Los Angeles through community action. The fact that the land had been donated by three men, none of whom were Methodist, was symbolic of the tolerant cooperation characteristic of the 1870's. Orzo W. Childs, a native of Vermont and an Episcopalian, John G. Downey, Irish and Catholic, and Isaias W. Hellman, a German Jew, had banded together to aid in other community projects. In many ways, they considered the University the capstone.[78]

For the Protestant community, however, the laying of the corner stone held greater significance. "The work begun by that great hero for the faith, James Woods," said the Reverend John W. Ellis of the First Presbyterian Church, "may now continue. The day of prayerful preparation is over. Our Methodist brothers have taken the first steps in the wider Work to which we are called as Christians."[79] Other sermons indicated that the University would provide a common meeting ground for the formation of Temperance, Benevolence, and Tract societies.[80] It would be an overstatement to suggest that the founding of the University was the end of the pre-Protestant period and the beginning of voluntaristic Los Angeles. It does have some symbolic importance, however. It was built in the manner most familiar to the townsmen. To non-Protestant citizens it did not seem unlike founding a social organization, helping build a synagogue or church, or organizing a Chamber of Commerce. It was quite different, however, for it reminded Protestants of their mission in the community. Not for reasons of bigotry or exclusivity, but because this mission was beginning to be realized, very few Jews or Catholics would be asked to share equally in any civic task of this dimension during the next forty years.

There were other symbols throughout the 1870's: the shift from social to service organizations, the increasing reporting of Protestant sermons in the local press, and the construction of permanent Protestant church structures. These were signs of rapid change in a hectic decade, which was part of a more basic transformation between 1850 and 1880. The Mexican community had become so powerless and insignificant that no public event took the decline of the *Californios* into account. One private and atypical act gave mute testimony to thirty years of historical development. On July 15, 1878, Arcadia Stearns, daughter of Don Juan Bandini, widow of the great *ranchero* Don Abel Stearns, and primary benefactor to California convents from 1845 to 1869, became a Protestant and married Robert S. Baker, a Baptist merchant from Rhode Island.[81]

NOTES

[1] United States Census Office, *Census Reports: Statistics of the Population of the United States at the Tenth Census* (Washington, 1883), p. 107.

[2] See Appendix IV for a summary of changing land usage in Los Angeles.

[3] "Farm and Orchard Lands, 1850," Archives of the Common Council, City of Los Angeles, Office of the City Clerk, City Hall, Los Angeles, California; United States Census Office, *Census Reports: Report on the Statistics of the Production of Agriculture at the Tenth Census* (Washington, 1883) pp. 287-293.

[4] Based on a comparison of the location of farms listed in *Los Angeles City Directory, 1880*, and the reconstruction of the 1850 land usage summarized in Appendix IV.

[5] Juan Temple to Abel Stearns, November 10, 19, 22, December 25, 1857, Stearns MSS.

[6] Pitt, p. 109.

7 Cleland, *Cattle on a Thousand Hills*, pp. 102-116.

[8] Los Angeles *Star*, April 27, July 20, August 3, 1861.

[9] United States Census Office, *Census Reports: Statistics of the Wealth and Industry of the United States at the Ninth Census* (Washington, 1873), pp. 89-91.

[10] Pitt, p. 251.

[11] Cleland, p. 207.

[12] *Ibid.*, pp. 208-233.

[13] Fogelson, pp. 46-51.

[14] *Ibid.*, pp. 53-54.

[15] Los Angeles *Daily News*, September 5, 8, 13, 14, 1872; R. N. Widney, *Los Angeles County Subsidy, Which Subsidy Shall I Vote for—or—Shall I Vote Against Both? Discussed From a Business Standpoint for the Business Community* (Los Angeles, 1872), Fogelson, pp. 52-56.

[16] Cleland, p. 121.

[17] Farm and Orchard Lands, 1860" - "*Ibid.*, 1869, "Archives of the Common Council.

[18] "*Ibid.*, 1867," - "*Ibid.*, 1871."

[19] United States Census Office, *Census Reports: Statistics of the Wealth and Industry of the United States at the Tenth Census* (Washington, 1883), p. 418; *Los Angeles City Directory, 1880, passim.*

[20] *An Historical Sketch of Los Angeles County, California* (Los Angeles, 1876), p.145.

[21] *Ibid.*, p. 146.

[22] *Ibid.*

[23] Los Angeles *Daily News,* August 1, 1873; Marco R. Newmark, "A Short History of the Los Angeles Chamber of Commerce," HSSCO XXVII (June, 1945), 57.

[24] *Ibid.*, p. 62.

[25] Cleland, p. 207.

[26] Newmark, "A Short History of the Los Angeles Chamber of Commerce," 68.

[27] Stearns to Juan Temple, January 17, 1850, Stearns MSS. Stearns was echoing the words of a correspondent on this subject, Alexander W. Hope to Stearns, December 22, 1849, Stearns MSS.

[28] *Daily Alta California,* February 10, 1851.

[29] Declaration of a Convention to Divide the State of California, Los Angeles, November 10, 1851," Henry E. Huntington Library, San Marino, California.

[30] *Ibid.*

[31] William B. Rice, *The Los Angeles Star, 1851-1864: The Beginnings of Journalism in Southern California,* ed. John Walton Caughey, (New York, 1947), p.14.

[32] *Ibid.*, p. 17.

[33] Los Angeles *Star,* July 23, 1851.

[34] Rice, *The Los Angeles Star,* pp. 46-47.

[35] Los Angeles *Star,* March 26, 1853.

[36] Los Angeles *Star,* February 2, 1856.

[37] *Ibid.*, May 30, 1864.

[38] Pitt, p. 276.

[39] Articles of Incorporation, 1850," Archives of the Common Council, City of Los Angeles.

[40] See Pitt, pp. 231-271; Bell, *On the Old West Coast,* pp. 164-180.

[41] Los Angeles *Star,* October 1, 1871; Marco R. Newmark, "Calle de los Negros and the Chinese Massacre of 1871," HSSCO XXVI (June-September, 1944), 97-98.

[42] Vorspan and Gartner, p. 18.

[43] *Ibid.,* p. 57.

[44] Los Angeles *Star,* August 19, 1871.

[45] *History of Los Angeles County, California* (Oakland, 1880), pp. 106-129.

[46] Newmark, *Sixty Years,* p. 383.

[47] *History of Los Angeles County,* p. 117.

[48] *Ibid.,* pp. 122-123.

[49] *Ibid.,* p. 120.

[50] *Ibid.,* p. 129.

[51] *Ibid.,* p. 107.

[52] *Ibid.,* p. 110.

[53] Los Angeles *Daily News,* March 7-16, 1872.

[54] *History of Los Angeles County,* p. 129.

[55] Pitt, p. 211.

[56] "Miscellaneous Records: Los Angeles County Almshouse." Special Collections, University of California, Los Angeles.

[57] *History of Los Angeles County,* pp. 119-121. There was one Unitarian and on Christian Science Church. The Unitarians were later included in many of the cooperative Protestant activities.

[58] *Ibid.* p. 120.

[59] Los Angeles Star, July 23, 1873.

[60] On the traditionalism of mid-western church architecture in the early nineteenth century, see Rexford Newcomb, *Architecture of the Old Northwest Territory* (Chicago, 1950).

[61] Los Angeles *Semi-Weekly News,* February 20, 1869.

[62] Newmark, "The Story of Religion in Los Angeles," 41.

[63] *Ibid.,* 45.

[64] *Ibid.,* 47; Manes Main Dixon, "A Presbyterian Settlement in Southern California," HSSCO X (1915-1917), 43-45.

[65] "Westminister Church Papers, 1871-1890," Library, San Francisco Theological Seminary, San Anselmo, California.

[66]Ostrander, p. 70.

[67]Rist, p. 457.

[68]*Ibid.,* p. 458.

[69]Leland D. Hind, *Baptists in Southern California* (Valley Forge, Pennsylvania, 1966), p. 31.

[70]*Minutes of the Los Angeles Baptist Association, 1869-1880.*

[71]Los Angeles *Daily Herald,* September 6, 1880.

[72]Manual P. Servin and Iris Higbe Wilson, *Southern California and Its University* (Los Angeles, 1969), pp. 3-4; Edward Drewry Jervey, "The Methodist Church and the University of Southern California," HSSCQ XL (March, 1958), 58; Leslie F. Gay, Jr., "The Founding of the University of Southern California," HSSCQ VII (1909-1910), 37-50.

[73]"Articles of Foundation of the University of Southern California, 1880," Archives of the University of Southern.

[74]Servin and Wilson, p. 5.

[75]"Articles of Foundation. . ."

[76]This phrase was deleted in 1887, apparently because there seemed to be too many "sick" that needed attending: Los Angeles *Times,* October 7, 1887.

[77]Los Angeles *Daily News,* September 15, 1880.

[78]See Vorspan and Gartner, p. 71.

[79]Los Angeles *Daily News,* October 3, 1880.

[80]*Ibid.,* September 6–November 4, 1880.

[81]*Ibid.,* July 16, 1878.

CHAPTER 3

A CITY OF CHURCHES

I

In September of 1881, a group of transplanted Easterners and Mid-Westerners, most of whom had been in the community for less than a decade, celebrated the centennial of the founding of Los Angeles. Like the festivities attending the one-hundredth anniversary of the signing of the Declaration of Independence five years before, the promise of the future rather than the glories of the past was the keynote of the day. The local citrus industry seemed destined to become at least as successful as the cattle ranches of the 1850's.[1] Plans were under way to introduce electric lighting and the telephone in the city, and local commerce, stimulated by the Southern Pacific Railroad, was expanding.[2] The many speeches delivered for the occasion made it clear that the "sleepy Spanish village" had been awakened by the migration of Americans. The contrast between the Mexican pueblo and the American town was constantly emphasized, and one orator went so far as to claim that the Centennial was in reality a "second founding of Los Angeles—a more prosperous, dynamic, and virtuous city."[3]

In a commemorative edition of the Los Angeles *Times*, the lead article named Los Angeles "A City of Churches."[4] The title was appropriate. For seven decades it had been a community of one church, both figuratively and literally. By 1882, the Roman Catholic Church was only one of seven denominations and comprised only two-fifths of the churchgoing population. To some, the change in the religious structure of the city signaled a better future for the community. Los Angeles was "rapidly developing into a highly moral town," declared a *Times* editorial, "from which it must perforce be inferred that its character had not hitherto been above suspicion."[5] The new Protestant elements made a deliberate effort to make Los Angeles their community. The most obvious method was through overt action; there were more subtle forms, however. The church building activity in the 1880's and earl 1890's was hardly less intense than the land speculation boom that accompanied it. Traditional voluntaristic organizations and church-related schools were founded. Other organizations with less formal ties to the Protestant community, but none-the-less Protestant in ethos and constituency, proliferated in late nineteenth-century Los Angeles.

The incipient tendencies of the 1870's were rapidly escalated between 1880 and the mid-1890's in such a way that to many national churchmen, the city at the turn of the century was an ideal Protestant community. The usual explanation for the "Protestantization" of Los Angeles is the migration of Mid-Western Americans in the late nineteenth century.[6] Certainly, there was such a migration, and the increased Protestant strength was a product of this migration. The population statistics are useful in explaining the presence of Protestant activity, but they do not explain the fervor with which the new Los Angelenos remade a community. Changes in the relation between community and religion in areas east of the Rockies from which these Protestants came help clarify the concept of community that Los Angeles Protestants held.

TABLE 11

RESIDENTS OF LOS ANGELES BY NATIVITY
1880-1900
(IN PERCENTAGES)

Region	1880	1890	1900
Pacific	31.3	32.5	35.1
Mid-West	32.4	34.0	35.5
Mid-Atlantic	12.2	12.4	11.3
Other	24.1	21.1	18.1

NOTE: This table is limited to the Native American Population. The Foreign-Born Population reached its pre-1940 zenith in 1890, 22%, and declined steadily thereafter. The Mid-Western influence was greater than indicated by the figures. By 1890 and 1900, a significant proportion of those born in the Pacific region were of Mid-Western parentage.

Source: U.S. Bureau of the Census, Tenth Census, 1880, Enumerator's Rollbook, Los Angeles County; U.S. Census Office, *Report on Population of the United States at the Eleventh Census: 1890. Part I* (Washington, 1895), pp. 580-583. U. S. Census Office, *Census Reports. Volume I. Twelfth Census of the United States: 1900. Population. Part I* (Washington, 1901), pp. 706-709.

II

The reasons why people in nineteenth-century America moved from one place to another are varied and complex, but most students of migration have found economic motivation of primary importance.[7] In late nineteenth-century Los Angeles there were a few individuals who migrated to the area for religious reasons, a few more who migrated for a combination of economic and religious motives, but most fit the standard pattern of economic motivation.[8] There were definite economic advantages to be gained by moving to Southern California in the late nineteenth century, especially during the "Boom Decade" of the 1880's.[9] Protestant migrants to Los Angeles, however, rapidly realized an opportunity to build a community which would perpetuate American Protestantism based on the voluntaristic system which was declining in communities to the east.

The fading of voluntarism was only one of many factors associated with basic changes in American Protestantism during the last quarter of the nineteenth century. There had, of course, been constant change since the founding of the Republic, and revivalism and reform movements occurred with fairly constant regularity.[10] They most often took place within the context of the voluntaristic system, however, and various regional anomalies, such as Mormonism and the Oneida experiment, were associated with more basic changes in the social and economic structure occasioned, for example, by the introduction of non-local forces such as the trade expansion through canal construction.[11] The dynamics of American Protestantism at the end of the century reflected a response to the development of national structures rather than regional mutations and shifted the context from voluntaristic communities to religious bureaucracies.

American Protestantism had roots which were rural, but it had become an important part of the differential structure of town and city life. The late nineteenth century brought new elements in population and institutions which altered the context of church life. Industrialization, the beginnings of the corporation, and the introduction of greater numbers of primarily non-Protestant immigrants required many churchmen to reassess the role of their organizations in community life. Unlike Beecher earlier in the century, men such as William T. Stead and Charles Loring Brace were required to adapt the churches to a new social reality rather than seek alternative avenues of perpetuating the centrality of religious organization in community life.[12] Social criticism, which had been relatively absent from religious discussion for two decades following the Civil War, formed an important element in Protestant apologetics by the 1880's. The rhetoric deplored the sorry state of society and criticized the churches for their lack of responsiveness to the changing conditions.[13] Intellectual responses ranged from a defense of the passing deferential society to Social Christianity, but it was rare to find a cleric who did not take the social dynamics into account.[14]

Institutional responses also varied. Established voluntaristic associations shifted their emphases from extending the concept of cohesive community across the nation to strengthening the status of Protestantism in other areas that had at one time been the bulwark of their movements. The New York Mission and Tract Society, for example, began a program of missionary activity among the laboring class in that city in the late 1870's.[15] In 1883, the American Home Missionary Society, which had been all but exclusively concerned with the "old-stock" population since its founding, organized German, Scandinavian, and Slavic departments to minister to the needs of immigrant populations in Eastern and Mid-Western cities.[16]

The greatest amount of Protestant activity in the late nineteenth century was not found in the older voluntaristic associations, however, but in new interdenominational organizations and denominational agencies. Some were openly reactionary, such as the American Protective Association, founded in Clinton, Iowa in 1887. The APA associated the urban political machines and general social upheaval with Catholic immigration and sought to stem the tide of population flow as well as contain the imaged power of the Roman Catholic hierarchy in government.[17] Although the anti-Catholic bias in American Protestantism in general should not be discounted, most of the new organizations expressed less paranoia and chose to direct their energies through social action The most prominent form of organization was the Institutional Church, such as the DeWitt Memorial or the Episcopal Church of St. George, both in New York City. These parishes were neither regular congregations nor missions, but an attempt to provide a variety of religious and social services in labor neighborhoods.[18]

Although limited to a small minority of churchmen, national organizations formed to extend American Protestantism to sectors of the population which had long been neglected gained the greatest attention. General public debate attended the establishment in 1887 of the Church Organization for the Advancement of the Interests of Labor by a group of Episcopal clergymen.[19] The controversy had not subsided when the issue was given added impetus by the organization of the Society of Christian Scientists in 1889. The purpose of the Society, according to its founder, W. D. P. Bliss of Grace Church in Boston, was to "awaken the members of the Christian Churches to the fact that the teachings of Jesus Christ lead directly to some specific form or forms of Socialism."[20] Denominational agencies established for similar purposes exercised greater restraint in the use of radical rhetoric, but they also were attempts to expand the constituency of American Protestantism. In 1891, the Congregational Church formed a Labor Committee, and the following year the labor-based Brotherhood of the Kingdom was established by

Baptist clergymen.[21] In 1894, individual congregations and more general organizations and agencies formed the Open and Institutional Church League.[22] By the turn of the century, all denominations associated with American Protestantism had created similar agencies.[23]

Institutional innovation was only one manifestation of the American Protestants' response to the changing society. While the churches as organizations were attempting to expand and diversify their constituencies, "old-stock" Protestants expressed their cohesion through extra-ecclesiastical structures. Some satisfied their desire for homogeneity by forming ancestral organizations, such as the Daughters of the American Revolution. The more affluent found temporary communities of cohesion through summer resorts, country clubs, and boarding schools. Others established a more permanent solution by moving to the suburbs, which, while never independent of the larger and more diverse society, provided residential cohesion.[24]

By 1890, almost one-half of the population of Los Angeles had migrated from states that were experiencing these basic changes. Over one quarter of the city's population were from seven states where tension between congregations and denominational agencies often took the form of bitter debate, reflective of a more general conflict between local exclusivism and national diversification.[25]

TABLE 12

NATIVITY OF LOS ANGELES RESIDENTS BY SELECTED STATES
1880-1900
(IN PERCENTAGES)

State	1880	1890	1900
New York	5.4	5.9	5.7
Ohio	4.8	5.1	5.3
Illinois	4.7	5.2	5.1
Missouri	3.8	3.3	3.2
Iowa	3.1	3.0	3.3
Pennsylvania	2.3	3.0	2.8
Indiana	.5	2.6	3.1
Total	24.6	28.1	28.5

Source: See Table 11.

Aside from the economic advantage to moving to Southern California, and perhaps the lure of the climate, it is impossible, with the lack of detailed biographical data on the thousands of migrants, to formulate the tempting hypothesis that Easterners and Mid-Westerners left their homes out of a frustrated desire for voluntaristic cohesion.[26] Once in Los Angeles, however, such a community was realized. 'Los Angeles as a reconstruction of a Mid-Western town has become a cliche, and one that received support from Los Angelenos themselves. One of the most prominent members of the community remembered the city in the late nineteenth century as a collection of "Good Templars from Sedalia; honest Spinsters from Grundy Center. . .the middle-aged from the middle class of the middle west."[27] Toward the end of the 1880's, the famous Iowa picnics attracted hundreds of Mid-Westerners, and by the end of the century thousands were in attendance.[28] The migrants rapidly formed a community and made every effort to keep it from becoming similar to the diversified and changing communities they left. In 1886, Harrison Gray Otis of the Los Angeles *Times* listed the social types who were not welcome in the city: "Dudes, loafers, paupers, those afraid to pull off their coats, cheap politicians, business scrubs, improprietous clerks, lawyers, and doctors."[29]

The town which only three decades before could not keep ministers for more than a few months was now faced with the possibility of an oversupply. Some clergymen followed their former parishioners to Los Angeles, but William Stewart Young, a Presbyterian minister, suspected unholy motives on the part of some clerics. "He is sending some excellent workers into His vineyard," wrote Young, "but it must be whispered here, just now there seems to be an unusually large number of preachers willing to sacrifice for the Lord in this climate."[30] For whatever reasons, churches had no difficulty filling their pulpits. Stable congregations and local denominational institutions, the central agencies of the voluntaristic system, could now be built.

III

The Los Angeles *Times* made the first estimation of the religious population of the city in 1882. It was determined that approximately 2,140 citizens of the community were church members, or roughly nineteen percent of the local population.[31] Eight years later the city had almost quintupled in size, and the religious population increased by more than six hundred percent, to the benefit of the American Protestant churches. By the turn of the century, over forty percent of Los Angelenos were church members, and the voluntaristic Protestant increase was the most impressive.

The infusion of population from the Mid-West and Mid-Atlantic states and the growth of the Protestant churches were highly related. By 1890, over half of the membership of the fourteen congregations for whom records remain consisted of recent migrants. Most of these migrated as families, but a few came as factions of former congregations in the Mid-West. In 1887, for example, a bank of thirty-one former members of the Second Baptist Church of Des Moines, Iowa, left their community for Los Angeles. They felt "a great yearning for a Christian experience free from the turmoil of these bitter days."[32] The immediate cause of their alienation from the congregation seems to have been

TABLE 13

RELIGIOUS MEMBERSHIP IN LOS ANGELES
AS PERCENTAGE OF THE TOTAL POPULATION
1882-1890

Denomination	1882	1890	1900
All Voluntaristic	7.4	12.5	17.6
Roman Catholic	17.7	17.3	17.2
Other	4.5	6.2	6.4
Total	39.6	36.0	41.2

Source: See Appendix I. The 1882 estimates are from the Los Angeles *Times*, June 14, 1882.

the decision by the Second Baptist Church to support Institutional Church experimentation in Des Moines. After a detailed search for a new congregation, and eventually a new community, the group decided to move to Los Angeles and become members of the First Baptist Church in that city. They had been impressed with the assurances from the Deacons of that congregation that "the Christian life, supported by uncompromising Christian doctrine, is of greatest importance to our church, and promises to be the guiding principle of this city."[33]

Congregations in Los Angeles were still actively involved in founding local churches and constructing buildings in the 1880's, but a loose federation of cooperation between the American Protestant denominations emerged almost immediately. The First Baptist Church, for example, completed

TABLE 14

NATIVITY OF MEMBERS OF VOLUNTARISTIC PROTESTANT CHURCHES, LOS ANGELES: 1890-1900 (IN PERCENTAGES)

State	1890	1900
New York	11.3	11.0
Ohio	10.9	11.1
Illinois	18.6	17.3
Missouri	5.1	5.4
Iowa	12.3	12.5
Pennsylvania	9.4	7.9
Indiana	14.5	16.5
Other	17.9	18.3

Source: See Appendix I.

its building in April of 1884, and in the following month invited representatives of local Presbyterian, Methodist, Episcopal, and Congregational churches to a "Meeting to share in prayerful discussion of common purposes in this vineyard."[34]   All invited congregations sent representatives who seem to have been satisfied with the constituency of the meeting, but Roger W. Elsworth, a young Congregational minister, suggested that other denominations be invited in the future.   The proposal was immediately dismissed without discussion by the assembly.[35]   Other denominations in Los Angeles, such as the Unitarians and Lutherans, made few attempts to enter into the corporate activity of the American Protestant churches.   The Lutherans remained fairly isolated for the next four decades, but the Unitarians made some attempt to construct alternative structures of religious cooperation. The First Unitarian Church hosted an interfaith Thanksgiving Day service in 1886 to which members and clergy of all congregations of all denominations in the city were invited. Only the more liberal clergy of the Congregational Church and Rabbi Emanuel Schreiber of the local Jewish community attended, however.[36]   To emphasize the broader concept of religious cohesion expressed by the service, Dr. William Fay, pastor of the host church, remarked, "Dr. Schreiber's pulpit cap may be square and flat at the top and mine may be oval and round at the top, but the people are beginning to see and feel that the form of our caps is not the invention of God."[37]

Fay's hopeful prognosis for a more flexible and inclusive concept of religious community in Los Angeles proved to be quite inaccurate. Perhaps because the members of their congregations migrated from areas where their traditional assumptions of social organization were being seriously questioned, the American Protestant denominations of Los Angeles had no desire to extend the parameters of the voluntaristic community. These denominations held their own cooperative Thanksgiving service in 1886 at St. Athanasius' Episcopal Church. Although the gathering at the Unitarian Church on the same day had, in theory, a broader constituency, the voluntaristic Protestant service was attended by almost five times as many worshippers, and represented more denominations.[38] The numerical strength of the American Protestant churches allowed them to practice their principle of homogeneity.

The First Baptist Church of Los Angeles became the primary agent of American Protestant activity in the 1880's. Most of the cooperative meetings and worship services were held there, and the congregation gave generously to Presbyterian, Methodist, Episcopal, and Congregational groups as well as to fellow Baptists, to aid in the construction of new church buildings.[39] In 1887, an assistant pastor, A. W. Rider from Ohio, was appointed by the First Baptist Church, and among his duties was the coordination of interdenominational activities.[40]

Just as the ecumenical activities of the First Baptist Church emphasized homogeneity and exclusivity, the congregational life of the church was concerned primarily with the communal life of the parishioners and the homogeneity of religious ideology. As early as 1875, the congregation required a Reaffirmation of Covenant from prospective members to insure "the purity of faith," and the practice was continued until the end of the century.[41] On a few occasions, individuals were excluded from the congregation for "unscriptural views." Ironically, five of the migrants from the Des Moines Baptist Church were denied membership in the congregation for this reason. Prayer meetings, held once a week, provided an expression of religious community beyond the Sunday worship services, and during the 1880's and 1890's, at least one-third of the congregation was always in attendance.[42] Other Baptist churches in the Los Angeles area also experienced relatively high participation in prayer meetings.[43]

The voluntaristic denominations expressed congregational cohesion in a variety of ways. In 1889, the Southern California

Conference of the Methodist Episcopal Church, North, organized a regional committee for the Epworth League and encouraged local congregations to establish affiliates.[44] The League, organized to serve the youth of the church, became an important part of Los Angeles Methodism by 1894. In that year, the First Methodist Church of Los Angeles instituted the Epworth Guards to lead the teenaged boys in the congregations "through the drill and practice of soldiering for the Prince of Peace."[45] A few Congregational churches organized similar organizations in the early 1890's.[46]

The establishment of a local diocese accounted for most of the activity in the congregations of the Protestant Episcopal Church between 1880 and 1895. A division of the Diocese of California had been suggested as early as 1871, and the General Convention (the national assembly of the Protestant Episcopal Church) created four Convocations in California in 1877. The Convocation of Southern California first met in 1883, under the direction of Dean A. G. H. Trew, who made it clear that he and other clerics considered the assembly "an incipient Diocese."[47] Many laymen were also anxious to have a local bishop more clearly responsive to the needs of Los Angeles and Southern California. The Churches of St. Athanasius and St. James in Los Angeles petitioned the Diocese of California for permission to bring the matter before the General Convention in 1888. They complained that the San Francisco-based bishopric "though certainly guided by the spirit of Christ, has demonstrated a greater concern for the plight of our fellow churchmen in those places of spiritual unrest than for the Christian and Ecclesiastical needs of Southern California."[48] As early as 1884, the Bishop of California began supporting Institutional Churches in the East, and by 1886, a labor-based parish in San Francisco was established.[49] Los Angeles Episcopalians were convinced that their share of diocesan funds could be spent more effectively for their own needs. A few laymen sent letters in support of the petition for separation to the Bishop of California which suggested that the needs of the northern city were more similar to those of industrial cities in the East than to Los Angeles. George Hills, an attorney and vestryman, of St. Athanasius, praised the Diocese for innovative action in the context of the condition of San Francisco, but stressed the necessity for the church in Los Angeles to establish its own program.[50]

In 1888, the General Convention established a committee to consider the creation of a Southern California bishopric. The following year the Diocese of California was directed to propose a plan for its own division.[51] The major problem facing Los Angeles Episcopalians was the selection of a Bishop who would serve the local interests of the religious community and who would also be acceptable to the General Convention—a rather difficult task. The bureaucratization of religious institutions had a more profound effect on the Episcopal Church than on other voluntaristic Protestant denominations. The control of the consecration of bishops had always been in the hands of the General Convention, but in the late nineteenth century this organization became more sensitive to the national implications of the selection of bishops. In 1886, the General Convention adopted a policy statement which declared, "The Protestant Episcopal Church in the United States of America is a national Province. Our Bishops, whether ruling, Suffragan, or Coadjutor, are prelates of the national church as well as the regional dioceses."[52]

Trew and a committee of laymen, all from Los Angeles, conducted an extensive search and finally settled on the Rev. Joseph H. Johnson, rector of Christ Church in Detroit, Michigan.[53] Johnson had previously filled pastorates in New York State, and had been on a number of committees of the General Convention; therefore he had a national reputation. After a detailed correspondence with Johnson and a personal interview at the 1895 meeting of the General Convention, the Trew committee felt that Johnson would be able to fill the needs of Southern California Episcopalians and satisfy the requisites of the national church.[54] A few local clergymen were also nominated at the diocesan convention in January of 1896, but Johnson was elected Bishop on the first ballot. On May 26, 1896, the Rt. Rev. William F. Nichols, Bishop of California, and three other prelates of the Protestant Episcopal Church consecrated Johnson as the Bishop of the Diocese of Los Angeles in St. Paul's Church. Johnson had chosen St. Paul's as the Cathedral Church, he explained in his inaugural sermon, because he had been ordained as a priest in a Cathedral of that name, and because St. Paul had best captured the sense of commitment that he brought to his priesthood and to his new role as prelate. "St. Paul instructed us to be all things to all men. At all times I am mindful of the Church Universal, but I have served my parishes as a citizen of Westchester, New York, and Detroit, Michigan. It is in this spirit that I will serve you as Bishop of Los Angeles."[55] During the early years of his Episcopate, Bishop Johnson concentrated his energies almost exclusively on matters concerning the Diocese.

The Presbyterian Church in Los Angeles also concerned itself with the establishment of an institution in the late nineteenth century. The Presbytery of Los Angeles had already been formed, and San Francisco Theological Seminary was established by the General Assembly to train ministers for the West Coast.[56] A few clergymen and laymen, however, felt that it would be advantageous to build a denominational college in Los Angeles to prepare young men for seminary, and the Presbytery began investigating this possibility in 1882. The report of the Committee on Higher Education gratefully recognized the efforts of the Methodist Church to "provide all Protestants with a Christian University," but expressed the sentiment that "The Kingdom of Christ can only be strengthened by a variety of colleges sharing the same Christian concerns."[57]   On a more practical level, the report cited the advantage of "providing a Christian education for those young men in our community who may be fortunate enough to receive the Call to the Lord's Work."[58]   William Stewart Young, Chairman of the Committee, privately expressed the hope that "a Presbyterian college in Los Angeles might provide us with future clergymen from our own community. We should not have to depend on ministers who see our town as a retreat from less desirable places."[59]

Young was the moving force behind the establishment of a denominational college and most of Presbyterian activity in general in the late nineteenth century Los Angeles. Born in Pennsylvania, and a graduate of Union Theological Seminary in New York, Young held his first pastorate in Portland, Oregon, in 1883. A year later he was called to the First Presbyterian Church of Los Angeles.[60] He was immediately impressed by the Christian character of the community. In other parts of the West, the city still had a reputation as a rough and violent society. Young came to the City of Angels with such prejudices and worked to correct the image.   "Every now and then somebody with more imagination than knowledge, tells you the name means *lost angels*. Not so," he informed his fellow Presbyterians, "It is the rendezvous for angles, but the lost ones are some place else—farther down."[61] He found Los Angeles esthetically as well as spiritually pleasing and claimed that the town was located "between the East and Heaven."[62] His enthusiam for the community and his tireless activities in the Presbytery led to his election, in 1892, to the position of Stated Clerk of the Presbytery of Los Angeles.[63] Until his retirement in 1934, Young continued to hold positions of prestige in the Presbytery and Synod.

Young's proprietary interest in maintaining local control over ecclesiastical institutions can be clearly seen in the founding of Occidental College. Responding to the desire of the Presbytery of Los Angeles for a denominational college, the Synod of the Pacific established Sierra Madre College in South Pasadena in 1884.[64] The Board of Trustees included only one Southern Californian, however, and the Presbytery's Committee on Higher Education refused to support the new school. In a report of the committee, Young referred to Sierra

Madre as "the Southern extension of the San Francisco Theological Seminary."[65] The Young committee launched a campaign to enlist the support of other voluntaristic Protestant denominations in Los Angeles to build an institution that would be as much a part of the community as a part of the network of Presbyterian schools across the nation. The University of Southern California had been built by representatives of a broadly defined American community. Occidental was founded by representatives of the new voluntaristic community. On April 29, 1887, Occidental University opened its doors to the first class, and the Board of Trustees consisted of three clergymen and seven laymen, all from the Presbyterian, Methodist, Baptist, Episcopal, and Congregational churches, and all residents of Southern California.[66]

All Presbyterian congregations in the city, and a few churches of the other voluntaristic Protestant denominations, held suppers, bake sales, bazaars, and special collections to raise funds for the new school.[67] The University of Southern California offered support in building the library.[68] It is unclear whether Young and other foresaw a larger educational institution in the future offering a wider variety of courses indicated by the title "University," but the name was changed to Occidental College in 1892, at the suggestion of E. C. Roy, Secretary to the College Board of the General Assembly. Roy accentuated the benefits of "a small Christian Liberal Arts College, which seems best to describe Occidental."[69] Although the difference in size and course offerings between the University of Southern California and Occidental College at this time were negligible, Los Angeles clergymen and prominent laymen congratulated each other for having created two institutions which served "different but mutual purposes for the Kingdom of Christ and the City of Los Angeles."[70]

Each denomination in the late nineteenth century, therefore, had specific programs around which congregational life could be built. None became isolated from the others, however. The Presbyterians actively enlisted the support of other denominations. The Trew committee for establishing a local Episcopal Diocese was constantly in contact with leaders of the other four denominations to determine areas of cooperation.[71] The Epworth League of the Methodist Church provided a youth organization that was attended by members of the other denominations.[72] Congregationalists had few programs within their own denominations, but were active in the foundation of the Epworth League and Occidental College. The Baptists' quest for doctrinal purity could have made them the most peculiaristic of the voluntaristic denominations in Los Angeles, but they emerged as leaders in interdenominational activity. As new religious elements were added to the city, they either expressed no desire to enter into the voluntaristic community or were never offered an invitation.   The one exception was the Disciples of Christ, which appeared in Los Angeles in 1891.[73]

References to the interdenominational nature of many congregational activities can be found in the letters and memoirs of church members during this period. A more precise measure, but one that does not capture the full extent of voluntaristic Protestant cooperation, is the practice of pulpit exchanges. The Congregationalists, who seem to have been the least active members of the voluntaristic community, provided some of the most popular pulpit orators who were frequently invited to preach in other churches.   Indeed, two Congregational ministers, C. J. Hutchins and A. J. Wells, were invited to fill the pulpits of other denominations more often than all other clergymen in late nineteenth-century Los Angeles together. The pattern of pulpit exchanges between 1880 and 1895 clearly demonstrates the integral nature of American Protestantism.

In addition to these various programs which intensified the community life of the voluntaristic denominations, new churches were being built. By 1895, the Baptist Church had nine congregations in Los Angeles, five Presbyterian and four Congregational churches had been built, seven Episcopal parishes had been established, and two new Disciples of Christ church were erected.[74] Most often the establishment of new congregations resulted from the migration of church members to Los Angeles.   From the records that remain for six voluntaristic congregations, it seems likely that the migration also accounted for the growth of established parishes. It also would seem that ex-members of churches in the East most often joined churches of the same denomination in Los Angeles in the late nineteenth century.   This general pattern persisted until the second decade of the twentieth century.   (See Appendix I.)

TABLE 15

PULPIT EXCHANGES IN LOS ANGELES
1880-1895

	Baptist	Congre-gational	Episcopal	Methodist	Presby-terian	Other
Baptist	-					
Congregational	42	-				
Episcopal	9	13	-			
Methodist	31	17	7	-		
Presbyterian	28	21	11	24	-	
Other	0	3	0	0	0	6

Source: Reports of pulpit exchanges in the Los Angeles
Daily News, and the Los Angeles Times, and the records of
various congregations: See Appendix I.

In two cases new congregations were created by dividing an established church which had grown too large. There was general agreement among the voluntaristic Protestant denominations that no congregation should be larger than four hundred communicant members. In 1889, the Congregational Association of Los Angeles suggested a division of the First Congregational Church.[75] The congregation refused to act on the suggestion, and the Association funded the creation of a new parish and requested the First Church to accept no new members. The request was honored, and within three years the Congregational Church of the Good Shepherd had more than two hundred members.[76] The decision to divide Westminster Church by the Presbytery of Los Angeles, which had greater power than the Association, caused a bitter debate which was ultimately carried to the General Assembly and State Supreme Court. The congregation was ultimately divided, but a small group of members withdrew from the Presbyterian Church and formed a small independent congregation which remained on the periphery of the voluntaristic community.[77] This unfortunate experience led to a policy of "non-intervention" on the part of local denominational agencies, and in the early twentieth century congregations of one thousand and more became a common feature of Los Angeles.[78]

Aside from these two examples, the congregational and interdenominational life of voluntaristic Protestants in Los Angeles appears to have been rather tranquil in the late nineteenth century. The crises of the churches in the East seemed far away, and there is nothing from the remaining sermons or budgetary support to suggest that Los Angeles Protestants were willing to give either moral or financial support to the efforts of their brethren to adjust to new social realities.[79] The one exception to the community orientation of church life in Los Angeles was the appearance of various women's missionary associations in many congregations. Often, however, the organizational impetus had roots in local concerns. William Stewart Young's wife, Janette, for example, formed a Women's Foreign Mission Society in the Presbytery of Los Angeles after she had observed a group of Chinese immigrants worshiping the "boat god. . .an ugly little wooden idol."[80] For similar reasons, the First Methodist Church established a Foreign Mission Association in 1887 and created a Chinese Mission in the city in the same year.[81] Similar organizations were begun in the 1880's by Episcopalians and Baptists.[82]

A few extraecclesiastical services were begun by religious organizations in Los Angeles before 1895, such as the Episcopalian Hospital and Home for Invalids, founded in 1884 and staffed by the Order of the Good Shepherd.[83] Most religious activities were limited to the development of congregational, denominational, and interdenominational institutions, however, Although these institutions were the bulwark of the voluntaristic Protestant culture, the effectiveness of the system depended upon the willingness and ability of church members to establish or capture the secular and nonecclesiastical institutions of the community. It has already been seen that this process was begun in the 1870's. In the '80's and '90's, while limiting the constituency of the voluntaristic community, Los Angeles Protestants sought to extend the influence of their culture to the broader society.

IV

Extraecclesiastical organizations provided three interrelated functions in the voluntaristic system: a sense of cohesion beyond the church organization for the American Protestants, control over local community organizations, and a custodial role in local affairs which had its roots in the concept of Christian Stewardship and facilitated community control. Some of these organizations in Los Angeles were transitory and provided interim community services before more formal permanent associations were established. Various temporary musical committees appeared in Los Angeles, for example, before the formation of the Los Angeles Choral Society in 1893. Most of those associated with these movements were also prominent laymen in one of the voluntaristic denominations.[84] Often, churches hosted musical presentations. In 1887, the First Congregational Church set the precedent of giving a concert to celebrate the acquisition of a new pipe organ.[85] Other churches in the voluntaristic tradition followed the example, and by 1895, the demand for organs was great enough that the firm of Fletcher and Harris was established in Los Angeles to satisfy the need.[86]

In 1893, musical performances moved from the church buildings to new auditoriums, under the sponsorship of the Choral Society. All of the founding members were members of one of the American Protestant denominations.[87] The following year, the society presented Handel's *Messiah* in the Club Theatre.[88] A few concerts for the entire community continued to be performed in churches, however. In 1896, the First Methodist Church presented its new paid choir conductor, Charles S. Cornell, leading a 150 voice assembly from churches in the community in a program of antiphonal singing.[89] In 1897 and 1898, the First Congregational Church gave weekly concerts featuring their Sunday School Orchestra.[90] By the end of the century professional entertainment began to replace amateur productions. The concerts varied from John Philip Sousa's Military Band to Jan Paderewski's interpretations of Chopin, but the arrangements remained firmly in the voluntaristic hands of the Choral Society.[91]

Other organizations provided less a service to the larger community than a sense of cohesion among the voluntaristic Protestants. An aura of instant tradition attended the establishment in 1883 of the Historical Society of Southern California. Noah Levering, a Congregational layman who migrated to Los Angeles from New York, met with twelve others in that year to found the society.[92] John Downey, ex-governor of the state, a founder of the University of Southern California, and Catholic, was the only member of the group who was not also affiliated with one of the voluntaristic denominations.[93] The emphasis of the *Annual Publication*, begun in 1884, was not on the history of Southern California so much as it was a celebration of those American Protestants who came to the area. Biographical sketches of pioneer merchants, ministers, and farmers in Los Angeles comprised the bulk of the publication until the turn of the century.[94] When the Catholic past was mentioned, it was usually in a comparison of the missionary efforts of the Spanish with the courageous work of early

Protestant clergymen.   John Downey suggested the publication of the Stearns papers in 1885, but the Board of Directors decided that Don Abel was not a part of their past.[95]

Although a few Protestants did hold public office in Los Angeles in the 1880's, it was not until the mid-1890's that a concentrated effort was made to capture the city government. In part, this can be accounted for by the efforts of churchmen to establish stable institutions in the early years, but there seems to have been very little reason for Protestants to enter into local government until the last few years of the nineteenth century. They were the primary voting group in the city, and decisions made by the City Council were strongly influenced by the Chamber of Commerce, which was under Protestant control. Voluntaristic Protestants also controlled a variety of agencies within the city, such as the Los Angeles Free Dispensary, the School Board, and the Board of Trustees of the Los Angeles Public Library.[96]

A few organizations, such as the YMCA founded in 1881, combined service and subtle control functions. During its first decade of existence in Los Angeles, the "Y" provided a boarding house for single young men in the city. Most of these were recent migrants, and the "Y" had an active program of various social activities in cooperation with local voluntaristic churches.[97]   Many of the residents of the boarding house became members of a local congregation.[98]   In the early 1890's, the "Y" provided vocational training and continued its program of recruitment for the voluntaristic churches.[99]

One organization was less subtle in the quest for social control. The Women's Christian Temperance Union established a California office at San Francisco in 1881, and the following year a Los Angeles chapter was formed at the First Methodist Church. With the exception of three Unitarians, all of the thirty-seven charter members were affiliated with one of the voluntaristic denominations.[100] The WCTU was able to gain the passage of a moderate dry ordinance in late 1882, and then turned its attention to other assorted vices in the city.[101] It is a testimony to the rather rapid "Protestantization" of Los Angeles that it had some difficulty in finding dens of iniquity. There were many forms of "Sabbath Breaking" and "riotous behavior" in the Mexican community, but the Mexicans were residentially segregated from the rest of the city, and the voluntaristic Protestants did not really consider them as residents of their community.[102]   Finally in August of 1883, the WCTU found an immoral act being performed in the center of the city. As part of the festivities surrounding an exhibition bout by John L. Sullivan, William G. Douglas, a San Francisco promoter, provided a bevy of dancing girls at a local theatre. Upon hearing that the great pugilist had "wantonly tossed silver dollars at the daughters of Jezabel," the

WCTU demanded immediate action from the City Council and the Los Angeles *Times*. The following day an editorial appeared in the *Times* calling the affair a "prostitute's carnival."[103] By the time the City Council met again, Sullivan had departed for Boston, Douglas was in San Francisco arranging a Shakespearian production, and the dancing girls, presumably, sought a more hospitable environment in which to practice their art.[104]

The WCTU next turned its attention to gambling. A few boarding houses near the center of the city provided informal card games in the evenings. The Union approached the City Council about the matter in July of 1884.[105] The question was shelved until September of the next year when, after a vigorous campaign by the WCTU, the Council adopted an ordinance which forbade fan-tan, stud poker, and a score of other games. At the insistence of the Union, supported by the petitions of five congregations, the ordinance also included a general condemnation of those who worshipped the "Goddess of Fortune."[106] The WCTU continued its existence long after the victory of 1885, but there seemed to be little purpose to the organization with so many other agencies in the community working so effectively to limit the possibility of vice. The charter of the Union forbade the organization from becoming a social club, and other forms of cohesion among Protestant women in the city emerged. Few women discontinued their membership in the WCTU, but most sought additional forms of communal life through women's missionary societies and civic organizations, such as the Friday Morning Club.[107]

There had been a Women's Club in Los Angeles as early as 1878. Caroline Severance, who migrated to Los Angeles with her husband from Boston in 1875, had been an active abolitionist in that city, and after the Emancipation Proclamation, she turned her attention to local civic affairs. In 1868, she helped found the Boston Woman's Club,[108] and three years after she arrived in Los Angeles she founded a Woman's Club which collapsed in 1880.[109] Severance found that the issues that concerned Bostonians did not necessarily concern Los Angelenos. During the next few years, Mrs. Severance devoted her energies to organizing a Unitarian church.[110] In 1890, having learned a bit more about her new community, she again thought about forming a woman's society.[111] It may seem strange that a Unitarian would be the founder of one of the voluntaristic organizations of Los Angeles, but Mrs. Severance was no stranger to voluntarism. Her abolitionist activities were in that tradition, and the Unitarian Church in Boston had been included in voluntaristic activities for some time.[112] On April 16, 1891, Mrs. Severance, four fellow Unitarians, twenty-two members of voluntaristic denominations, and three women whose religious affiliation, if any, cannot be identified, formed the Friday Morning Club, "to form a center of united thought and action for women who desire the consideration and discussion of all subjects of general interest."[113] At the organizational meeting the members adopted as their motto, "In Essentials, Unity, in Nonessentials, Liberty, in all things, Charity."[114] The ladies would have been shocked to learn that they had accepted a formulation of Unitarian doctrine, but the motto could also serve as a statement of the voluntaristic culture that was by this time central to the social life of Los Angeles.

V

Although the social life of Los Angeles was stabilized by the voluntaristic organizations, the social structure of the city was anything but stable. The land boom, which was common to all of Southern California in the 1880's, increased the population of Los Angeles almost five-fold. The speculation frenzy not only benefited the voluntaristic Protestant denominations through the migration of Anglo-Saxon Americans, it also temporarily altered the nature of religious rhetoric. Sermons were preached which compared the movement of Protestants to Los Angeles with the "journey of the Hebrew nation to the Promised Land."[115] Dr. Fay of the Unitarian Church exhorted his congregation to be virtuous that they might gain "choice lots" in the "New Jerusalem."[116] One prominent Presbyterian minister announced the text for his sermon as "Lot W, Block 5 of St. Matthew's Subdivision of the New Testament."[117]

The more lasting effect of the boom, however, was in the increase of voluntaristic Protestants in Los Angeles. There was more to this group of like-minded denominations than ideological cohesion. Indeed, the variety of concerns which characterized the differences between the six denominations cannot be overemphasized. Underlying the voluntaristic community—and perhaps giving it the greatest, although unarticulated cohesion—was a social homogeneity that differentiated them from the rest of the citizenry of Los Angeles and caused them to be more concerned about the nature and future of the community than their fellow townsmen. It has already been stated that the majority of the voluntaristic Protestants came from a cluster of seven states, and that most of these had similar experiences with the changing relation between religion and community. The occupational distribution of Los Angeles Protestants was also a cohesive factor. The vast majority of these were either farmers or merchants, and over eighty percent of the merchants and large orchard owners in Los Angeles were members of a voluntaristic congregation. The membership of the Chamber of Commerce, which had a great influence on the City Council, primarily consisted, of course, of American Protestants.[118]

At the time when a cohesive segment of Los Angeles was gaining control of the social life of the community, the economic, political, and ethnic diversity of the city was on the increase. This is a seeming contradiction, but it should not divert attention from the level of homogeneity indicated by the more impressionistic sources. In the first place, the introduction of American population and social structures in a Mexican pueblo immediately raised the level of diversity. In American cities in the East and Mid-West, the diversity indices were raised by immigrant groups who threatened the established order. In Los Angeles

TABLE 16

OCCUPATIONAL STRUCTURE OF LOS ANGELES PROTESTANTS
1880-1900
(IN PERCENTAGES)

	1880	1890	1900
Merchant[a]	38.5	38.1	42.6
Agriculture	22.1	23.0	13.8
Professional	17.3	17.0	18.7
Clerk	13.5	13.6	17.1
Labor	8.6	8.3	7.8

Source: U.S. Bureau of the Census, Tenth Census, 1880, Enumerator's Rollbook, Los Angeles County; *Los Angeles City Directory*, 1880-1900. These sources were used in conjunction with the directories discussed in Appendix I.

[a] Includes a few small industrialists.

it was old-stock Americans who were the new elements, and they concentrated their energies on the establishment of familiar life styles in their new community. If the same indices were applied to the Boston area in 1629 and 1639, the introduction of the English population would immediately raise the level of diversity, but no one would argue that Boston, therefore, was not a cohesive society in the early seventeenth century. The Mexican population of nineteenth-century Los Angeles were hardly considered part of the community by voluntaristic Protestants. Second, the majority of denominations and church members in the city were included in the voluntaristic tradition. The index of religious diversity during this time, therefore, is something of an overstatement. It should also be mentioned that aside from these qualifications, the diversity indices for Los Angeles were lower than the norm for all cities of similar size and function in the United States in 1880 and 1900. The proportion of the population belonging to religious organizations was higher then the norm for cities of similar size (See Appendices V and VI).

TABLE 17

POPULATION GROWTH AND SOCIAL CHANGE
IN LOS ANGELES, 1880-1920

	Size	Diversity Index		
		Ethnic	Religious	Economic
1880	11,183	.43	.22	.21
1890	50,393	.45	.26	.32
1900	102,479	.46	.25	.44
1910	319,198	.50	.28	.53
1920	576,673	.52	.31	.57

Source: See Appendix VI.

The voluntaristic Protestants in Los Angeles not only shared a common heritage, social and economic cohesion, and membership in similar organizations, they also shared common residential areas. While the data for membership for the late nineteenth century is somewhat sketchy, the location of church buildings can be used as a rough guide. The voluntaristic Protestant churches were clustered in the center of the city and in a few neighborhoods west of Main Street, primarily on Adams and Wilshire Boulevards.[119] For the twelve congregations which can be reconstructed for the 1890's, it is clear that members tended to live within ten blocks of the church building, and the proportion of voluntaristic Protestants living in the same neighborhood was extremely high.

TABLE 18

RESIDENTIAL CLUSTERING FOR
12 VOLUNTARISTIC CONGREGATIONS
1880-1900
(IN PERCENTAGES)

Cohesion Factor	1880	1890	1900
In Neighborhood with Other Members of Same Congregation	62.1	73.4	74.6
In Neighborhood with Members of Other Voluntaristic Congregations	78.3	80.9	83.2

Source: See Appendix I.   "Neighborhood" is defined here as an area of four square blocks.   If the definition is extended to ten square blocks, the figures are greatly increased.   The factor is 50.1% or more in the neighborhood in this classification.

The Mexican community of Los Angeles lived east of Main Street, and their four parish churches were located in the area.[120]   The Unitarian and Lutheran churches, and a handful of smaller denominations were clustered south of the civic center.   Only one membership directory remains for any of these churches.   The members of the First Unitarian Church were rather widely dispersed over the southern and western sectors of the city.[121]   The routes of expansion of the Protestant and Catholic populations over the next four decades were east and west.

As the city grew larger and became more complex and diverse in the early twentieth century, it took on the aspects of more traditional American cities in the East.   There was a considerable industrial labor force in Los Angeles by 1920, and non-Protestant elements had begun migrating in greater numbers after 1910.[122]

Along with other large cities, Los Angeles experienced rather rapid population flow in and out of the area.[123]   The voluntaristic community remained stable, however, and the pattern of residential clustering continued.[124]

The City of the Angels was indeed "A City of Churches" in 1881, and the title became even more appropriate in the early twentieth century.   The growth of Los Angeles in size and diversity did not deter the voluntaristic Protestants, buttressed by a stable and cohesive social basis, from continuing and extending their particular sense of community through the first two decades of the twentieth century.   Although there was a general decline in the proportion of Los Angelenos who were

members of religious organizations just after the turn of the century, the
increase in gross religious membership of the voluntaristic Protestant
denominations continued.   In some ways, comparative membership
statistics were of very little importance to the American Protestants. The
real question was whether they were in control of the local culture.   A
good start had been made in the late nineteenth century, and the
voluntaristic Protestants continued to solidify their position in the city.

TABLE 19

RELIGIOUS GROWTH IN LOS ANGELES
1900-1920

	1900	1910	1920
All Religious Organizations	44,026 (41.2)[a]	93,603 (29.4)	203,613 (35.6)
Voluntaristic Protestants	17,387 (17.6)	36,198 (10.6)	91,698 (16.0)

Source: See Appendix I.

[a] Proportion of total population.

NOTES

[1] Newmark, *Sixty Years in Southern California*, pp. 281-293; Emma H. Adams, *To and Fro in Southern California* (Cincinnati, 1887), pp. 37-41; Los Angeles Chamber of Commerce, *California Citrus: A Real Opportunity* (Los Angeles, 1881).

[2] Fogelson, pp. 43-62; Glen S. Dumke, *The Boom of the Eighties in Southern California* (San Marino, 1944), pp. 24-25; Glen Chensey Quiett, *They Built the West: An Epic of Rails and Cities* (New York, 1934), p. 275.

[3] "Speech delivered by John Cole, September 27, 1881, to the Republican Club of Los Angeles," Cole Family Papers, Special Collection Division, University Library, University of California, Los Angeles. Other speeches can be found in the Los Angeles *Times* and the Early Los Angeles History Collection, Special Collections Division, University Library, University of California, Los Angeles.

[4] Los Angeles *Times*, September 4, 1881.

[5] *Ibid.*, September 11, 1881.

[6] See Fogelson, pp. 63-84; McWilliams, pp. 113-182; Vorspan and Bartner, pp. 71-107.

[7] The literature on this subject is summarized in Stephan Thernstrom and Peter R. Knights, "Men in Motion: Some Data and Speculations on Urban Population Mobility in Nineteenth-Century America," *Journal of Interdisciplinary History*, I (Fall, 1970), 23-41.

[8] This statement is based on an analysis of the aggregate data for Los Angeles migrants correlated with data from Simon Kuznets and Dorothy Swaine Thomas, *Population Redistribution and Economic Growth: United States, 1870-1950* (3 Vols.; Philadelphia, 1957).

[9] See Dumke, *passim*; Theodore S. Van Dyke, *Millionaires of a Day: An Inside History of the Great Southern California "Boom"* (New York, 1890).

[10] See Timothy L. Smith, *Revivalism and Social Reform 1890)* (New York, 1957); William G. McLaughlin, *Modern Revivalism: Charles Grandison Finney to Billy Graham* (New York, 1959); and Bernard Weisberger, *They Gathered at the River* (Boston, 1958).

[11] See Whitney R. Cross, *The Burned-Over District: The Social and Intellectual History of Enthusiastic Religion in Western New York, 1800-1850* (Ithaca, New York, 1950); Richard T. Dorney, "The Oneida Experiment and Social Change," (Unpublished Doctoral Dissertation, Union Theological Seminary, New York, 1953). Robert W. Doherty, *The Hicksite Separation: A Sociological Analysis of Religious Schism in Early Nineteenth-Century America* (New Brunswick, New Jersey, 1967) is a functional analysis of more subtle effects of social change on religious organization.

[12] A good selection of the various adaptations can be found in Cross, *The Church and the City, passim*. The best general summary of the problem remains Schlesinger's "A Critical Period in American Religion."

[13]See Abell, *passim*; May *passim*; and Hopkins, *The Rise of the Social Gospel in American Protestantism, passim.* On the lack of social criticism between the Civil War and 1880, see Clifford E. Clark, Jr., "The Changing Nature of Protestantism in Mid-Nineteenth Century America: Henry Ward Beecher's Seven Lectures to Young Men," *The Journal of American History,* LVII (March, 1971), 832-846.

[14]A survey reported in the North American Review (April, 1883), 107-118, indicated that for the twelve American cities canvassed, only a handful of clergymen had not made the response of the churches to social change a major sermon topic.

[15]Abell, pp. 112-115.

[16]*American Home Missionary Society, Report, 1883,* pp. 4-18.

[17]T. J. Jenkins, "The A. P. A. Conspirators," *Catholic World,* LVII (June, 1893), 685-693; Washington Gladden, "The Anti-Catholic Crusade," *Century,* XLVII (July, 1894), 789-795; W. H. J. Traynor, "The Aims and Methods of the A. P. A.,: *North American Review,* CLIX (February, 1894), 69-83; Humphrey Joseph Desmond, *The A. P. A. Movement, A Sketch* (Washington, D. C., 1912); Donald Louis Kinzer, "The American Protective Association: A Study in Anti-Catholicism," (Unpublished Doctoral Dissertation, University of Washington, 1954); John Higham, *Strangers in the Land: Patterns of American Nativism, 1865-1925* (New Brunswick, New Jersey, 1955), *passim.* For earlier anti-Catholic biases inherent in voluntaristic Protestantism, see Ray Allen Billington, "Anti-Catholic Propaganda and the Home Missionary Movement, 1800-1860," *Mississippi Valley Historical Review,* XXII (December, 1935), 361-384.

[18]Abel, pp. 137-165; George Herbert Mead, *Modern Methods of Church Work* (New York, 1897), pp. 337-339; Clyde C. Griffen, "An Urban Church in Ferment: The Episcopal Church in New York City," (Unpublished Doctoral Dissertation, Columbia University, New York, 1960), *passim.*

[19]Although not limited to these two periodicals, the debate can best be followed in *Century* and the *North American Review.*

[20]*The Dawn,* I (January, 1889), 3.

[21]The Northern Baptist Association, *Report of the General Association, 1891,* p. 37.

[22]Abell, pp. 114.

[23]The last was the Presbyterian Church in the United States of America, in 1896.

[24]Baltzell, pp. 114-142.

[25]This statement is based on a systematic reading of denominational reports for states in the Mid-West and the North-East: see Appendix V. The seven states were New York, Pennsylvania, Ohio, Indiana, Illinois, Iowa, and Missouri.

[26]On climate as an inducement to migrate to Southern California, see John E. Baur, *The Health Seekers of Southern California* (San Marino, California, 1959), and William A. Edwards and Beatrice Harraden, *Two Health Seekers in Southern California* (Philadelphia, 1896).

[27]Quoted in Remi A. Nadeau, *Los Angeles: From Mission to Modern City* (New York, 1960), p. 75.

[28]Ostrander, p. 69.

[29]Los Angeles *Times*, June 12, 1886.

[30]The *Occident*, January 14, 1888.

[31]Los Angeles *Times*, March 21, 1882.

[32]Letter to the Deacons of the First Baptist Church of Los Angeles, March 17, 1887, Cole Family Papers.

[33]Letter to Simon Johnson, April 3, 1887, Cole Family Papers.

[34]Minutes of the First Baptist Church, April 14, 1884, First Baptist Church, Los Angeles.

[35]Minutes of the First Baptist Church, April 26, 1884.

[36]Los Angeles *Times*, November 30, 1886.

[37]*Ibid.*

[38]*Ibid.*, November 28, 1886.

[39]Minutes of the First Baptist Church, 1880-1895, *passim*.

[40]Minutes of the First Baptist Church, March 29, 1887.

[41]Minutes of the First Baptist Church, 1880-1900, *passim*.

[42]*Ibid.*

[43]Hine, pp. 73-73.

[44]Methodist Episcopal Church, North, Southern California Conference *Report, 1889*, pp. 21-22.

[45]Minutes of the First Methodist Church for 1894, First Methodist Church Collection, Special Collections Division, University Research Library, University of California, Los Angeles. The activities of the Methodist Episcopal Church, South, in Los Angeles were closely associated with those of the northern denomination. Their congregations and membership were much smaller in the city, and they are included in the Methodist figures for religious membership; see Edward Drewry Jervey, *The*

History of Methodism in Southern California and Arizona (Nashville, 1960), *passim.* A survey of social and economic indices revealed no appreciable differences between the membership of the two Methodist denominations.

[46]Congregational Church, *Minutes of the Association of Southern California* (Los Angeles, 1891), pp. 36-53.

[47]Minutes of the Convocation of Southern California, 1883, Archives of the Protestant Episcopal Diocese of Los Angeles.

[48]*Journal of the Protestant Episcopal Diocese of California* (San Francisco, 1888), pp. 173-190.

[49]*Ibid.*, (San Francisco, 1880-1887), *passim.*

[50]Letter from George Hills to the Bishop of California, August 7, 1888, Archives of the Diocese of California, San Francisco, California.

[51]Frederick G. Bohme, "Episcopal Beginnings in Southern California: The Centennial of Los Angeles' First Parish," HSSCQ, XLVII (June, 1965), 171-190.

[52]*Journal of the General Convention of the Protestant Episcopal Church* (New York, 1886), p. 107.

[53]Lionel Ridout, "Foundations of the Episcopal Church in the Diocese of California, 1849-1893," (Unpublished Doctoral Dissertation, University of Southern California, 1953), pp. 183-206.

[54]Letter from Trew to the Bishop of California, November 8, 1895, Archives of the Protestant Episcopal Diocese of California.

[55]"Sermon by the Rt. Rev. Joseph H. Johnson, May 26, 1896," Archives of the Protestant Episcopal Diocese of Los Angeles.

[56]There had been a minor disagreement over the location of the seminary. William Stewart Young, and others, had argued in Synodical meetings for a more southerly location.

[57]"Report of the Committee on Higher Education, 1893," Archives of the Presbytery of Los Angeles.

[58]*Ibid.*

[59]Letters to Lyman Stewart, May 3, 1883, William Stewart Young Papers, San Francisco Theological Seminary, San Anselmo, California.

[60]Nellie May Young, *William Stewart Young, 1859-1937: Builder of California Institutions* (Glendale, California, 1967), pp. 1-9.

[61]*The Occident*, December 11, 1884.

[62]*Ibid.*, November 17, 1886.

[63]Minutes of the Presbytery of Los Angeles, 1892, Archives of the Presbytery of Los Angeles.

[64]*Minutes of the Synod of the Pacific of the Presbyterian Church in the United States of America* (San Francisco, 1884), p. 35.

[65]"Report of the Committee on Higher Education, 1884," Archives of the Presbytery of Los Angeles. Two other colleges established in Los Angeles without the support of the voluntaristic churches came to rather abrupt ends also: Ellis College and the Los Angeles College for Women, founded in 1884 and 1885; see Newmark, *Sixty Years in Southern California*, p. 566.

[66]The original Trustees are listed in the "Occidental University Prospectus," Archives of Occidental College, Los Angeles. Denominational affiliation was determined by the sources listed in Appendix I.

[67]References to these activities were found in the Los Angeles *Times*, and the Records of the Immanuel Presbyterian Church, Special Collections Division, University Research Library, University of California, Los Angeles.

[68]Los Angeles *Times*, January 23, 1888.

[69]"Report of the Secretary of the Presbyterian College Board," in the *Minutes of the General Assembly of the Presbyterian Church in the U.S.A.*, III (Philadelphia, 1893), p. 639.

[70]Los Angeles *Times*, October 7, 1894. In two smaller voluntaristic communities in Southern California, the founding of denominational colleges became important community projects. The Congregationalists sponsored Pomona College, built in 1887, and the Baptists founded Redlands University in 1909.

[71]Letters from Trew expressing this general spirit of cooperation were found in the records of the First Baptist Church, the First Methodist Church, the First Congregational Church, Immanuel Presbyterian Church, and Trinity Methodist Church.

[72]The Records of the First Methodist Church of Los Angeles, Special Collections Division, University Research Library, University of California, Los Angeles, for the period under discussion, contain many references to the interdenominational composition of that chapter of the Epworth League.

[73]The Disciples of Christ congregation was immediately invited to join interdenominational activities: Minutes of the First Baptist Church, March 17, 1891. The Disciples had originally been a pietistic sect in the early nineteenth century, but gradually took on the socio-economic, institutional, and ideological characteristics of voluntaristic denominations. See Winfred Ernest Garrison, *Religion Follows the Frontier: A History of the Disciples of Christ* (New York, 1931) and Winfred Ernest Garrison and Thomas DeGroot, *The Disciples of Christ, A History* (St. Louis, 1948).

[74]Determined from the *Los Angeles City Directory, 1895,* and regional denominated reports; see Appendix III.

[75]"Minutes of the Congregational Association of Los Angeles, 1889," Files of the United Church of Christ, Los Angeles District.

[76]*Ibid,* 1892.

[77]"File on the Westminster Church Division," Archives of the Presbytery of Los Angeles.

[78]All six denominations adopted specific policies of non-intervention at the regional level. The Presbytery of Los Angeles was the first in 1899.

[79]Determined from a survey of the sources mentioned in Appendix I and Appendix III.

[80]Janet Young, Diary, October 27, 1885, Young Papers.

[81]"Minutes of the First Methodist Church, 1887," Records of the First Methodist Church of Los Angeles.

[82]"Diocesan Report, 1888," Archives of the Protestant Episcopal Diocese of Los Angeles; *Report of the Los Angeles Baptist Association, 1889,* p. 17.

[83]Diocese of California, *Diocesan Report on Charitable Works* (San Francisco, 1885), pp. 93-94. Further information on the congregational and community activities of the voluntaristic Protestants in Los Angeles can be found in Louis C. Sanford, *The Province of the Pacific* (Philadelphia, 1949); Elizabeth Ritter, "The History of the Protestant Episcopal Church in Southern California," (Unpublished Master's Thesis, University of Southern California, Los Angeles, 1936); Edward Arthur Wicher, *The Presbyterian Church in California, 1849-1927* (New York, 1927); Elizabeth Harness, "A History of the Presbytery of Los Angeles, 1850-1928," (Unpublished Master's Thesis, University of Southern California, Los Angeles, 1929); Robert Hamilton, "The History and Influence of the Baptist Church in California, 1848-1899," (Unpublished Doctoral Dissertation, University of Southern California, Los Angeles, 1953); G. W. Haskell, "Formative Factors in Life and Faith: Southern Congregationalism, 1850-1908," (Unpublished Doctoral Dissertation, University of Southern California, Los Angeles, 1947), in addition to regional denominational histories cited elsewhere.

[84]Determined from a correlation of the listed membership of the various groups listed in the Los Angeles *Times,* with congregational membership sources mentioned in Appendix I.

[85]Los Angeles *Times,* May 17, 1882.

[86]*Ibid.,* January 13, 1883; March 29, 1883; October 30, 1883; December 3, 1883; February 24, 1884; April 12, 1884; November 18, 1884; July 2, 1887; September 20, 1891; June 7, 1894; March 11, 1895.

[87]The membership list is reproduced in Henry Winfred Splitter, "Music in Los Angeles, HSSCQ, XXXVIII (December, 1956), 307. The list was correlated with the sources mentioned in Appendix I.

[88]Splitter, 330.

[89]Los Angeles *Times,* June 27, 1896.

[90]Splitter, 331.

[91]*Ibid.,* 335. The constituency of the membership of the Choral Society to the end of the century was determined from the periodic listings in the Los Angeles *Times* and correlated with the sources mentioned in Appendix I.

[92]Anna Begue de Packman, "A Brief Society History," HSSCQ, XL (September, 1958), 223.

[93]The list of founding members was obtained from the Historical Society of Southern California, *Annual Publication,* I (1884), 3, and correlated with the sources mentioned in Appendix I.

[94]Based on a survey of the *Annual Publication,* 1884-1900.

[95]Historical Society of Southern California, *Annual Publication,* II (1885), 307.

[96]Determined from a correlation of the sources mentioned in Appendix I with the members of civic organizations mentioned, and others listed in the Los Angeles *Times,* the Los Angeles City School Board, *Report,* 1882-1900, and Laura C. Cooley, "The Los Angeles Public Library," HSSCQ, XIII (March, 1941), 5-23.

[97]Manuscript Reports of the Los Angeles YMCA, 1882-1900, Los Angeles Young Men's Christian Association.

[98]The records that remain of all voluntaristic congregations from this period contain frequent reference to members so recruited.

[99]Rudy Abrecht, *The YMCA on the Western Frontier: A Brief History of the California State Young Men's Christian Association* (Los Angeles, 1964), pp. 92ff.

[100]The charter members are listed in the *Annual Report of the Women's Christian Temperance Union of California* (San Francisco, 1882), p. 114. The membership was correlated with the sources mentioned in Appendix I.

[101]Based on a systematic reading of materials relating to the Los Angeles chapter in the Records of the California Woman's Christian Temperance Union, Bancroft Library, University of California, Berkeley. The more interesting aspects of this early campaign can be found in the Los Angeles *Times,* May 15-August 6, 1882.

[102]Sabbatarian laws had been passed in California as early as 1855. After many court battles and revisions, George Stonehouse made the repeal of these laws a major issue in his gubernatorial campaign in 1882. After his election, and at his request, this was

accomplished. See Ronald R. Nelson, "The Legal Relationship of Church and State in California, Part II," HSSCQ, XLVI (June, 1964), 146-154. Stonehouse lost Los Angeles by a margin of three to one: Los Angeles *Times*, September 13, 1882.

[103]Los Angeles *Times*, August 18, 1883.

[104]*Ibid*, September 1, 1883.

[105]Minutes of Meeting, July 23, 1884, Los Angeles Common Council Files, City Hall, Los Angeles.

[106]*Ibid*, September 8, 1885.

[107]The membership of the woman's missionary associations grew rapidly after the 1885 WCTU "victory." For specific citations see the materials listed in Notes 81 and 82 in this chapter.

[108]Thelma Lee Hubbell and Gloria R. Lothrop, "The Friday Morning Club: A Los Angeles Legacy," HSSCQ, L (March, 1968), 59-61.

[109]*Ibid.*, 62.

[110]*Ibid*, 63-65.

[111]Letter from Caroline Severance to Angela Gerson, March 7, 1890, Theodore Percival Gerson Papers, Special Collections Division, University Research Library, University of California, Los Angeles.

[112]See Octavius Brooks Frothingham, *Boston Unitarianism, 1820-1850; a Study of the Life and Work of Nathaniel Longdon Frothingham* (New York, 1890) and George Ellis, *Half-Century of the Unitarian Controversy* (Boston, 1857).

[113]"Founding Statement," Files of the Friday Morning Club, Special Collections Division, University Research Library, University of California, Los Angeles.

[114]Hubell and Lothrop, 62.

[115]"Sermon by the Rev. A. J. Wells, February, 1884," First Congregational Church Collection, Special Collections Division, University Research Library, University of California, Los Angeles.

[116]H. D. Barrows, "Early Clericals of Los Angeles," HSSCQ, V (1901), 133.

[117]Williams Stewart Young, "Historical Address Commemorating the Twenty-Fifth Anniversary of the Founding of Occidental College, March 6, 1914," Young Papers.

[118]From a correlation of the membership found in the Los Angeles Chamber of Commerce Minutes, 1889-1900, Los Angeles Chamber of Commerce, with the sources mentioned in Appendix I.

[119]Determined from locations given in the *Los Angeles City Directory*, 1880-1900.

[120]*Ibid.*

[121]Determined from a correlation of membership found in the "First Unitarian Directory," First Unitarian Church, Files, Special Collections Division, University Research Library, University of California, Los Angeles, with addresses given in the *Los Angeles City Directory*, 1880-1900.

[122]See Chapter 5.

[123]On the national implications of these migration patterns, see Thernstrom and Knights, *passim.*

[124]See Chapter 4. On residential persistence, see the summary in Appendix IV.

CHAPTER 4

PURE FAITH, PURE MORALS, PURE GOVERNMENT

I

By the last decade of the nineteenth century Los Angeles Protestants thought of their community as an organic society. Urban growth, which had caused so many problems for Protestants in the East and Mid-West, was seen as an opportunity by voluntaristic Los Angelenos. As early as 1891, Harrison Gray Otis exclaimed, "The progress of Los Angeles during the past ten years has been great; but he is indeed blind who does not see that this progress has but begun." Surveying the increase of fruit tree orchards and the expanding market, Otis concluded, "it needs no high order of prophetic vision to see, in the near future, a city."[1] In order to preserve the newly established voluntaristic social order, members of the Immanuel Presbyterian Church called for a loose federation of citizens concerned about the civic welfare of the community. Under their sponsorship, the *California Independent* began publication in 1896, carrying the banner line, "Pure Faith, Pure Morals, Pure Government."[2] There is a great deal of impressionistic evidence to suggest that their goal was achieved.

Dana W. Bartlett, a local Methodist minister, boasted of his community in 1907: "It is a city of churches and schools and civic bodies, deeply interested in the best. The type is that of the highest moral and ethical citizenship."[3] A prominent Los Angeleno, recalling the first two decades of the century, marvelled that a city could be so prosperous, yet so virtuous.[4] Between 1900 and 1920, sixteen national organizations affiliated with voluntaristic protestant denominations cited Los Angeles as an "Ideal Protestant City," and a "Model Christian Community."[5] Even the detractors of Los Angeles gave evidence of the influence of Protestant culture in the city. Willard Huntington Wright claimed, "The current belief in Los Angeles is that there is something inherently and inalienably indecent (or at least indelicate) in that segment of the day between twelve midnight and five a.m." The city, he wrote, "is overrun with militant moralists, connoisseurs of sin, experts on biological purity."[6]

The Protestant spirit so evident in Los Angeles is somewhat remarkable. Although the City of the Angels had a greater proportion of the population in American Protestant churches than other cities of comparable size, this segment of the citizenry was limited to less than one-fifth of the total. Even if non-voluntaristic Protestants are included, the proportion never rose to more than thirty percent.[7] However, the control of local institutions, including the city government by 1907, was firmly in voluntaristic hands.

In their quest to perpetuate the cohesive, organic sense of community, American Protestants were active in four related general areas: the local congregation, denominational and interdenominational institutions, community organizations which were not directly related to church activity, and the city government. Although these areas continued to depend on one another, each took on a life of its own. A few individuals served at all four levels. Lyman Stewart, for example, was an Elder of Immanuel Presbyterian Church, a delegate of the Presbytery of Los Angeles to the Synod of California, a Trustee of the Union Rescue Mission and the Bible Institute of Los Angeles, a member of a number of civic organizations, and a Commissioner of Water.[8] Most Protestants, however, tended to be involved in a more limited sphere of activities.

By 1920, the rhetoric of sermons, the local press, and public speeches implied a cohesive and organic Protestant community.[9] While there are elements of truth to this image, a basic change had taken place in the structure of the voluntaristic system. Perhaps in response to the growing size and diversity of the city, the Protestant establishment adopted a division of labor commensurate with the four levels of civic activity; and within each of these levels, bureaucratic structures emerged. By the end of World War I the configuration of voluntaristic Protestantism in Los Angeles resembled a corporation more than a community.

TABLE 20

LEVELS OF INDIVIDUAL PROTESTANT ACTIVITY, 1900-1920 (IN PERCENTAGES)

Protestant Leaders Involved in	1900-1904	1905-1909	1910-1914	1915-1920
1 Level	29.6	55.1	58.7	59.2
2 Levels	15.4	13.3	17.8	18.1
3 Levels	36.7	17.5	16.9	16.5
4 Levels	18.3	14.1	6.6	6.2

Source: See Appendices I, III, and IV.

II

Congregational life in Los Angeles varied greatly from denomination to denomination between 1900 and 1920, but two common trends became more clearly developed.   On the one hand, denominational distinctions, which at the turn of the century had been rather severe, became somewhat blurred after two decades.   This seemingly should have strengthened the cohesiveness of voluntaristic Protestantism, but the trend was counteractive.   In the late 1890's and early 1900's church buildings were located in the neighborhoods they served and the congregations were small enough to provide a neighborhood organization. By 1920, voluntaristic Protestants still tended to be clustered in well-delineated residential areas (see Table 21), but their church buildings and congregations had lost neighborhood integrity. Individual churches were allowed to grow into mammoth organizations, often with membership spread over the entire city. These changes had an effect on the structure of congregational life.   They also affected the place of the basic unit of the voluntaristic system in the larger community.

These trends can be seen most clearly, but most superficially, through an analysis of the aggregate membership statistics. In 1900, the average size of voluntaristic congregations in Los Angeles was 184 members, with the largest parish containing 418 communicants. By 1920 the average congregation consisted of approximately 600 members, and a few of the larger churches numbered several thousand souls.[10] Although the regional denominational agencies had abandoned all hope of controlling congregational size, they continued to be concerned. William Stewart Young, in 1911, despaired, "I wonder what use the Immanuel Church has for the rest of us. They are large enough to form their own Presbytery there now."[11] It is not clear why some congregations grew to such immense size, but former members indicate a variety of plausible explanations.[12]   The dozen largest voluntaristic churches in the city, which were also the largest religious congregations in Los Angeles, were all noted for excellent programs in one of the three areas: preaching, religious education, or social activities.

TABLE 21

RESIDENTIAL CLUSTERING OF VOLUNTARISTIC
PROTESTANTS
1900-1920
(IN PERCENTAGES)

Cohesion Factor	1900	1910	1920
In Neighborhood with Other Members of Same Congregation[a]	74.6	71.7	68.9
In Neighborhood with Members of Other Voluntaristic Congregations[a]	83.2	81.4	81.1

Source: See Appendix I. for definition of "neighborhood", see Table 18.

[a] Living in neighborhood with 50.1% or greater in this classification.

Trinity Methodist Church, First Congregational, First Presbyterian, St. James' Episcopal Church, and Wilshire Christian Church (Disciples of Christ) all had reputations for having fine pulpit orators. The Rev. Frank D. Talmadge, pastor of First Presbyterian from 1904 to 1908, was often asked to be guest preacher at neighboring congregations. In 1906, the Session of that church resolved to find a gifted speaker to serve as assistant pastor.[13] "There is no reason," wrote one Elder, "why we should hear the Word preached less eloquently while Rev. Talmadge is whirling around the city."[14] The founding vestry of St. James' Episcopal parish made preaching ability the prime requisite in their search for a rector.[15] After a three year investigation, the vestry acquired the Rev. A. W. Noel Porter, a noted Boston pulpit orator.[16]

The First Baptist Church, Immanuel Presbyterian, and Wilshire Presbyterian Church were all known for the quality of their Sunday Schools. As their enrollment increased, First Baptist and Wilshire Presbyterian hired full-time Ministers of Religious Education and established a number of committees to select educational materials, determine the qualifications of teachers, and establish yearly programs of coordinated religious instruction for everyone from first graders to the retired.[17] Immanuel Presbyterian Church also adopted a large bureaucratic structure for religious education, but the congregation was spared the expense of hiring a professional coordinator. Lyman Stewart, a relative of William Stewart Young and together with his brother Milton a major shareholder in the Union Oil Company, had been interested in religious education as early as 1897, when he first elected to the Session of Immanuel Presbyterian.[18] When it became evident by 1906, that the Sunday School Department needed ongoing and intensive leadership, Stewart volunteered to act as Superintendent until professional help could be found. After three years, he announced his decision to serve as permanent voluntary head of the church's religious education program.[19] He withdrew in 1911 to devote his energies to the Bible Institute of Los Angeles, and Joseph M. Irvine, a wealthy realtor, assumed the position, which he held until 1951.[20]

Temple Baptist Church, First Methodist, St. John's Episcopal parish, and St. Paul's Cathedral had specific social programs which attracted a large number of parishioners. First Methodist Church continued to have the most active chapter of the Epworth League in Southern California.[21] St. John's and St. Paul's both had active charitable organizations, such as rest homes and children's hospitals, which were staffed by volunteers from the congregation. Temple Baptist had perhaps the most active social program of any church in early twentieth-century Los Angeles. Groups such as the Men and Religion Forward Movement hosted many fund raising concerts in the sanctuary, which was built in the style of an auditorium.[22] On February 8, 1915, the Women's Missionary Alliance of Temple Baptist Church increased their funds considerably by renting the sanctuary and providing ushers from the congregation for the World Premier of the movie "Birth of a Nation."[23] These churches, though large, were atypical. Most congregations had very little in the way of auxiliary organizations. Social, charitable, and civic organizations in the city were Protestant institutions by extension, and further organization would have been redundant.

The more average churches experienced a much greater population turnover, usually associated with residential change. Very few of the members of the twelve largest congregations changed their affiliation when they changed their addresses, even when the move was of considerable distance. Perhaps the smaller parishes never were able to establish larger programs because of the population turnover, but there was, in each congregation, a stable faction of long-time residents in the neighborhood.[24] In 1900, families usually changed congregational affiliation when a move was made from one neighborhood to another. Most often, their new congregation was of the same denomination. By 1920, the pattern was more complex. A person was as likely to join another voluntaristic denomination in his new neighborhood, or one of the larger congregations of the same denomination. Although specific denominational integrity declined, the affiliation almost always changed within voluntaristic denominations.[25] (See Appendix I).

The members of voluntaristic denominations continued to be advantageously differentiated from other Los Angelenos in the early twentieth century. The variance from denomination to denomination was very slight. In 1900, the greatest variance in social structure could be seen between congregations, regardless of denominational affiliation. First Baptist, Immanuel Presbyterian, and First Methodist, for example, all had a greater share of the wealthier merchants than other congregations. In none of the smaller congregations, however, did the configuration reflect the larger community of Los Angeles, and all were advantageously differentiated.[26]

At the turn of the century, therefore, congregations were cohesive neighborhood units that were a part of a larger organic voluntaristic community, but by 1920, the integrity of the neighborhood and denomination had been seriously eroded. This change had an effect on the function of the congregation. In the 1890's, individual congregations were involved in the founding of voluntaristic and civic associations. By 1920, it was the Protestant leadership in denominational and civic organizations that provided the impetus for social action.[27] With the exception of the dozen largest churches in Los Angeles, the congregation provided only worship services. The Protestant community was still a vital part of the larger city, but the leading members were no longer active at the congregational level. Prominent churchmen had been active in the leadership of individual churches as well as civic and interdenominational organizations at the turn of the century. By 1920, the churchmen with greatest status in the community tended to assume positions at the denominational, civic association, or city government levels. Leadership in the congregations was exercised by small merchants, minor professionals, and clerks. (See Appendix I.) With the exception of the largest parishes, the neighborhood church was reduced to a supportive role. Collections were periodically taken for agencies, such as the Orthopaedic Hospital or the Christian Home for the Aged, which were no longer controlled by the congregation. In most cases, they were not controlled by the denominations, either.[28]

Perhaps because the voluntaristic Protestant community began to develop a "hierarchy" of lay control, denominational integrity declined. In addition to the statistics indicating an increase in changes in denominational affiliation, sermons and the pattern of interdenominational activity suggest the adoption of an American Protestant attitude which tended to obscure the subleties of traditional divisions. The Rev. John R. Salton, of the Episcopal Church of the Ascension, for example, preached many sermons on the sacramental function of the priesthood until his retirement in 1909. In searching for a new rector, the Vestry received specific instructions from the

TABLE 22

SOCIAL STRATIFICATION OF PROTESTANT CONGREGATIONS
1920
(IN PERCENTAGES)

| | Membership | | | |
	499	500-999	1000+	All Los Angeles
Entrepreneur	2.6	7.3	14.2	5.3
Merchant	30.8	27.9	37.6	9.2
Professional	11.5	14.1	12.3	13.4
Clerical	43.7	39.4	28.4	23.4
Labor	11.4	11.3	7.5	48.7

Source: See Appendix I.

Note: Voluntaristic Protestants accounted for approximately the following percentages of each occupational group in Los Angeles: Entrepreneur, 28%; Merchant, 53%, Professional, 15%; Clerical, 45%; Labor, 9%. These denominations accounted for 15% of the population of the city.

congregation to disregard any candidate who "has a greater love for Anglican tradition than the spirit of Christian community."[29] Although not as conservative as the High-Church Salton, most Episcopal clergymen in the first decade of the twentieth century refused to take part in an interdenominational activity of a sacramental nature. Baptists refused to participate in any organization that might tend to subordinate the autonomy of the congregation, and Presbyterians were reluctant to support statements of "General Christian Belief." By 1920, Episcopal Priests were participating in interdenominational communion services, Baptists had urged their national denomination to join the Federation of Churches, and Presbyterians participated in the drafting of vague statements of common belief.[30] Within the context of the changing nature and function of voluntaristic congregations and denominations, a stable Protestant leadership provided the integrative functions of a seemingly cohesive community. The corporate structure that evolved in Los Angeles Protestantism was, in many ways, the most efficient means of maintaining and extending the influence of voluntarism, but it also changed the configuration of the community. The story of Protestantism in Los Angeles in the early twentieth century, therefore, must be found beyond the congregations.

III

Between 1890 and the turn of the century, the primary activity of denominational agencies in Los Angeles had been the raising of funds to support the building of new churches. In addition to the traditional sources, wealthy layman donated real estate lots to be auctioned for this purpose. The Diocese of Los Angeles held banquets in 1898 and 1903, charging twenty dollars a plate.[31] The specific devices were diverse, but by the early 1900's, all six denominations had established adequate building funds. The pattern of giving by wealthy layman was altered during this time. H. G. Wylie, a local oil magnate, for example, had donated large amounts to individual Presbyterian churches in the late 1890's. Beginning in 1902, he gave directly to various funds of the Presbytery of Los Angeles, where the money could be "put to the most effective use."[32] Wylie's case was not unique. Congregational income remained relatively stable between 1905 and 1920, but the funds of the denominational agencies rose steadily.[33]

With the financial health of the denominations secure, Protestant leaders began investigating potential areas of social action. In some cases, existing congregational programs were incorporated and enlarged by denominational agencies. The First Baptist Church of Los Angeles, for example, considered the possibility of operating a city mission for the indigent in 1890.[34]   After a great deal of discussion, and as the downtown area became more clearly a resting place for the indigent, the Baptist City Mission was founded in 1898.[35] Until 1906, the mission was staffed by volunteers from the First Baptist Church. In that year the Los Angeles Baptist Association, recognizing the "valiant efforts of our Brethren at, the First Church," suggested that the mission be administered by the Association and under the direction of an experienced missionary. "The complexities of the modern city demand complex solutions," read the report of the Association.[36]   In the following year, the First Baptist Church, "rejoicing in the wider service the Christian community of Los Angeles will now be able to render," turned the operation of their volunteer-staffed mission over to professionals.[37]   Nine years later, Shailer Mathews of the Northern Baptist Convention praised the Los Angeles Association for its cooperative effort.[38]

Other denominations had similar experiences. First Methodist had instituted a program of training Mexican youths for non-agricultural jobs in the late 1890's. It was hoped that "if they are removed from the bean fields, and placed in more modern occupations, they may be more able to adopt the Protestant faith."[39] In 1909, seventeen other Methodist Churches in the area joined the First Church to expand the program into the Industrial Training School for Boys.[40] (It is dubious that the school achieved the desired conversions, but it did provide a needed local supply of skilled and semi-skilled labor.[41]) Presbyterians and Congregationalists saw a series of homes for children or the aged change from voluntary congregational operations to denominational institutions. In all cases, the laymen most active in the founding or operation of these charitable agencies became members of denominational boards which had directional responsibilities. In very few cases did these lay leaders remain officers of the local congregation.[42] In the case of the Episcopal Church, an established hierarchy facilitated the flow from congregational to denominational control. The office of Deaconess and the various nursing orders within the national church provided trained professionals. The Hospital of the Good Samaritan, the Episcopal Church Home for Children, and the Home for the Aged had all been volunteer-staffed agencies of Episcopal parishes at the turn of the century. By 1920, they were all large and professionally run institutions.[43]

Denominational activity was heightened in 1903 and 1915. In these years the city hosted the General Assembly of the Presbyterian Church, U.S.A., and the meeting of the General Conference of the Northern Baptist Convention.[44] All of the local voluntaristic denominational agencies arranged schedules for "the preaching talent that will be available to us," and the Presbytery of Los Angeles had to hire seven more staff members to process the requests.[45] Even the Disciples of Christ, the denomination with the least formal regional and national structure, appointed a committee to help with arrangements.[46]

Perhaps the best measure of the growth in the importance of denominational agencies is the amount of money that congregations were willing to donate to the local bureaucracies. In 1900, the proportion of congregational funds designated for the support of the regional agency was eight percent. By 1920, one dollar out of every four put in collection plates was sent to the local denominational headquarters.[47] At the turn of the century, the staff of the Diocese of Los Angeles consisted of the Bishop and two secretaries. Twenty years later, eight secretaries, a bishop Co-adjutur, four Deans, seven Cannons, three Deaconesses, and nine priest-administrators had been added.[48] Other denominations experienced similar expansion. Many laymen were also included in the enlargement of the central agencies. As the denominations took on more responsibilities, committees involving lay membership were created. This, of course, drained the leadership talent from the local congregations, and insured that future innovations would come from the central agencies.[49]

With the strengthening of the local denominational unit in Los Angeles, it would appear that the decline in denominational integrity was a contradictory trend. As the central agencies gained more vitality, however, the inter-communication between them increased. In 1900, there were no joint committees existing between congregations or denominations. The usual pattern for cooperation had been the calling of a meeting for a specific purpose by one congregation which was open to all voluntaristic Protestants. If long range action were required, non-ecclesiastical organizations, such as the WCTU, would be formed. Within a few years, however, committees of the various denominations were often in correspondence and occasionally met jointly to discuss areas of common concern.[50]   It was in this way that many interdenominational agencies were begun which were invariably limited to the voluntaristic denominations. The Los Angeles Federation of Churches, for example, was first suggested by the council of the First Unitarian Church in 1899. The suggestion was politely ignored by all but one Congregational church.[51] In order to demonstrate solidarity and coordinate "the spiritual effort of our forces," the Federation was formed in 1906 as part of the Good Government Campaign.[52] Membership was extended to any congregation in the city which supported the Good Government candidates, but after the election the constituency was limited to those "Trinitarian Churches of the American Tradition," which were, oddly enough, the six voluntaristic denominations.[53]   The Federation served primarily as a coordinating agency for the various denominational programs.

The seeming contradiction between the decline of denominational integrity and the increasing importance of the denominational agencies can be further dispelled by an understanding of the provincial nature of denominational activities. The centralistic impulse did not extend beyond Los Angeles. The Presbytery and Methodist District, for example, demonstrated greater interest in the community than in their respective national associations.[54] During the early twentieth century, Los Angeles Protestants gave much less than other Protestants in major cities to their national organizations. Indeed, they gave considerably less than average for the nation in all six denominations. Donations from the local congregations to the various missionary agencies were comparatively high, but very little money flowed from Los Angeles to support the Institutional Churches and social ministries of the national churches. (See Appendix III.) Harvey Bender, chairman of the Budget Committee of the Los Angeles Congregational Association may have given voice to a general spirit when he wrote in 1914, "Maintaining Christian standards in a modern city is not an easy task. If we spend all our money on the needs—and they are real—of Christians in other cities, how can we continue the job we have started here?"[55]

Within this context, it is easy to understand how an informal, though highly restricted, interdenominationalism came to exist in Los Angeles. Somehow, being a Los Angeles Presbyterian, a resident of a Christian city, was more important than being a Presbyterian who lived in Los Angeles. Indeed, the spirit of interdenominationalism was so strong that a number of important religious institutions emerged in early twentieth-century Los Angeles which began neither in congregations nor denominational committees, but through the interaction of churchmen who had become acquainted with each other through more formal interdenominational channels. The most important of these were the Union Rescue Mission and the Bible Institute of Los Angeles.

The Union Rescue Mission had its origins in the desire of a group of laymen of the Congregational, Methodist, and Disciples of Christ Churches to provide a service for "our fellow Christians who have suffered misfortunes in relocating to this community."[56] They were impressed by the work of the Pacific Gospel Union, founded in San Francisco in 1891; and Silas Martin, Congregational Deacon and dry goods merchant, began an active correspondence with the Bay Area organization.[57] By December of 1891, seven laymen (including Lyman Stewart), all members of the voluntaristic denominations, formed the founding Board of Trustees of the Union Rescue Mission. Major George Hilton, director of the Central Union Mission in Washington, D.C., was appointed Superintendent.[58] From the beginning the mission had denominational ties only through the constituency of the Board of Trustees, but it received the general support, financial and moral, of the voluntaristic community.[59] In the early 1900's, Protestant ministers preached enthusiastic sermons about the organization. Popular clerics, such as Frank Dewitt Talmage, Robert McIntyre of First Methodist, and Hugh K. Walker of Immanuel Presbyterian, praised the mission for "bringing those of our brethren who may have lost their way to Heaven on the route to Los Angeles back into the fold."[60] Indeed, the assumption on the part of most Protestants in the City of the Angels seems to have been that the major work of the mission was to revitalize voluntaristic souls rather than to win new ones.

The mission actually ran a large variety of programs including a "soup kitchen" and job training for local industrial occupations.[61] Every so often, however, publications of the mission indicated that, behind the general program, a ministry to the lost sheep of the voluntaristic community was being conducted. "A mistaken idea is entertained by a very large class of the Christian Church-going people", complained the Superintendent in 1906, "that the men reached in our work are invariably those who through dense ignorance and vicious surroundings have found their way into the gutter."[62]   To counteract this assumption, he listed a "sampling" of men, most of whom had suffered various misfortunes: "lawyers, doctors, pharmacists, druggists, editors, capitalists, ranchers, and men in almost every walk of life."[63]   The mission made every effort to remind local churches of its organic unity with the spirit of voluntaristic Protestantism.   Reports constantly emphasized the "auxiliary" nature of the mission. "We are not a separate organization," insisted the Superintendent in 1908." "What the churches cannot do directly through their services, they do through the instrumentality of their consecrated wealth in this Mission."[64]   By 1920, the union Rescue Mission was still guided by voluntaristic Protestants, and was the largest city mission in the nation.[65]

The Bible Institute of Los Angeles was founded under a different set of conditions that indicate both dissatisfaction with the loose structure of Los Angeles Protestantism, and the ability of that structure to submuse many varieties of faith and practice. As early as 1904, Lyman Stewart, layman *extraordinaire* of Immanuel Presbyterian Church, expressed discontent about the nature of religion in the City of the Angels. On the surface it looked like the ideal Protestant community it was noted for, Stewart wrote his clerical relative, William Stewart Young, but "I don't see much of the operation of the real spirit of Christ in this town"[66]   Stewart felt that a stronger emphasis on the Bible in religious and general education could remedy the situation. It was this notion that led him to devote so much time to the Immanuel Presbyterian Sunday School.[67]   In 1905, he gave $3,000 to Occidental College to endow a series of Bible courses.[68]   After two years, it became apparent that there was enough interest to support only one general course, and Stewart withdrew his funds.

In 1907, Stewart and Thomas C. Horton, a local minister and educator, laid out plans for a Bible school in Los Angeles which would provide undergraduate education and seminary training. On February 25, 1908, a charter was drawn for the Bible Institute of Los Angeles, and all of the signers were voluntaristic Protestants.[70]   It seems clear, however, that Stewart intended BIOLA to be a counter-institution in Los Angeles religious life.   He hinted as much in a good deal of his correspondence during the foundation stage.[71] Stewart also retreated from the larger Protestant community.   Although he retained his membership in the Immanuel Presbyterian Church, Stewart withdrew his financial support from congregational and denominational activities and spent most of his time in the more conservative atmosphere of BIOLA.[72] The school would have become the symbol of early Protestant friction in Los Angeles if it had not been for the activities of Stewart's close friend and successor at Immanuel Presbyterian, Joseph M. Irvine. A member of the Board of Trustees of BIOLA, Irvine made every effort to involve the voluntaristic community in the new enterprise. In 1909, he sent letters requesting funds to all American Protestant congregations and the response was enthusiastic.[73] One pastor, who had heard very little of the new school, exclaimed, "Look at the Board! Why, every name on there is a testimony to its Christian character."[74] The trustees found themselves unable to disassociate themselves from the lucrative involvement in the voluntaristic community of Los Angeles.[75] At Irvine's urging, and much to the chagrin of Stewart, Ruben Archer Torrey entered into the cooperative spirit.[76] Stewart had recruited Torrey for his reputation as a literalist revival preacher, and had built the Independent Church of the Open Door for Torrey. Irving, however, soon made Torrey and his church a part of the voluntaristic community.[77]

To end the discussion of denominational and interdenominational activity in early twentieth-century Los Angeles with the most anomalous example is to demonstrate both the precise structural definitions *and* the amorphous nature of the Protestant culture in Los Angeles. It transcended the congregation, but was confined to the city. If national spokesmen for the church were calling for a new Christian social order, their words fell on deaf ears in the City of the Angels. Los Angeles Protestants were interested in an older social order in which the Christian element firmly controlled the life of the community. Although denominational and interdenominational activity was significant, it hardly was the most important level of Protestant action.

The way Los Angeles Protestants went about securing and maintaining "Pure Faith, Pure Morals, Pure Government" suggests the persistence of voluntarism in the face of changes in its own structure. Faith was left to the religious organizations, but the purity of the larger community was achieved not through congregational, denominational, or interdenominational action, but through the actions of voluntaristic Protestants in social organizations, civic associations, and local government. The membership of the most active civic organizations and the most prestigeous social clubs were overwhelmingly voluntaristic Protestants.[78] Most of the social organizations, such as the Johnathan Club and the Moose, were not innovative, but provided support for programs developed by the more civic associations. Many Los Angelenos, of course, were members of both social and civic clubs.[79]

Some of the social organizations supported charitable institutions that had originally received ecclesiastical support. The California Club, for example, became the primary benefactor of the Orthopaedic Hospital of Los Angeles in 1918. The institution had its origins as a clinic operated by volunteers from the First Congregational Church under the direction of Charles Lowman, a young physician who became interested in community medicine through the YMCA.[80] By 1915, the operation had expanded to the Crippled Children's Guild of Los Angeles under the sponsorship of a more general group of voluntaristic churches. In 1918, the Orthopaedic Hospital became an independent corporation, and the California Club was glad to find a "worth-while cause in which to discharge our responsibility of social stewardship."[81] Charitable action was the most prominent vehicle for civic concern on the part of the social clubs.

It was in the activities of the civic associations that a clearer picture of voluntaristic social attitudes emerged. The Woman's Club, Chamber of Commerce, the Merchants and Manufacturers Association (M and M), and others took part in and indeed often initiated periodic attacks on vice in the city. After the passage of the ordinance prohibiting fan-tan, the M and M, Woman's Club, and the WCTU petitioned the City Council to act upon the provisions of the ordinance immediately. Complaining that they lacked the manpower for enforcement, the Council begged the representatives of the three organizations to wait for "reasonable" implementation.[82] The spokesmen demanded that all members of their organizations be deputized, and a citizen's "police force" had closed down all of Los Angeles' gambling houses by the end of 1896.[83] Similar pressure was used in the ordinance of 1899, which limited the number of saloons in the city to two hundred, "regardless of future population growth," and the 1909 crusade to close down the pitifully small and ineffective vice district near the civic center.[84]

Although periodic crusades against various forms of vice were an important element of voluntaristic Protestantism in Los Angeles, it should not be assumed that the eradication of sin was the central element of the civic consciousness. If vice, even in limited forms, caused a great deal of concern, it was only because it represented a divisive and unholy force in the cohesive Christian community. It was the integrity of that community that was the major concern of the voluntaristic Protestants. More representative is the founding of the Civic Association of Los Angeles in 1899. The founding membership, which differed from the standard pattern of local civic organizations only in the fact that *every* member was also a member of a voluntaristic Protestant church, included the President of the Los Angeles Orphans' Home Board and a member of the Board of Education.[85] The purpose of the organization, according to the charter, was to cooperate with a host of civic and charitable organizations, which were mentioned by name, "to make this the most beautiful, intellectual, moral and sanitary city in the land; a city where slums may never enter. . . .a city where moral, physical and industrial training may go hand in hand with mental training."[86]

Obviously, "Pure Morals" was considered more a matter of creating the proper Christian environment than a protracted vice crusade. A number of local ministers greeted the founding of the Civic Association as "a more encouraging form of community improvement than well-intentioned Christian dragons searching out evil-doers."[87] The major concern of all civic organizations, whether charitable, economic, or general, was with the proper atmosphere for the progress of the cohesive community.

The Protestant-dominated Chamber of Commerce supported economic policies commensurate with the social attitudes of the community they represented. The Chamber had been primarily a "booster" organization in the 1880's, and the M and M was founded in 1893 for a specific promotional purpose. A group of merchants, primarily associated with the citrus industry, petitioned the City Council to sponsor a Trade Carnival to stimulate business in Los Angeles.[88] The immediate inspiration for the idea came from the Midwinter Fair being held in San Francisco. It was assumed that the Trade Carnival would capitalize on the tourist trade to the northern city.[89] In order to attract as many visitors as possible, Harry E. Brook, one of the founding members of the M and M, compiled a promotional booklet "Containing Reliable Information for the Homeseeker, Tourist, and Invalid."[90]

By the time that plans were being formulated for the Trade Carnival, the M and M had established a council of leading citizens to direct the activities. It was decided that the Carnival should, "reflect more of the community than just the trade."[91] All of Los Angeles was to be represented, or at least all of the voluntaristic community. Churches, clubs, and charitable associations all provided booths and attractions based on the theme of Spanish California. Thus it was that in 1894, the first annual *La Fiesta de Los Angeles* was held. There was nothing Spanish or Mexican about the occasion except the name. All members of the guiding committee and all of the participating institutions were *gringo*.[92] A Baptist minister delivered the "Blessing of the Animals," and the Protestant Mrs. Ozro Childs was crowned *La Reina de La Fiesta*.[93] The festival continued to be an important part of

Los Angeles social life, and until well into the thirties, Protestants dominated the celebration of the Spanish past.[94]

Los Angeles boosterism was fairly successful in the late nineteenth century, and both the •M and M and the Chamber of Commerce were able to turn their attention to more serious considerations of local economic policy. The late 1890's was a time of general prosperity in Los Angeles, especially among the Protestant merchants. Of the many comments by visitors to Southern California in this time, the most frequent were about the high prices. "There is little trade competition," wrote one tourist, "and consequently prices are maintained at an arbitrary standard."[95]   Both the Chamber and the M and M adopted loose plans for the voluntary coordination of local enterprise in order to perpetuate the prosperous times.[96]

Out of this blend of participation in the voluntaristic community and desire for continued economic success the "open shop" policy of Los Angeles emerged, which was to persist until World War II[97] The usual picture that is drawn of the Los Angeles entrepreneur between 1890 and 1941 is that of a greedy man with a sinister slim mustache, well dressed, and with one foot planted firmly on the back of labor.[98]   While the image is not is not entirely incorrect, it is suggests an antipathy towards the laboring class that did not exist in so simple a form.   In 1897, for example, the Chamber and the M and M joined with the City Council, under the sponsorship of the First Congregational Church, to provide coordinated relief and public work for the unemployed.[99]   Increased migration had created a significant rise in unemployment that year, and both commercial organizations indicated a feeling of responsibility for having lured workmen to Los Angeles with a promise of economic success.[100]

The attitude of the Los Angeles business community (the same Protestants in another role) towards organized labor was quite another matter. The problem first arose in 1897, when the workers at the Maier and Zobelein Brewery attempted to organize a local chapter of the Council of Labor. The M and M, primarily Protestant and on friendly terms with the WCTU, pledged their support to the two beer makers in an effort to halt a trend toward organized labor.[101] Officially the M and M announced their opposition to "any form of control—over business, politics, or labor—from those outside our community."[102] One of the most prominent members added privately, "What in God's name are we doing helping a couple of Jew booze manufacturers. I know I would not have supported the resolution if I did not think that a union would ruin the town."[103]   There was some early clerical support for the anti-union policy which equated organized labor with the social upheaval in cities to the East.[104]

In the early twentieth century, anti-unionism was wedded with a fear of radicalism. There was never a significant leftist element in the city, but the appearance of the Los Angeles *Socialist* in November of 1901 drew an hysterical response from the Chamber, the M and M, and the pulpit. The newspaper folded three years later, but the fear remained.[105] Beginning in 1905, the M and M hired "investigators" which were deputized by the Los Angeles Police Department to "discover the sources of radicalism in this city."[106] Radicalism was not discovered, but many incipient labor organizations were exposed by the M and M deputies.[107] In 1908, the Association began to apply pressure to banks to refuse loans to any companies which made concessions to organized labor forces. In the same year, the Chamber of Commerce suggested that the business community cease advertising Los Angeles as an economic heaven. "If we can reduce the migration of unwanted elements in this way, it may be worth the minor losses we may incur," wrote the President of the Chamber.[108]

It was within this atmosphere that the bombing of the Los Angeles *Times* building occurred in October of 1910. The *Times* had long been anti-union, and Harrison Gray Otis, the publisher, was an outspoken defender of the "open shop" system.[109] Fearing that radical labor may have had a stronger case than had been thought, the Chamber of Commerce and the M and M offered financial assistance to the city government in the investigation of the incendiary action.[110] It was found that the incident was unrelated to the general labor movement in Los Angeles, but the two commercial organizations used the bombing as another example of the sinister implications of unionism. The matter took on added significance when Clarence Darrow arrived in town to defend the incendiaries. "The unions bring lawyers from Chicago," exclaimed the President of the Chamber of Commerce, "Who knows what other people for what other purpose they will bring in next from who knows where."[111] In order to stem the dual tide of unionism and radicalism, the M and M and the Chamber organized mass meetings during the trail, and petitioned the City Council to increase the police force by two hundred. The Council immediately authorized the hiring of one hundred additional officers.[112] Antiunionism was the most prominent, but not the major, effort of the two commercial associations. Most of their energies were directed to various civic projects, usually cooperation with other organizations. Often, of course, the Chamber and M and M presented proposals for economic legislation to the City

Council, and the measures were usually adopted.[113]   Whether engaged in "open shop" promotion, civic projects, or proposing city ordinances, the two associations constantly demonstrated localist tendencies.   Their programs of Los Angeles boosterism and the maintenance of the "open shop," and their effective campaigns to exclude outside economic control in the form of corporate industry, were all part of a consistent pattern of voluntaristic attitudes which gave prime importance to the integrity of the cohesive community.[114]   It was at the level of the city government that voluntaristic Protestants gained control of the agencies which could transmute this general attitude into public policy.

V

Until the late 1890's, Los Angeles voluntaristic Protestants, as a group, demonstrated little interest in politics.   Between 1880 and 1898, over half of all elective and appointive positions in the city and county were held by members of one of the six major denominations (see Table 23), but this was more the result of the selection of office holders from a rather limited pool of civic leaders than a manifestation of a Protestant "party."   Occasionally religious and civic groups of the Protestant community engaged in political activities to achieve specific ends, such as the crusades of the WCTU and the 1895 petition by local churches to limit the number of saloons in the city.[115]   Most often, however, specific desires of the voluntaristic communities were satisfied, and no need was perceived for more concentrated political action.

In 1898, a revised charter for the city government was defeated. The document had received the unqualified support of the voluntaristic Protestant community.[116]   The major revisions included provisions for referendum, initiative, and recall, and a prohibition against city officials holding offices in the state of national political parties.[117]   Protestants were clearly enthusiastic about the community cohesion implicit in the new charter.   In addition to the unanimous support of the voluntaristic civic organizations, a few congregations voted to endorse the new charter.[118]   Said the Rev. William J. Keller of Trinity Methodist Church, "I rejoice that we have before us an instrument of government that can so admirably administer our Christian city."[119]   Perhaps because everyone assumed that the charter would receive overwhelming support, the revisions were defeated.   Voters in Protestant neighborhoods turned out in very low numbers, and the small labor community returned a very substantial vote against the measure, which had not included labor requests to establish a minimum wage for the city.[120]   It would be the last time for two decades that the voluntaristic community would face such a dismal defeat at the polls.

Immediately after the charter was defeated, the loose federation of active laymen who sponsored the *California Independent* drafted a slate of voluntaristic civic leaders for the upcoming city elections. "If our city is to truly be a 'City of Churches,'" declared James R. Toberman, Methodist layman and candidate for Mayor, "it must be governed by Christians."[121] Of course, most of the existing office holders were not only Christian, but also Protestant. Obviously the campaign was an attempt to awaken the voluntaristic community to its potential political power, and to make the logical extension of the voluntaristic system into the city government. All of the candidates on the *California Independent* slate were elected, and all were announced as "Protestant Candidates."[122] It is no overstatement to say that during the next twenty years, voluntaristic Protestants controlled the elective and appointive offices. Less than ten percent of these positions were filled by men who cannot also be identified as members of a voluntaristic congregations.

Although the city was strongly Republican from 1880 to 1930, the local concerns of city officials made party identification within the national context superfluous.

TABLE 23

VOLUNTARISTIC PROTESTANT OFFICE HOLDERS AS PERCENTAGE OF ALL LOS ANGELES CITY OFFICIALS

	1880-1898	1899-1920
Elective	51.7	93.4
Appointive	43.6	86.9
School Board[a]	79.3	98.1
All Offices	52.5	91.0

Source: Municipal Reference Department, City of Los Angeles, *A Chronological Record of Los Angeles City Officials, 1850-1938* (Los Angeles, 1938); Los Angeles City School Board, Manuscript Records; Sources listed in Appendix I.

Indeed, this can be extended to the voting voluntaristic community in general. Neighborhoods of high Protestant concentration tended to vote heavily and in consistent patterns in local elections, and more sparsely and with greater diversity in state and national elections.[123] In the first few years of conscious Protestant control of the city government, public office was not considered a career, and the concerns of the transitory office holders were local.   James Toberman, for example, served one term as mayor and was nominated for a second, but declined in order to reopen his Venetian-blind factory and devote his attention to the founding of the Methodist Convalescent Home.[124] Until 1906, most of the city officials served for only one term, and many still held positions of leadership in congregations and civic organizations. After this time, however, offices tended to be held for a number of terms, and the distributions of positions took place within an increasingly limited community of elective and appointive office holders.[125] They were still overwhelmingly voluntaristic Protestants, and their concerns continued to be local. Before the 1920's, less than five percent of the local office holders made any observable effort to enter state or national politics.[126]

In part the change in the structure of local politics was a result of the tendency of Los Angeles Protestant leaders to become specialized in one particular area of the maintenance of the Christian community. In the political life of the city, however, the year 1906 had a specific effect on local government. Since the 1870's, the Southern Pacific entertained baronial notions about its relation to the city (which it correctly believed that it helped build). In 1887, a group of local clergymen concerned about the "unhealthy indigent population" which staffed the local offices and yards of the railroad tried to organize a campaign to end the power of the Southern Pacific in Los Angeles.[127] For the most part however the Protestant merchants and farmers were direct beneficiaries from the presence of the railroad, and the corporation did very little to interfere in local affairs. Ordinances which the Southern Pacific wanted passed were most often those that were also supported by the voluntaristic community. The action of the city government in the areas of vice and the control of alcoholic beverages were of no concern to the corporation.[128]

Between 1895 and 1906, however, a series of developments caused the voluntaristic community in Los Angeles to perceive the Southern Pacific as a dangerous corporate machine in local politics. In 1895, the Direct Legislation League of Los Angeles was formed to "create a city government that will be an expression of our community."[129] It was through this organization that the charter revisions suggested in 1898 were initiated. By 1903, the new charter was adopted. The citizenry used the provisions the following year to remove J. P. Davenport from the councilmanic seat, and Los Angeles thus became the first city in the United States to recall a city official.[130] Davenport was probably removed from office because his voting record was consistently against the voluntaristic majority.[131] The stated reason for the action was his connection with the Southern Pacific. As an employee of the corporation, it was charged, Davenport was not a representative of the people of Los Angeles.[132]

Voluntaristic businessmen in the community had already formulated a policy against outside interference in local affairs through labor unions, and the Chamber of Commerce was becoming suspicious of corporations controlled from other areas.[133] Prominent Los Angelenos created an informal civic reform group in 1905 to investigate the extent of the control of the city government by the Southern Pacific.[134] John R. Haynes, Congregationalist businessman and philanthropist, announced a general campaign to make the city government more clearly responsive to the citizenry rather than serving special interests of corporations "in other parts of this state, if not this nation."[135] The "incorrupt people" of the City of the Angels, he argued, had the power to "purify the city government and achieve civic progress."[136] The informal group named itself the Good Government Association and declared political war on "Boss" Walter Parker, local representative of the Southern Pacific, and his unnamed "lackies."[137]

The Good Government Association was unable to find any evidence of the corruption of local office holders, but it was discovered that the city had allowed the Southern Pacific to select the surgeons that settled disputes involving passengers injured on the railroad in the area.[138] It was this and similar practices of the corporation that the Good Government Association attacked. Indeed, it would have been embarrassing for the Protestant businessmen to criticize fellow Protestant businessmen, often from their own congregations. What was needed was not a purging of public offices, but a "fresh approach to city government, administered by local citizens who can devote their full attention to the problems of a modern city."[139] Privately, Haynes expressed his conviction that "our city officers have been, and are, good and decent men. This business of one or two years in office and then back to the store just will not work. We need a group of long term statesmen from our community."[140]

In the 1906 city election, the Good Government Association cooperated with the Municipal League to post a slate of twenty-three candidates for local offices, of whom seventeen were elected.[141] Their candidate for Mayor, Lee C. Gates, a Methodist real estate broker, lost the election. Gates had long been active in temperance movements, and at the urging of the WCTC campaigned on a prohibition platform, to the exclusion of remarks on the Southern Pacific.[142] The reform movement received the support of press and pulpit, as well as the endorsement of civic organizations and congregations.[143]   The composition of the city government after 1906 remained overwhelmingly Protestant, but a small proportion of the community was involved. Professional politics at the local level had begun, and the stratification of the voluntaristic community into levels of activity was increased.

A few minor reform movements emerged after 1906, all relating to local affairs. After the *Times* bombing in 1910, for example, George Alexander, former Presbyterian Elder and warehouse owner and now a professional politician, formed the Good Government Organization (as distinct from the Good Government Association) to rid the community of any socialist elements. He was elected Mayor on this platform, but he found no socialists. His political career was eventually harmed by his obsession. At his urging, a conservative faction of the Chamber of Commerce formed the Los Angeles Municipal League to prevent two "Socialist-labor" candidates from being elected in 1913.[144] In order to present a strong slate, the Municipal Conference decided to support a stronger candidate than Alexander, and nominated John W. Schenk, a conservative councilman.[145] Edwin T. Earl, a more progressive publisher and member of the organization, had urged the nomination of William Mulholland, and engineer and contractor who had been brought to Los Angeles to supervise public building projects. Mulholland could bring to the office, Earl argued, a knowledge of the physical complexities of the city and could provide efficient leadership.[146]   Mulholland, a non-Protestant, free-thinker, idiosyncratic, and something of a technocrat, was completely unacceptable to the other members of the Municipal Conference.[147]   In order to gain support for their candidate, the organization made an appeal to the dreaded corporate interests in the city. Earl, and his paper, immediately withdrew their support from the Conference slate. "This alliance with the First National Bank and other Corporated interests to deliver the city government into the hands of the money power," declared Earl, "is a most amazing act of treachery to the people."[148]   After the election, it became clear that the two radical candidates had posed no real threat, and that the corporate interests were to have no influence in the new administration. Alexander was out of office and suffered the condemnation of his fellow Los Angelenos for having created an atmosphere of distrust in a community that was based on cooperation.[149]

The localistic influences so evident in other levels of Protestant activity were an important part of city politics. "Urban Progressivism" in Los Angeles was not no much a part of a more general Progressive movement in the state or nation as it was yet another expression of the voluntaristic principle as it came to be practiced in the City of the

Angels. Elements in the city and in state and national politics were working to make the city part of a larger sphere of political action, but until 1920, the Los Angeles city government was most concerned with maintaining the integrity of the local community.

VI

For over two decades, a fairly stable voluntaristic community existed in Los Angeles. Although it never consisted of more than seventeen percent of the total population, the general principles associated with it were extended into the social and political life of the city. If the voluntaristic spirit is a vague and general concept, it is because neither the formulators nor the perpetuators of the system had any desire to specify the concept beyond "a Christian sense of community." The system, after all, had to embrace those who believed that the local congregation was the definition of the Church and those who held that the Church had been historically transmitted through the apostolic succession of the episcopacy. From this broad base of doctrine and practice, nineteenth-century Protestants sought to extend their concept of community across the expanding nation. In early twentieth-century Los Angeles, voluntaristic Protestants attempted to preserve their tradition in the face of the decline of the system in other communities. They did so by limiting their loose federation of denominations to a relatively homogenous population and using their solidarity to serve and control the larger community.

Beyond the activities outlined in this chapter, the extension of the Protestant community took more subtle forms. Every minister invited to speak at commencement services for Los Angeles high schools was affiliated with one of the six voluntaristic denominations.[150] In 1915, the School Board instituted Americanization and Citizenship Classes in predominantly Mexican schools, using materials provided by voluntaristic denominations.[151] Missionary activity among the Mexican population most often took the form of job training for local occupations, but optional religious instruction was also provided. The desire for homogeneity probably inhibited any impulse to proselytize the Mexican population. When a Mexican did convert, and that was a rare occasion, he usually received a clerical job from one of the wealthier members of his new congregation, moved to a predominantly Protestant neighborhood, and improved his economic status appreciably.[152]

There were, of course a few events and movements in the early twentieth century which did not fit into the general pattern of stability outlined here. In the 1890's for example, Los Angeles had the most flourishing Nationalist movement in the nation.[153] Although Lyman

Stewart's BIOLA was brought into the voluntaristic community, the oilman withdrew his support from local religious institutions and financed the writing of *The Fundamentals,* which was written by conservative theologians across the nation and was the intellectual justification for the Fundamentalist movement.[154]   The Church of the Nazarene was founded by a group of ex-Methodists in Los Angeles in 1895. The Methodist Church was too concerned with the community and gave too little attention to the soul, they complained.[155]   A small group of Presbyterians claimed that Los Angeles was not enough of a Christian community and founded the Los Angeles Voluntary Association in 1913.[156]   On one occasion, a handful of Congregationalist ministers joined Unitarian pastors in Los Angeles to protest an allegedly unfair trail of radial labor leaders in San Francisco.[157]   None of these things, however, detract from the stability of the larger Protestant community. In all cases they were limited to a small faction. The fact that the life of the voluntaristic community usually ignored such anomalies is testimony to the integral nature of the system.

The stability of the community was somewhat misleading, however. The fragmentation of Protestant leadership into four levels of activity created a structure which performed the functions of the voluntaristic community, but used the methods of the corporation. The gradual shift in innovations from the congregation to the local denominational agencies was indicative of a more general breakdown in the integrity of the congregation. In addition to losing control over specific institutions, the neighborhood parishes had to contend with the more professionally run large churches. This had an effect on the Protestant family. In 1900, entire families were members of the neighborhood congregation. By 1920, eighteen percent of the children of members of the smaller parishes were members of one of the twelve largest churches in the city.[158] It is impossible to reconstruct with any accuracy the specific age groupings, but one long-time resident of the City of the Angels recalls, "A lot of us in high school didn't want to stay around the same old church. It was easy to get a trolley to Immanuel Presbyterian. The preaching was better. There were more people to meet. There was more to do."[159] Another recalled, "I have always been a member of Calvary Baptist, but sometime about 1909 or 1910, I started attending First Baptist. It was more fun and more active."[160]

The change in the specifics of Protestant life in Los Angeles was the result of the corporate structure that became necessary to sustain Protestant power. The rhetoric of the period, however, still emphasized the concept of a cohesive organic community. In 1919, voluntaristic churches in the City of the Angels held joyous celebrations of the passage of the Prohibition Amendment. Temple Baptist Church held a mock funeral for "John Barleycorn."[161] One minister expressed the hope that "the implementation of this great amendment may bring communities together in all parts of the nation. What a blessing it would be if Philadelphia or Chicago could experience the communion of Christian Brotherhood we have in this city."[162] William Stewart Young, preaching at the First Presbyterian Church, congratulated the rest of the nation for having "caught up with the moral awareness of Los Angeles,"[163] To the contrary, Los Angeles was catching up with the rest of the nation. Just as the Protestant community experienced a change in structure, the city as a whole changed with urban growth. Basic and often unperceived developments further altered the configuration of the voluntaristic community, and radially changed the place of Protestantism in the life of the city.

NOTES

[1] Los Angeles *Times*, December 4, 1891.

[2] Minutes of Meeting of the Congregation, April 3, 1896, Immanual Presbyterian Church, Los Angeles, California; *Ibid.*, May 9, 1896; *California Independent*, June 27, 1896.

[3] Dana W. Bartlett, *The Better City* (Los Angeles, 1907), p. 134.

[4] Jackson A. Graves, *My Seventy Years in California, 1857-1927* (Los Angeles, 1927), pp. 467-470.

[5] The citations from Baptist, Methodist, Congregational, Episcopal, Presbyterian, and Disciples of Christ national agencies are most easily found in summary form in Dana W. Bartlett, *The Christian City* (Los Angeles, 1923), pp. 18-27.

[6] Willard Hunt Wright, "Los Angeles—The Chemically Pure," *The Smart Set Anthology*, eds. Burton Rascoe and Gradd Conkin (New York, 1934), p. 91. The article first appeared in 1913.

[7] See Appendix I for citation of religious censuses.

[8] The specifics of Lyman Stewart's unique involvement, until 1909, in the four levels of Protestant activity in Los Angeles were obtained from the Lyman Stewart Papers, Bible Institute of Los Angeles.

[9] Determined from a systematic reading of the Los Angeles *Times*, *Examiner*, and the various sermon collections mentioned in Appendix III.

[10] Determined from a reconstruction of Protestant parishes from data discussed in Appendix I.

[11] Young to Melvin J. Howard, October 17, 1911, Young Papers.

[12] Based on interviews listed in the Bibliography.

[13] Minutes of the Session, February 13, 1906, First Presbyterian Church, Los Angeles.

[14] James D. Dawson to William Stewart Young, February 17, 1906, Young Papers.

[15] Report of the Vestry of His Excellency, the Bishop of Los Angeles, 1905, Archives of the Diocese of Los Angeles.

[16] *Ibid.*, 1908.

[17] Minutes of the Committee on Religious Education, 1903-1905, First Baptist Church, Los Angeles, *passim*. "Summary Report on the Development of the Sunday School Program of the Wilshire Presbyterian Church of Los Angeles, Prepared as a Study Guide for the Committee on Educational Programs of the Presbytery of Los Angeles," (Typescript, 1909), Archives of the Presbytery of Los Angeles.

[18]The letters written from Stewart to William Stewart Young immediately following his ordination as an Elder (Stewart Papers and Young Papers) constantly refer to Stewart's interest in religious education.

[19]Minutes of the Session, July 8, 1909, Immanuel Presbyterian Church, Los Angeles.

[20]Stewart to William Stewart Young, August 19, 1911, Young Papers; Minutes of the Session, August 24, 1911, Immanuel Presbyterian Church, Los Angeles; "A Tribute to Joseph M. Irvine," *Southern California Presbyterian* (December, 1957), 348.

[21]Methodist Episcopal Church, North, *Southern California Conference Minutes* (Los Angeles, 1900-1920), *passim*, in "Report of the Epworth League."

[22]"Budget Reports," 1900-1920, Files of Temple Baptist Church, Los Angeles.

[23]"Budget Report," 1915, *Ibid.*

[24]Based on parish reconstructions from sources discussed in Appendix I.

[25]Determined from the application of a multi-parameter repeating program to the reconstruction cited in Note 24.

[26]*Ibid.*, compared with a reconstruction of the social stratification of Los Angeles based on published census data in the *Los Angeles City Directory*. A rough estimate of wealth was determined by data from the Office of the Tax Assessor, Hall of Records, County of Los Angeles.

[27]The founding of the Civic Association, the Women's Club, and the Merchants and Manufacturers Association can all be traced to origins in the First Congregational, Immanuel Presbyterian, and First Methodist Churches.

[28]The general pattern was determined from a computer analysis of denominational and congregational budgets from sources discussed in Appendices I and III.

[29]Minutes of the Vestry, January 28, 1909, Church of the Ascension, Los Angeles. Salton's sermons were read in the collections listed in Appendix II.

[30]Based on a systematic reading of the reports of church activity in the Los angels *Times*, and the relevant materials in the archival sources for local denominational activities discussed in Appendix II.

[31]Fogelson, p. 105; Budget Summaries, 1898-1903, Archives of the Diocese of Los Angeles.

[32]Wylie to the Stated Clerk of the Presbytery of Los Angeles, March 30, 1902, Young Papers.

[33]See Note 8.

[34]Minutes of Meeting of the Congregation, September (?), 1890, First Baptist Church, Los Angeles.

[35] *Ibid.,* May 21, 1898.

[36] Los Angeles Baptist Association, *Report,* 1906, p. 129.

[37] Minutes of Meeting of the Congregation, July 8, 1907, First Baptist Church, Los Angeles.

[38] Northern Baptist Convention, *Annual Report* (New York, 1916), p. 283.

[39] Minutes of the Board of Stewards, November (?), 1897, First Methodist Church, Los Angeles.

[40] Southern California Conference Minutes (Los Angeles, 1909, pp. 74-83; Los Angeles *Times,* June 11, 1909.

[41] Only two boys who were listed as students in the school in the *Southern California Conference Minutes* between 1909 and 1920 appear on the master list of voluntaristic Protestants prepared from sources discussed in Appendix. I.

[42] Determined from a reconstruction of Protestant leadership, and levels of activity, based on the sources discussed in Appendices I and III.

[43] "Summary Reports on Institutions," 1900-1920, Archives of the Diocese of Los Angeles, *passim.*

[44] Los Angeles *Times,* May 13, 1903; September 4, 1915.

[45] *Ibid.,* May 17, 1903.

[46] *Ibid.,* May 16, 1903; September 5, 1915.

[47] See Note 28.

[48] "Summary Report on Diocesan Operations," 1900 and 1920, Archives of the Diocese of Los Angeles.

[49] See Note 42.

[50] Based on the relevant data from the local denominational archival sources discussed in Appendix III.

[51] Los Angeles *Times,* January 12, 1899; January 19, 1899.

[52] *Ibid.,* May 10, 1906.

[53] *Ibid,* September 23, 1906.

[54] Based on an analysis of budgetary emphasis and response to (or really lack of response to) debates and issues at the national level, from appropriate sources discussed in Appendices I and III.

[55]Harvey Bender to the Secretary of the Los Angeles Congregational Association Budget Committee, March 27, 1914, Files of the United Church of Christ, Los Angeles.

[56]Minutes of Organizational Meeting, 1891, Files of the Union Rescue Mission.

[57]Lyman Stewart to William Stewart Young, November 3, 1891, Young Papers.

[58]Los Angeles *Times*, December 15, 1891.

[59]The budgetary reports in the Files of the Union Rescue Mission indicate that over seventy percent of the operating funds came from local voluntaristic denominations.

[60]*Fuller Notes.*, VI, p. 163. See Appendix III for a description of this source.

[61]See Helga Bender Henry, *Mission on Main Street* (Boston, 1955.

[62]Union Rescue Mission, *Report*, 1906 (unpaginated).

[63]*Ibid.*

[64]*Ibid.*, 1908.

[65]Membership of the board was obtained through the *Report* 1892-1920, and correlated with the sources in Appendix I; Henry, p. 136.

[66]Stewart to Young, June 14, 1904, Young Papers.

[67]*Ibid.*, October 17, 1907.

[68]File on Lyman Stewart and Curricula in Biblical Literature, Archives of Occidental College.

[69]*Ibid.*

[70]Charter of the Bible Institute of Los Angeles, in the Archives of that institution.

[71]Stewart Papers, *passim*, especially Stewart to Thomas C. Horton, January 12, 1909.

[72]*Ibid.*

[73]Letter of Joseph Irvine to the Churches of Los Angeles, March 21, 1901, Archives of the Bible Institute of Los Angeles, Report of Donations, 1909-1920, *Ibid.*

[74]Fuller *Notes*, VII.

[75]This was made repeatedly clear in the letters of other board members of Stewart, Stewart Papers.

[76]Torrey became a member of the Los Angeles Ministerial Association in 1912; Los Angeles *Times*, March 30, 1912.,

[77]Ernest R. Sandeen, *The Roots of Fundamentalism: British and American Millenarianism, 1800-1930* (Chicago, 1970), pp. 182-185.

[78]Prestigious" and "active" organizations were determined rather impressionistically from the local press, published memoirs, interviews, and the papers of prominent Los Angelenos, Protestant and non-Protestant, listed in the Bibliography.   See the summary of this data in Appendix IV.

[79]Determined from a correlation of data from sources discussed in Appendix I. The activities of the social clubs had to be gleaned from newspaper references, with the exception of the California Club Papers, Special Collections Division, University Research Library, University of California, Los Angeles.

[80]Charles LeRoy Lowaman, "The Orthopaedic Medical Center—A Los Angeles Achievement, 1903-1962," HSSCQ (June, 1962), 133.

[81]*Ibid.,* 135-139.

[82]Minutes of Meeting, December 19, 1895, Los Angeles Common Files; George E. Mowry, *The California Progressives* (Berkeley, 1951), p. 38.

[83]*Ibid;* Los Angeles *Times,* November 28, 1896.

[84]Ostrander, pp. 77 and 131.

[85]M. Burton Williamson, "The Civic Association as a Factor in Greater Los Angeles, " HSSCQ VIII (1911), 180-187; List of Members, 1899, Files of the Civic Association of Los Angeles, Special Collections Division, University Research Library, University of California, Los Angeles, correlated with data from sources in Appendix I.

[86]Williamson, 183.

[87]Los Angeles *Times,* March 26, 1899.

[88]Minutes of Meeting, January 23, 1893, Los Angeles Common Council Files.

[89]Los Angeles *Times,* March 3, 1893.

[90]Harry Ellington Brook, *The Land of Sunshine: Southern California, an Authentic Description of Its Natural Features, Resources and Prospects, Containing Reliable Information for the Homeseeker, Tourist, and Invalid; Compiled for the Southern California World's Fair Association and Southern California Bureau of Information* (Los Angeles, 1893).

[91]Los Angeles *Times,* April 24, 1893.

[92]This list of the guiding committees, and participating institutions was obtained from Isabel Wiclus, "La Fiesta de Los Angeles: A Survey of the Yearly Celebrations, 1894-1898," (Unpublished Master's Thesis, University of California, Los Angeles, 1946) p. 94.

[93]*Ibid.*, 81; Marco R. Newmark, "La Fiesta de Los Angeles of 1894," HSSCQ XXIX (June, 1947) 107.

[94]Laurence L. Hill, "A Great City Celebrates Its One Hundred and Fiftieth Anniversary," HSSCQ XC (1931), 7-55. By 1931, the Mexican community finally gained some representation in the celebration of their past. Of the seventy-two leading citizens appointed to the guiding committee, one had a Spanish surname. For the first time, the Catholic Church was invited to participate in a formal way. The Baptist Mary Youngworth was crowned *La Reina de la Fiesta* by the Irish born Archbishop of the Roman Catholic Archdiocese of Los Angeles, William May Garland.

[95]Edwards and Harraden, pp. 97-98.

[96]Los Angeles Chamber of Commerce Minutes, 1890-1900, Los Angeles Chamber of Commerce, *passim.*

[97]The general outline of the development and maintainance of the "anti-union" attitude can be found in Ira B. Cross, *A History of the Labor Movement in California* (Berkeley, 1935), *passim;* Grace Heilman Stimson, *Rise of the Labor Movement in Los Angeles* (Berkeley and Los Angeles, 1955); and Louis B. and Richard S. Perry, *A History of Los Angeles Labor Movement, 1911-1941* (Berkeley and Los Angeles, 1963). All three sources are written from the perspective of labor history, and the cultural context of the development of the "open shop" policy is not analyzed.

[98]This is the image that was presented by labor periodicals at the time (see Stimson, pp. 352-355), and it has found its way into such generals works as Joseph G. Rayback, *A History of American Labor* (rev. ed.; New York, 1966), p. 685.

[99]Stimson, p. 190; Los Angeles Chamber of Commerce Minutes, May 9, 1897; Minutes of Meeting, May, 1897, Los Angeles Common Council Files.

[100]Los Angeles *Times*, April 2, 1897; April 5, 1897.

[101]Stimson, p. 189.

[102]Los Angeles *Times*, August 28, 1897.

[103]George Dawson to John Randolph Haynes, September 4, 1897, John Randolph Haynes Papers, Special Collections Division University Research Library, University of California Los Angeles.

[104]Los Angeles *Times*, October 17, 1897; November 3, 1897; November 10, 1897.

[105]Los Angeles *Socialist*, 1901-1904; Los Angeles *Times*, March 13, 1901-January 30, 1902, contains many editorials statements by the M and M, Chamber of Commerce, and other civic groups, and extracts from sermons which demonstrate this general fear.

[106]Mowry, pp. 48-49.

[107] Los Angeles *Times,* April 19-July 5, 1905.

[108] Stimson, pp. 319-320; Los Angeles Chamber of Commerce, *Members Annual,* (1908), p. 84.

[109] Stimson, pp. 366-406; Louis Adamic, *Dynamite* (New York, 1931); Los Angeles *Times, The Forty Year War for a Free City: A History of the Open Shop in Los Angeles* (New York, 1929).

[110] Stimson, p. 376.

[111] Los Angeles *Times,* December 6, 1910.

[112] Stimson, pp. 375-376.

[113] Based on a survey of action on proposals presented by the Chamber of Commerce and the Merchants and Manufacturers Association in the Minutes of Meetings, 1900-1920, Los Angeles Common Council Files.

[114] For an interesting analysis of the effects of localism in urban areas in the early twentieth century, see Samuel P. Hays, "The Politics of Reform in Municipal Government in the Progressive Era," *Pacific Northwest Quarterly* LV (October, 1964), 157-169. Hays generally equates "locals" with political machines and "cosmopolitans" with reform elements. The fact that Los Angeles reformers were extreme localists is evidence of the difference between that large voluntaristic community and the structure of other cities at the same time.

[115] Betty Woods, "An Historical Survey of the Woman's Christian Temperance Union of Southern California (Unpublished Master's Thesis, Occidental College, Los Angeles, 1950), pp. 67-73.

[116] Stimson, p. 221; Los Angeles *Times,* February 25, December 7, 1898. Almost every issue carried a story, editorial, or the announcement of organizational support.

[117] Proposed Charter Amendments of 1898, Los Angeles Common Council Files.

[118] Handbills in support of the revised charter printed by seven voluntaristic congregations are collected in the Los Angels Churches Collection, Special Collections Division, University Research Library, University of California, Los Angeles.

[119] Los Angeles *Times,* October 7, 1898.

[120] Precinct returns obtained from Los Angeles *Times,* December 9, 1898, and compared with a reconstruction of Protestant residential areas from sources discussed in Appendix I, and areas of high labor concentration reconstructed from a random sample of residents in the Los Angeles *City Directory,* 1898.

[121] *California Independent,* December 12, 1898.

[122] Los Angeles *Times* March 14, 1899; *California Independent,* February 17-25, 1899.

123See Chapter 5, Section IV.

124Jervey, p. 43

125Determined from Municipal Reference Department, *A Chronological Record of Los Angeles City Officials, 1850-1938*   (Los Angeles, 1938).

126Based on tracing careers of office holders from *Ibid.* and *Men of California: Western Personalities and their Affiliations* (San Francisco and Los Angeles, 1924-1930).

127Mowry, p. 39.

128Albert Codius, "The Quest for Good Government in Los Angeles, 1890-1910," (Unpublished Doctoral Dissertation, Claremont Graduate School, 1953), pp. 97-113; Lola Kassell, 'A History of the Government of Los Angeles, 1781-1925," (Unpublished Master's Thesis, Occidental College, 1929), p. 106.

129Los Angeles *Times,* August 21, 1895.

130Stimson, pp. 282-285.

131Davenport's record in contrast to that of the majority of the Council was determined from Minutes of Meetings, 1903-1905, Los Angeles Common Council Files.   One of the leaders of the recall movement privately indicated that the aberrant voting behavior was a basic reason for the campaign to unseat Davenport: C. V. Barton to John Haynes, Haynes Papers.

132John R. Haynes, "The Recall of Councilman Davenport," Unpublished manuscript, n.d., Haynes Foundation, Los Angeles; C.V. Barton, "The Recall," Unpublished manuscript Haynes Foundation, Los Angeles; Los Angeles *Times,* August 16, 1904; Los Angeles *Times,* August 16, 1904; Los Angeles *Examiner,* August 18, 1904.

133See Chapter 5, Section II.

134Los Angeles *Times,* January 14, 1905.

135*Ibid.,* February 26, 1905.

136*Ibid.;* see Spencer C. Olin, Jr., *California Prodigal Sons: Hiram Johnson and the Progressives, 1911-1917* (Berkeley and Los Angeles, 1968), pp. 2-11.

137Los Angeles *Times,* March 3, 1905.

138Mowry, pp. 38-39.

139Los Angeles Angeles, *Times,* March 5, 1905.

140John R. Haynes to Franklin Hichborn, March 7, 1905, Franklin Hichborn Papers, Specials Collections Division University Research Library, University of California, Los Angeles.

[141]Mowry, pp. 44-45.

[142]Ostrander, p. 106.

[143]Based on a survey of the relevant articles in the Los Angeles *Times* for 1906, congregational sources listed in Appendix I, and *Fuller Notes,* IX.

[144]Stimson, pp. 398-400.

[145]Municipal Conference of Los Angeles, *Bulletin,* April 19, 1913.

[146]Earl to Leo B. Lesperance, April 2, 1913, Leo B. Lesperance Papers, Special Collections Division, University Research Library, University of California, Los Angeles.

[147]Municipal Conference, *Bulletin,* April 19, 1913.

[148]Los Angeles *Express,* April 23, 1913.

[149]Los Angeles *Times,* May 1, 1913; Los Angeles *Examiner,* May 3, 1913. Alexander privately complained about his mistreatment by civic leaders: Alexander to Fremont Ackerman, April 23, 1913. Fremont Ackerman Papers, Special Collections Division, University Library, University of California, Los Angeles.

[150]From a survey of announcements of commencement participants in the Los Angeles *Times,* 1900-1920.

[151]Ruth Callendar, "A Study of Special Day Americanization and Citizenship Classes in the Los Angeles City Schools," (Unpublished Master's Thesis, University of Southern California, 1949), pp. 32-47.

[152]Based on reports of missions to local denominational agencies in archival sources discussed in Appendix III, correlated with the master list of voluntaristic Protestants prepared from sources listed in Appendix I.

[153]Michael P. Rogin and John L. Shover, *Political Change in California* (Westport, Connecticut, 1970), p. 15.

[154]Sandeen, pp. 188-189; Stewart to A. C. Dixon, July 28, 1915, Stewart Papers.

[155]Jervey, pp. lllff; also see John Leland Peters, *Christian Perfection and American Methodism* (New York, 1956), pp. 208-211; M. E. Redford, *The Rise of the Church of the Nazarene* (Kansas City, 1951), pp. 28-34; Timothy L. Smith, *Called Unto Holiness: The Story of the Nazarenes: The Formative Years* (Kansas City 1962), *passim.*

[156]Fern Dawson Shochat, "The Voluntary Cooperative Association of Los Angeles, 1913-1922," HSSCQ XLV (June, 1963), 169-180.

[157]Robert Moats Miller, *American Protestantism and Social Issues, 1919-1939* (Chapter Hill, 1958), pp. 173-175.

[158]See Appendix I.

[159]Interview with George Postam, Presbyterian Home, Los Angeles, February 23, 1970. The effects of trolley transportation on the nuclear family may have been rather significant. See Spencer Crump, *Ride the Big Red Cars: How Trolleys Helped Build Southern California* (Los Angeles, 1962) for a simple description of the system in Los Angeles, and Sam B. Warner, Jr., *Streetcar Suburbs: The Process of Growth in Boston, 1870-1900* (Cambridge, 1962) for a social analysis of the effects of intraurban transportation.

[160]Interview with Jack Kincaid, United Christian Home, Los Angeles, January 17, 1970.

[161]Los Angeles *Times*, January 17, 1919; Gordon Riegler, "The Attitudes of the People of Los Angeles Toward Prohibition from the Recommendation of the Eighteenth Amendment to the Time of Its Adoption," (Unpublished Master's Thesis, University of Southern California, 1924), pp. 147-148. Similar services were held a year later when the amendment went into effect.

[162]*Fuller Notes*, X.

[163]William Stewart Young, "Sermon on the Occasion of the Passage of the Eighteenth Amendment at the First Presbyterian Church of Los Angeles," n.d., Young Papers.

CHAPTER 5

FROM PROTESTANT CITY TO SECULAR METROPOLIS

I

Few, if any, Protestants in Los Angeles at the turn of the century doubted that progress was synonymous with their community. Indeed, the concept became a doctrine of civic faith. The rest of the nation, they thought, had abandoned religious integrity for progress, but Los Angeles was an expanding city that had more churches per capita than any other urban area in America.[1] Protestant leaders across the nation reinforced this self-conception of the voluntaristic community.[2] In no city of the same size or larger, and in few that were smaller, were religious organizations and attitudes so closely associated with the political, economic, and social life of the community. For twenty years, the six major Protestant denominations were able to maintain control of the city government, and the voluntaristic civic organizations established in the 1880's and 1890's continued to exercise influence over the life of the larger community.

"Los Angeles can show the rest of the nation that Christian faith and practice do not hinder progress," said the Reverend John R. Stimpson of Grace Methodist Church to a meeting of the Chamber of Commerce in 1901. "In fact, we can expand with fewer problems if our city is guided by Christ."[3] Other ministers used similar public occasions to make the same point. Any sign of increase was interpreted as the continuance of God's favor. "This city is destined to be the largest in the state by 1930," claimed a local cleric assuming the role of prophet in 1903.[4] Migration patterns rather than Divine Will, however, determined that Los Angeles should overtake San Francisco by 1920.

Certainly, the most obvious and striking example of growth in the city was the population increase from 50,000 in 1890 to 1,283,000 in 1930—a rate far more rapid than the population of the nation or urban areas in general. Among cities with populations over 50,000 in 1890, the growth-rate for Los Angeles was exceeded only once in one decade by Denver between 1910 and 1920.[5] The population increase in the city was the result of migration, territorial expansion, and, to a lesser degree, a slowly rising birth rate.

Los Angeles did not simply get larger, however, The population became more diverse religiously and economically, and existing ethnic groups became more aware of their own identity and separateness from the dominant Protestants. The political and economic organization of the state and nation were undergoing rapid change, and the largest city in an important state could not hope to remain a cohesive community of local interests.   The Protestants of Los Angeles did hope to remain so, however. When the city became a regional and national metropolis, local institutions were unable—often unwilling—to perform the administrative functions of an industrial society. The voluntaristic associations seemed curiously out of place in a state that was providing charitable and custodial services for large communities through complex bureaucracies. Ironically, voluntaristic institutions and agencies actively pursued policies that stimulated urban growth and enthusiastically greeted the changes that were to make them obsolete. Only occasionally did they question change, and then only the specifics of a particular change.   Without realizing it, Los Angeles Protestants were experiencing the same process that made cities to the East appear to un-Christian to them.[6]

TABLE 24

POPULATION GROWTH AND SOCIAL CHANGE
LOS ANGELES, 1900-1930

| | | Diversity Index | | |
	Size	Ethnic	Religious	Economic
1900	102,479	.46	.25	.44
1910	319,198	.50	.28	.53
1920	576,673	.52	.31	.57
1930	1,283,000	.57	.56	.68

Source: See Appendix VI.

II

The general migration to Los Angeles in the period following 1880, the year of the last available manuscript census schedules, cannot be analyzed with the degree of accuracy that one would like, but it would appear that the composition of Los Angeles did not change significantly between 1890 and 1930. The proportion of foreign born remained low—still under twenty percent in 1920.   Of these, approximately one-fourth were from England or Canada. The Mexican-American population, however, was perceived by the Protestant community as "immigrants."[7]   The migration of Spanish-speaking citizens to Los Angeles from other California counties gives evidence of less homogeneity in the city during the early twentieth century than is generally assumed.[8] If the proportion of the native population of foreign parentage is also considered, it is clear that a basis for non-Protestant (or non-Anglo-Saxon) communities within the city emerged.

Few of the immigrants or migrants of non-native parentage joined any of the major Protestant denominations in Los Angeles.[9] After the turn of the century, twenty-three foreign language newspapers were introduced into the city, and Eastern Orthodox, Uniate Catholic, and foreign-language Lutheran churches began to make their appearance. Until 1900, Los Angeles had only three synagogues and less than a dozen ethnic social organizations. During the next thirty years, these associations increased at a rate more rapid than the general population.

TABLE 25

FOREIGN-BORN AND NATIVE-BORN OF FOREIGN PARENTAGE
AS PERCENTAGE OF TOTAL POPULATION OF LOS ANGELES
1900-1930

	Foreign-Born	Native: Foreign Parentage
1900	18	11
1910	18	19
1920	19	24
1930	20	25

Source: U. S. Census Office, *Census Reports: Twelfth Census of the United States: 1900; Population, Part 1* (Washington, 1901), pp.134-135; U. S. Bureau of the Census, *Fourteenth Census of the United States: Population* (Washington, 1922), pp. 75-76; U. S. Bureau of the Census, *Fifteenth Census of the United States: Population* (Washington, 1932), II,. pp. 73-78.

Until the 1920's, these churches, synagogues, and organizations were not involved in political activity, but provided something of a counterpart to the social functions of the civic institutions of the dominant Protestant culture. The Armenian Patriotic League, for example, held banquets and festivals celebrating American holidays and major Saints' days.[10] The Mexican-American community, of course, was organized primarily through the Roman Catholic Church. As long as these groups did not challenge the power base of civic culture, or threaten community consensus, Protestants took little notice.[11]

The American-born migration did not significantly change the composition of Los Angeles by region or state of origin, but a larger segment was coming from urban areas. A random sampling of marriage licenses between 1890 and 1930 indicates an increase in the percentage of the immigrant population who were born in other cities rather than rural areas. The proportion is even higher among those who were married by Justices of the Peace or judges, and who were therefore probably not members of a religious organization.

The Black community of Los Angeles grew steadily, but slowly, during these years. Until 1923, however, the Blacks did not form social organizations. In that year Black churches became the meeting place for neighborhood social clubs and local affiliates of the NAACP and the Urban League.[12] The major migration and subsequent formation of political and community action groups in areas of high Black concentration did not occur until the depression years.[13]

Los Angeles grew not only in population and diversity, but also in area. In 1781, the pueblo covered only twenty-eight square miles, and it had increased by only one square mile by 1890. Through the annexation or consolidation of seventy-five surrounding communities, the area of Los Angeles increased over 1000 percent during the next forty

TABLE 26

ESTIMATION OF PERCENTAGE OF LOS ANGELES MIGRANTS
FROM RURAL AND URBAN AREAS
1890-1930

		URBAN		
	RURAL	2,500-50,000	50,000-250,000	250,000
1890	57.6	17.4	13.7	11.3
1900	48.9	18.6	10.8	21.7
1910	37.3	16.8	19.4	26.5
1920	30.1	18.9	12.8	38.2
1930	23.4	17.0	19.5	40.1

Source: Marriage License Files, Hall of Records, County of Los Angeles. A ten percent sample was used, controlled for migrant population only. Rural and Urban designations determined from place of birth, interphased with categorization appropriate to that year using data retrieval supplied by the Inter-University Consortium for Social and Political Research, Ann Arbor, Michigan: Population statistics, 1850-1910.

years. In many ways, the larger population and enlarged area of the city simply reflected the fact that a greater proportion of the residents of the county chose to avail themselves of various urban services offered by Los Angeles, especially and crucially the municipal water supply. This was certainly a factor in the annexation of Eagle Rock, Rosewood, Hancock, and Owensmouth. The lack of vocal opposition to annexation in any of these communities suggests that such a desire was the norm.[14] The population of the county grew at about the same rate as the city, and unincorporated areas adjacent to Los Angeles had long shared a common social and economic life.[15] The inclusion of those new areas was the greatest factor in the stability of the percentage of the native-born Protestant population.[16]

The expansion of the size and population of Los Angeles was related to the increase in economic diversity. By 1909 the city had extricated itself from bondage to San Francisco. Los Angeles banks were independently funded and handled over eighty percent of the city's business.[17] The kinds of services and variety of manufactured goods locally provided were on the increase, the import trade began to decline slightly after 1903, and exports rose steadily after 1921.[18] These changes indicate the transformation of the economic function of the city which was directly related to the changing social structure and migration patterns to Los Angeles. The Protestant community, in supporting an expansion of the economy, unwittingly encouraged a different genre of businessman and laborer to take residence in Los Angeles. The success of the changing economic base attracted even more visitors, usually permanent, and often from areas where twentieth-century industrialism was already a fact of life. The rise in the proportion of the population employed in manufacturing, clerical, and professional occupations, the increase in trade and transportation employment, and the decline in agricultural labor was paralleled in an exaggerated form by the changing concentration of capital in these economic activities. As industry continued to recruit a greater percentage of the labor force, it represented a disproportionate share of the Los Angeles economy.[19]

TABLE 27

ANNEXATION AND EXPANSION OF LOS ANGELES
1781-1930

	Number of Communities Annexed	Total Area of City (Sq. Miles)	Rate of Increase (Percentage)
1781		28	
1781-1890	1	29	3.6
1890-1895	1	31	6.4
1895-1900	3	43	38.8
1900-1905	-	43	--
1905-1910	6	101	134.9
1910-1915	4	288	185.2
1915-1920	17	364	26.4
1920-1925	32	415	14.0
1925-1930	14	442	6.5

From Fogelson, pp. 226-227.

Stimulated by the efforts of the Los Angeles Chamber of Commerce and the Merchants and Manufacturers Association to create a stable and independent local economy, a varied industrial community emerged from the early days of processing plants serving local agricultural interests. Under the leadership of Charles Dwight Willard, the Chamber actively encouraged the establishment of new manufacturing interests in the city. Beginning in 1897, Eastern and Mid-Western newspapers carried full page advertisements encouraging bright young industrialists to "Come to the land of SUNSHINE and PROMISE," free from "CORRUPTION and FINANCIAL IRREGULARITIES."[20] Those interested were asked to contact the Chamber, and likely candidates were given free passage to Los Angeles to discuss their plans and the city's needs.[21]

Whether membership in one of the voluntaristic denominations was a factor in selection is not known, but of the thirty-four men thus recruited, all but one immediately became members of one of the influential congregations.[22]   Most of the new industries were begun by local men, however. The general pattern was the expansion of a small shop to a small factory, usually employing twenty to thirty men, and eventual growth to a larger operation employing over one hundred men. Often these manufacturers would change the nature of their products, such as Richard Jeffson's cooperage shop, which served successively as a home furnishings repair agency, light fixtures factory, and construction tool manufacturing operation before his large tool and fixture factory was established, which incorporated all of these functions and more.[23]   By 1930, over twenty factories employed 500 or more workers.[24]

Henry Swather, owner of the city's largest shoe factory, was one of many Los Angelenos who rhapsodized the new industrial progress. In 1911, at a luncheon meeting of the Greater Los Angeles Business Men's Association, Swather claimed, "There's nothing that you could want that isn't made here. Why, there's no reason to look up the coast or over the mountains any more." Over the next two years, Swather repeated his extravagant claims before many church groups, adding, "You always know you'll be dealing with Christians."[25]   Although Swather and others did have a tendency to exaggerate, the diversity of goods being manufactured in the city had increased at a rapid rate. In 1890, fine furniture, plate-glass, carpeting, and other luxury items had to be imported from San Francisco or the East. By 1910, local manufacturing interests had sharply decreased the need for imports.[26]

Los Angeles industries recruited local labor when possible, but in 1907 the Chamber of Commerce and the Merchants and Manufacturers Association decided that certain industrial skills, not associated with national unionism, should be imported. In cooperation with owners and managers, the two organizations launched an advertising campaign in Chicago, Detroit, and New York.[27]   The effort was not as large as the quest for industrialists, nor were prospective employees given free passage. There is no way of estimating the effects of the campaign, but it is safe to assume that the emergence of industry itself may have stimulated some of the migration. A study of the Jewish community in the Boyle Heights region in 1927 suggests that the new garment industry in the area was a prime factor in increased Jewish migration from New York.[28]

Protestant church leadership was enthusiastic about industrial growth. William Stewart Young proposed to a Los Angeles Federation of Churches meeting in 1912 that "we support the efforts of the business interests of our city to make this a real city. The Christian influence we feel here every day could set a model for the nation."[29]   The resolution was unanimously adopted, and a few local parishes announced their support, which was spiritual rather than material.   The operating assumption seems to have been that the new migrants would simply join voluntaristic congregations.[30]

There was no reason to assume that such would be the case. The laboring class had comprised a disproportionately small percentage of these churches since their beginnings in Los Angeles. (See Tables 16 and 22.) Institutional and industrial churches had been in operation in other manufacturing cities for some time, but there seemed to be no reason for these ecclesiastical innovations in a voluntaristic city where the political, economic, and social life was part of a Protestant civic culture. As a result, a greater proportion of the population fell outside the Protestant churches and religious organizations in general.[31]

By 1915, the Los Angeles Federation of Churches received the results of a survey made by the Religious Studies Department of the University of Southern California which indicated that fewer Los Angelenos were churched than had been thought, and that the industrial neighborhoods in the city were the most neglected. The embarrassed officers of the Federation mildly urged congregations to begin work among the unchurched.   Vague plans were made for coordinated membership campaigns, including the use of evangelistic teams on loan from the University, Occidental College, the Bible Institute of Los Angeles, and Fuller Theological Seminary.[32]   The mobilization of churches for the moral support of the war effort, however, saved them from implementing these plans. In 1918, George McCauley, Pastor of the Eagle Rock Presbyterian Church, expressed what may have been a general feeling of relief in the Protestant community in a letter to the Dean of Faculty of San Francisco Theological Seminary: "I am grieved that we are not able, at this time, to carry forward the Work to the laboring class. Still, the men who control the destiny of Los Angeles are good Christians."[33] This attitude ignored a basic fact about the growing labor class—it was a symptom of basic changes in the economic and social structure of the city, which ultimately changed the focus of power.

III

One dominant feature of late nineteenth-century and early twentieth-century America was the rationalization of economic activity through the concentration of capital and power in regional and national corporations.   Individual corporations were not necessarily more rationalized than the smaller companies that preceeded them, but diversified activities were coordinated in a way they had not been before. A system of organization which standardized business and manufacturing activities throughout the nation made industrial cities part of a complex network of interlocking interests.[34]   In Los Angeles, the coming of industry and trade stimulated the interest of corporations in San Francisco, Chicago, and the East, which either brought existing factories and businesses into their own networks or established new operations. Although the Chamber of Commerce, the Merchants and Manufacturers Association, and the City Council were enthusiastic about economic expansion in Los Angeles, they viewed corporations with suspicion. The intrusion of the outside ownership and control of the city's economic life was considered a dangerous move toward the "Easternization" of the City of Angels.[35]   The agencies of the Protestant culture fought this intrusion for over twenty years, but an emerging corporate structure in the nation proved irresistible.

In the early 1880's, the local Democratic and Republican parties included in their platforms complaints against "corporate exploitation."[36] At that time the city was more an agrarian than a business community, and the focus of the attack was the Southern Pacific Railroad and a few of the local corporate land agencies of the Southern California "Boom." Outside investment was encouraged and actively sought, but Los Angelenos insisted that "foreign" capital either become part of the community or at least conform to local practices.   The railroad concentrated most of its efforts to dominate the economy of the state in the more prosperous agricultural region between Fresno and Bakersfield, and was less dependent upon Los Angeles than the city was upon it. Furthermore, the Southern Pacific gave a meaningless assent to local policies.   No real conflict, therefore, emerged.   Land corporations were highly dependent on the Chamber of Commerce and the City Council, and readily accepted local controls and practices.[37]

In the late 1890's, corporate activity of a different nature entered Los Angeles.   Colin Frisch, president of the Frisch Wagon Company in San Francisco, began manufacturing replacement fixtures for wagons and carriages in 1889, and had purchased or established plants in Fresno, San Diego, and Sacramento.   In 1896, he procured a shop from a Los Angeles blacksmith and imported an experienced worker from the San Francisco plant to manage the local branch.[38]

The Chamber of Commerce was initially enthusiastic about the founding of a new and needed industry.   H. J. Hanchette, former secretary of the Chamber, wrote Charles Dwight Willard, "This is a good start.   We need more people like Frisch, with skill and money, interested in the growth of the Southland."[39]   It soon became evident, however, that the Frisch organization was less interested in taking an active part in the development of Los Angeles than in utilizing the area of rapid population growth to expand its own market.   In 1901, the Chamber wrote Frisch about the failure of his local representative to attend meetings and "become part of our business life."[40] The San Franciscan replied, in no uncertain terms, that his company had a responsibility to provide parts for the entire California area, and his local managers were responsible only to him for the manner in which they performed this function.[41]   Other early corporate experiments in Los Angeles were equally as uninterested in community business associations.[42]

The desire for local control and community cohesion led Los Angeles institutions to fight the rise of corporate business and industrial organization in two ways: municipal ownership and the adoption of anti-corporation ordinances. Stimulated by experiments in the East, the City Council and the Chamber of Commerce had been mildly interested in, although slightly suspicious of, "Water and Power Socialism" since the mid-1890's.[43] The concern was slight enough, however, that local private corporations had no difficulties establishing control over all public utilities, including the San Pedro Harbor.[44]   Until 1906, prominent Los Angelenos discussed municipal ownership, at length, and often, in terms of efficiency and private initiative. Both the Council and Chamber were divided on the issue, but it was not considered important enough a matter to create long-lasting hostilities.[45] There were many impassioned speeches on the subject delivered in both bodies, but impassioned speeches, according to one long-time Councilman, were delivered on almost any topic.[46]

Municipal ownership became a more serious issue when local corporations were replaced by regional organizations. The first shift of ownership and power occurred in the telephone service. The Home Telephone Corporation, owned by local businessmen, was founded in 1902 to compete with the Sunset Telephone Company, also locally owned, but without new conveniences such as the dial system. In 1906, the Bell System, through its regional affiliate, Pacific Telephone, purchased Sunset. Home and Pacific were in open competition, and telephone service for the expanding city was inadequate. Both the Chamber and Council agreed that uniform services must be offered, but their sympathy was decidedly with the smaller corporation. "Only a local company, run by men who know Los Angeles, can serve our needs," claimed a Chamber of Commerce publication in 1912.[47]

By 1916 civic leaders were convinced that it was necessary for Los Angeles to become a part of a regional and national communications network. In that year, the Council allowed Home and Pacific to merge and become Southern California Telephone with the expressed hope that local institutions would maintain some control.[48]   The new company, however, was simply a sub-regional affiliate of the Bell System. In the same year, a new fight for municipal ownership was begun when Southern California Edison was established. The end result was the same.[49] By 1931, the last remnants of interest in local control were seen in the formation of the ineffective Municipal Light and Power Defense League, founded by thirty-eight local businessmen—all but one members of a voluntaristic denomination.[50]

The second threat from corporate activity—private business and industry—was more difficult to control and, ultimately, more disastrous for the Protestant civic culture. Following the initial disappointment after the founding of the local Frisch factory, the Chamber of Commerce was still enthusiastic about recruiting outside investment. The San Franciscan was considered an eccentric crank, and the Chamber was certain that more enlightened industrialists would be more cooperative.[51] Of the thirty-seven corporations with offices or plants in Los Angeles by 1905, however, only four were represented in the Chamber of Commerce, and three of these were local corporations.[52] In 1907 the Los Angeles Stock Exchange was founded, and was greeted with mixed feelings by civic leaders. James Willard, a local banker and councilman, stated that the exchange would undoubtedly aid the economic growth of Los Angeles, but wondered whether it could be brought under local control. His primary fear was that San Francisco investors might be able to control the local market.[53] It soon became evident that the Los Angeles Stock Exchange was simply a regional institution for national speculation, and that local control was out of the question. During the first ten years of operation over seventy percent of the Los Angeles investment activity was trade in national and regional securities.[54]

Beginning in 1911, the City Council initiated a series of zoning and tax measures to discourage the growth of corporations controlled from outside. The basic framework for all of this legislation was continued in the Industrial Zoning Code of 1911, which distinguished between corporations in which the majority of the ownership was held by residents of the county and those owned by persons living outside the county.[55] In practice, a majority of the ownership by Southern Californians was all that was necessary. National and regional corporations were restricted to isolated, often uninhabited, areas of the city. These corporations could receive a waiver of the zoning ordinances by agreeing to accept the Code of Business Ethics established by the Chamber of Commerce for this purpose. In addition to supporting the maintenance of an open-shop policy, the corporations were to eschew "unfair" competition with local enterprise.[56] John R. Newmark, a member of the executive council of the Chamber, expressed his hope that national corporations would come into the city under these conditions. "We need the large organizations if we are to be a city," he said, "but it has to be *our* city."[57]

Less than ten corporations accepted the agreement. Those that already existed were beyond the control of the legislation. Los Angeles was too important an area of growing concentration, however, for national organizations to ignore. The city was the logical choice for regional offices and plants. Oil drilling began on an extensive scale in the early twentieth century, and Standard Oil, among others, became increasingly interested in Los Angeles as a possible area for expansion.[58] A few corporations considered bringing suit against the city, but it was much easier to establish plants in adjacent unincorporated areas where the county, by state law, was prohibited from adopting zoning legislation.[59]   Many of these areas were eventually annexed, and the corporations could not be touched by ordinances enacted before annexation. By 1920, an increasing proportion of the Los Angeles labor force was employed by corporations, and many local industries, unable to compete, were bought by national or regional organizations.[60]

The period of most rapid industrial-corporate expansion was during World War I. Instead of a "return to normalcy," the business community accepted corporate life as a fact of life. In 1921, at the urging of the Chamber of Commerce and the Merchants and Manufacturers Association, the City Council drafted new ordinances which removed the clauses instituting discriminating zoning.[61]   The Los Angeles *Times*, long the advocate of Protestant civic culture and supporter of a cohesive Los Angeles business community, editorialized in 1927, "Los Angeles has existed too long with an economic base of local Real Estate and Building interests.   We need more factories, new industries, more interstate commerce and the development of foreign trade."[62]   The Protestant leadership may have retarded diversification and expansion for a while, but the city was becoming an industrial metropolis. The old leadership began to wane as soon as they lost a cohesive proprietary business community they could control.

IV

Los Angeles newspapers were the first local institutions to give evidence of the city's emergence from parochialism into state and national politics. Edward A. Dickson of the *Examiner* spent the first decade of the twentieth century as head of the Sacramento bureau, where he became interested in a more broadly defined politics.[63] His articles and activities on behalf of Los Angeles progressivism were "trial balloons" for state reform ideas.[64]   Harrison Gray Otis, publisher of the *Times*, became interested in state and national politics in the early 1900's. Until his death in 1917, however, the *Times* was still more of a local daily than the *Examiner*[65]. Otis' son-in-law, Harry Chandler, took over publication; and, stimulated by the war effort, the *Times* in the 1920's became a major urban newspaper.[66]

In some ways, the shift from a local to a broader emphasis reflected the predilections of the men who controlled the press, but Los Angeles, the fastest growing city in the state and the largest after 1920, was of increasing importance to the major political parties. California in general, experiencing a population increase of 380 percent from 1,485,053 in 1900 to 5,677,251 in 1930, and rising from the twenty-first most populous state to sixth, gained a greater share of the attention of national politicos.[67] In at least three national elections, the state's electoral votes were decided by a handful of ballots: in 1880, James Garfield was defeated by one hundred votes; Grover Cleveland carried the state by 212 votes in 1892; and two decades later the state went to Theodore Roosevelt, with only two hundred votes more than Woodrow Wilson.[68] Although other Presidential races were not as close in California, few resulted in landslide victories. Wilson, for example, carried the state by 4,000 votes in 1916, and this was considered a wide margin.[69] As the population of Los Angeles increased, the role of the city in elections became more critical. It was the only large urban area in the state that returned a majority for Roosevelt in 1912.[70] In state politics, the city had a similar role. Los Angeles alone among California cities remained faithful to Hiram Johnson until 1920.[71]

Taking cognizance of the political implications of Los Angeles voting patterns, U.S. Senators from California established offices in the city as early as 1904.[72] A parade of state and national political figures began to include Los Angeles as a regular stop in their campaign sweeps. Non-candidates, such as William Jennings Bryan and Clarence Darrow, came to the city to campaign for their party's candidates for state and national offices.[73] It was in the broader political community that Los Angeles first showed signs of diversification. The general consensus surrounding local issues was not reflected in state and national elections. One of the reasons was that different groups were involved in political behavior at various levels.

Elections for municipal and county offices and issues were the province of the established Protestant community. They were the longest residents, and the local issues and candidates had the most meaning to them. The Protestant culture was characterized by its proprietary concern for the community, and no attempt was made to "get out the vote" in neighborhoods that did not share this concern. The rhetoric of municipal campaigns contained the fear of alternative forms of social organization represented by outside interests and new elements in the city. The choice facing the voter in 1906, according to reform leader Marshall Stimson, was between "a government controlled by corporate interests,

Socialism, or if we have the courage, unselfishness, and determination, a government of individuals."[74]

The municipal government was maintained as the servant of the cohesive Protestant community for two decades after 1900 by a rather stable faction of voters. The areas of the city with the highest concentration of Protestant residents also experienced the highest participation in local elections. Areas with a low concentration of Protestant church members also were the zones of lowest participation. In state and national elections, however, the pattern was reversed. Although the Protestant neighborhoods voted regularly in these elections, non-Protestant areas demonstrated a slightly higher proportion of registered voters exercising the franchise. (See Table 28.)

TABLE 28

PROTESTANT AND NON-PROTESTANT
VOTING TRENDS, 1900-1930
(IN PERCENTAGES)

| | Ballots Cast, of Total Registered | | | |
| | Local | | State and National | |
	Protestant	Non-Protestant	Protestant	Non-Protestant
1900-1909	63.4	28.9	57.9	61.3
1910-1919	65.1	30.6	52.6	63.1
1920-1930	56.3	52.6	58.1	60.4

Source: Total registered for each ward used obtained from the County of Los Angeles, *Great Register*, 1900-1929. The ballots cast in each ward for each election were obtained from the Los Angeles *Times*.

Note: Because the data for the entire voluntaristic community is incomplete, only those wards with residential clustering of greater than fifty percent, or lower than ten percent, were used. Wards were chosen by applying their geographical boundaries against the configuration of the residential reconstruction made from sources discussed in Appendix I.

Certainly, the role of political organizers among the non-Protestant community cannot be overlooked as a causal factor. The Protestant community was extremely stable in the early twentieth century. While the persistence rate (the proportion of the population remaining from decade to decade) was rather low for the city generally, over eighty percent of the Protestant population remained each decade.[75] It was among the newcomers that political organizers worked most diligently.[76] As the mobile element of the community, their interest in state and national elections may have been greater than in local issues, but the lack of concern among political organizers for local affairs was crucial. City politics were not an extension of partisan politics, and few party functionaries saw any need to become involved in local elections.[77] The Democratic party was more active among new residents of Los Angeles than the G.O.P. until the 1920's.[78] Whether as the result of the Democrats' efforts, migration patterns, or other factors, the Republican strength in state and national elections declined between 1910 and 1920.[79] Republican party activity increased in response to this perceived threat.[80] By the end of World War I, the general social pattern of political participation in Los Angeles began to fade. The exercise of the franchise in national and state elections in predominantly Protestant areas equaled or surpassed participation in local voting. The level of voting on local issues increased in non-Protestant zones. These changing patterns were accompanied by smaller majorities in local elections.[81]

Some of the breakdown in consensus can be attributed to the introduction of new elements into city politics. Labor organizations were extremely weak in the first decades of the century, but provided a good basis for early Democratic organization.[82] Los Angeles labor gave its rather shaky support to Democratic candidates, except in those elections involving Hiram Johnson.[83] By 1919, labor organizations, with a collective membership of 40,000 began to endorse candidates. Usually these office-seekers were not members of the influential Protestant churches, nor did they receive the support of the Chamber of Commerce or the established civic organizations.[84] A few of the early endorsed candidates won offices, and in the municipal election of 1925, eight of the eleven labor candidates for city council were elected.[85]

Ethnic politics did not really exist until the 1920's in Los Angeles. When non-Protestants began participating in local elections, however, ethnicity was one of the more salient features. The Mexican-American community had never entered the political life of early Los Angeles, and was ignored in the building of local political traditions. Beginning in the early 1920's, Mexican areas of the city began voting—and for candidates that were not endorsed by the Protestant culture. These residents of East Los Angeles were organized by Jewish migrants from New York City who had had experience in politicizing various ethnic groups in the East. Areas of high Jewish concentration demonstrated a pattern of voting behavior similar to labor and the Mexican community.[86]

The new elements in city politics are only one factor in the decline of consensus, however. The Protestant community itself began to show signs of division. There were early indications of breakdown. In 1909, the Chamber of Commerce petitioned the state legislature to withhold passage of anti-Japanese legislation because it could hurt the important Oriental trade.[87]   A group of Los Angeles Protestant businessmen, who were not involved in the larger trade interests of the Chamber, organized the Los Angeles Anti-Asiatic Association in the early teens in order to gain passage of the exclusionary legislation.[88]   In 1913, the state-wide progressive interests of a group of businessmen under the leadership of Edwin T. Earl, publisher of the *Express*, formed a factional group of the Chamber known as the Los Angeles Municipal Conference.[89]   Until the 1920's, however, the consensus persisted.

By the end of World War I, the leadership of the Protestant community was divided between men who continued their local interests as proprietors and small businessmen, and those who had entered, sometimes reluctantly, into the larger corporate economy. Indeed, by 1930, the Protestant community was factionalized to the extent that it was hardly recognizable. Between 1900 and 1920, it was difficult to find an office-holder or candidate in the city government who was not a voluntaristic Protestant. By 1930, this group was still disproportionately represented in local politics, but it was only one of a number of factions that ran the city.

The issues that ultimately divided the Protestants and brought new elements into local politics were those associated with the facilitation of corporate expansion in the city and the inclusion of local agencies in statewide operations.   Candidates for councilmanic offices made the easing of restrictive zoning and taxation practices part of their campaign.[90]   Associated with this was an effort to reorganize the city government. As early as 1912, some of the more progressive and realistic elements of the Protestant leadership proposed a new charter which would combine the features of metropolitan administration with the elective element thought necessary to retain control by the community. Commissions for various urban services would be established, but would be administered by elected officials rather than professional managers.[91] The proposal and a revision of it in 1915 were roundly defeated. In 1924, a campaign was launched which identified a revised charter with industrial and commercial progress. It received the support of the press and corporate representatives, and was approved at the polls by an extremely large majority.[92]

TABLE 29

VOLUNTARISTIC PROTESTANT OFFICE HOLDERS
AS PERCENTAGE OF ALL LOS ANGELES CITY OFFICIALS

	1899-1920	1921-1930
Elective	93.4	47.3
Appointive	86.9	49.6
School Board	98.1	51.2
All Offices	91.0	48.1

Source: See Table 23.

Note: The implied stability in the 1899-1920 figures is correct, but for 1921-1930 it is misleading.   There was a general decline in voluntaristic representation during that decade.

Between 1916 and 1921, municipal governments in California were given the option of having offices of various state agencies located in their cities. Industrial Relations was the first department to offer its services, and the new Department of Social Welfare was the last. Most of these state agencies were adopted with fair ease, although the loss of local control was always mourned.[93] The acceptance of an office of the Department of Social Welfare was more bitterly fought, and was the last clear example of a cohesive Protestant vote in the decade. The Department emerged in 1921 as a reorganization of the Department of Charities, which itself had been a reorganization of the Department of Charities and Correction. The evolution involved not simply a change in nomenclature, but the development of a concept of state responsibility in areas that had once been left to local institutions, especially voluntaristic associations.[94] In 1921, the emphasis was shifted from charity to welfare, and Sophanisba P. Breckenridge, holder of advanced degrees in the scientific administration of social programs from Chicago and Columbia, became director of the new department.[95] Her proposed program involved the rationalization of many county and city operations, the effective coordination of private charities, and an efficient administration of the whole from Sacramento.[96]

A few Protestant ministers hailed the Breckenridge department as a step forward in the realization of Christian brotherhood in an industrial society. Most denounced her program as an attempt to replace church administered charities, which cared for the soul as well as the body, with a public dole. The unfortunate wretches who were forced to rely on others, the argument went, would, if presented the choice, take the form of charity that did not remind them of their wretchedness.[97] A few of the more aggressive ministers resorted to *ad hominum* arguments.[98] Some were more moderate and expressed a sense of despair that one of the most important functions of the Protestant culture might be replaced.[99]

Candidates for councilmanic offices campaigned vigorously on the issue. Long-term members of the council and new candidates of the Protestant community promised to thank the lady director and politely refuse the services offered by her department. Candidates who were not part of the Protestant establishment and were backed by the labor or ethnic interests pledged themselves to acquiring these services for Los Angeles.[100] The voting patterns in the city followed predictable lines. Perhaps because the small depression of 1921 had an adverse effect on the non-Protestant lower class, interest in this election was stimulated to the extent that for the first time in the century the council was not controlled by a majority of men clearly associated with the Protestant community.[101] By August of 1922, Los Angeles was benefitting from the services of the California State Department of Social Welfare.[102]

The city became a metropolis, and the political control slipped from the hands of the Protestant establishment as easily as had the organization of the economic life of the community. It was not a deliberate rejection of Protestant values; rather, it was the search for leadership and organization more suited to the new social and economic order in which efficiency and efficacy were higher values than the quest for "Pure Faith, Pure Morals, Pure Government." In a city that had been the citadel of temperance and prohibition rhetoric since the turn of the century, it was a sign of transformed culture that Milton Young, a Los Angeles Protestant seeing the Democratic nomination for the governorship of California, campaigning on a platform pledging himself to protect the laws prohibiting liquor and promote morality in general, could not carry his home town.[103]

V

From the 1890's to the 1910's, political, business, and social institutions in Los Angeles were extensions of the Protestant culture. The evolving corporate structures of the city which first threatened and then ended the control exercised by the Protestants, had a corresponding effect on the role of religious organizations in the structure of the city. In the economic life of the community, the Protestant churches lost their function as a place for businessmen of similar backgrounds and interests to make contacts. In 1905, the majority of the contracts in the city reported in the local press were made between independent businessmen who were members of the same congregation or who served on the same local denominational or interdenominational boards. By 1930, a majority of the reported contracts were negotiated by corporations, most often with firms located elsewhere. Obviously, this reflects a change in the focus of journalistic attention from proprietorships to corporations, but the indicated trend is important.[104]

Many local corporate managers and vice-presidents, of course, were also members of one of the major Protestant denominations, but they were slightly fewer in proportion than had been the case with early Los Angeles merchants and proprietors. The corporate churchmen of the 1920's were more heavily involved in denominational activities at the regional or national levels than were prominent Protestant businessmen earlier in the century.[105]

The absolute control of local politics by the Protestants declined rapidly in the 1920's, although they still held a disproportionate share of power. The greatest increase in the proportion of public office holders was among those who cannot be located on remaining church rolls and who stated no religious preference in the various biographical sources. The function of local offices in the careers of candidates began to take on added significance. There was a rapid increase, especially among the group for whom no religious affiliation can be found, in the proportion of local officials who later sought state or national office.[106] In both issues and function, Los Angeles city politics was no longer merely local. Coincident with the broadening scope and decline of power was the gradual disappearance of cohesive voting patterns in areas of high Protestant concentration. It is not clear, therefore, that councilmen from these areas represented a solidified faction.

At the turn of the century, Los Angeles had all of the characteristics of what one scholar has called "island communities."[107] No community in late nineteenth-century America, of course, could be an island. Great population movements, the extension of transportation technology, and an organizational impetus in national life made isolation virtually impossible.[108] Perhaps in response to these changes, however, some American communities attempted to become islands. Some adopted ineffective legislation against the transformation of their society by industrialization, others entered a period of exaggerated local boosterism, and at least one new community sought to combine an industrial economic base and a cohesive society by isolating the means of production and the labor force from the erosive influence of the big city.[109]

TABLE 30

VOTING COHESION IN VOLUNTARISTIC WARDS
IN LOCAL ELECTIONS
1900-1930
(IN PERCENTAGES)

	Less than 50%	50%-70%	More than 70%
1900-1909	12.3	62.1	25.6
1910-1919	11.6	64.7	23.7
1920-1929	38.5	50.6	10.9

Source: See Table 28.

Note: The figures for each column represent the percentage of total elections for each period in which the wards consisting of neighborhoods with over half the population appearing on the list from sources in Appendix I returned votes in blocks of more than seventy percent for one candidate or issue, between seventy and fifty percent, and when no candidate received a majority of votes cast.

Many of the Protestants who migrated to Los Angeles between 1880 and 1910 came from areas that were experiencing rapid social and economic changes which resulted in institutional and theological reorganization of the churches. A few of these migrants articulated their desire to escape the destruction of traditional American Protestantism. Los Angeles became the last bastion of voluntarism. Cohesive local institutions of civic order had been established, two church-related colleges had been built, and a Bible school for the training of the local clergy was founded. The nation and the Pacific Coast were increasingly relying on urban centers for broader functions, however, and Los Angeles was brought reluctantly into that framework. By the 1920's, the city was a metropolis, and the control, if not the ethos, of Los Angeles civic culture was increasingly secular. The loss of cohesion was accompanied by the loss of important social functions. Charity, once the exclusive domain of voluntaristic societies, was now administered by a vast bureaucracy. Higher education, once the exclusive domain of the churches, was asked to serve more secular functions. In 1924, the University of Southern California, the first major institution of the

Protestant culture in Los Angeles, under the leadership of the new President, Rufus von Kleinsmid, the first non-cleric to hold that post, extricated itself from Methodist control. It continued to be "affiliated" with the Methodist church, but the funding and administration were independent.[110] Occidental College established the same relationship with the Presbyterian church in 1927.[111] One year later, the secular University of California established a campus in Los Angeles.[112]

It was also during the 1920's that the motion picture industry became so clearly identified with Los Angeles. In part, the rise of the industry was another example of economic diversification. In 1910, the fledgling industry was located primarily in New York, but by 1925, approximately ninety percent of the total film production in the United States took place in Los Angeles in more than sixty studios employing over seven thousand people.[113] Unlike other corporations, which were extensions of businesses begun under voluntaristic control, the motion picture industry, and the people associated with it, migrated from the East Coast.[114] If any group can be said to have been dominant among them, it was the Jewish population.[115] People who would have been excluded from positions of prestige in the older voluntaristic structure of Los Angeles, such as Charlie Chaplin, became popular representatives of the Hollywood counter-culture. This new style of life, supported by economic power, was an example of the varieties of options in the once cohesive City of the Angels.

These changes would effect religion in any city. In Los Angeles the effect was even greater. In the early nineteenth century, Protestants concerned about social change they could neither understand nor reverse could move to the Old Northwest. Later in the century, those Protestants who wanted to escape the complexities and upheaval of industrialization could move to the Pacific Coast, especially Los Angeles. When a cohesive voluntaristic community was no longer a reality and could not be maintained as a fiction in the City of the Angels, there was no place left to run. The most ardent adherents of American Protestantism finally had to face urban and industrial society in Los Angeles by the 1920's. Their responses were no less innovative nor more bizarre than those of Bostonians or New Yorkers, who had gone through similar experiences earlier. If they are more notorious, it is only because the process occurred more rapidly in Los Angeles, and many of the faithful sensed that their city was the last of its kind.

NOTES

[1] Los Angeles *Times*, August 8, 1901; McWilliams, p. 157.

[2] See Chapter 4, Section I.

[3] Los Angeles Chamber of Commerce, *Members Annual*, 1901, p. 73.

[4] Los Angeles *Times*, September 13, 1903.

[5] U.S. Bureau of the Census, *Fifteenth Census of the United States: 1930; Metropolitan Districts* (Washington, 1932), pp. 10-12.

[6] Constant references to the "lack of Christian spirit" in other cities were made in the Los Angeles *Times* and *Examiner*, Municipal League of Los Angeles, *Municipal Affairs* and *Bulletin* and the sermons from the sources listed in Appendix II.

[7] See Carey McWilliams, *North from Mexico: The Spanish-Speaking People of the United States* (Phildelphia, 1949), pp. 138-153.

[8] Until 1930 the Mexican population was classified as "white" by the Bureau of the Census. Work now being done on ethnic groups in Los Angeles, using city directories and marriage licenses should result in a clearer picture of the composition of Los Angeles society.

[9] From the random sample of marriage licenses mentioned in Table 26, and correlated with the list of voluntaristic Protestants from sources listed in Appendix I. Only three percent of the foreign-born or non-native parentage group could be found as members of the American Protestant churches.

[10] From a systematic reading of the Files of the Armenian Patriotic League, Los Angeles, California. The Armenian community became economically and politically important in Los Angeles in the 1940's and 1950's.

[11] Codius, pp. 67-73. With the exception of specific reports of those few institutions that dealt directly with the Mexican population, it would be difficult to infer from local denominational sources that anyone but WASPs lived in Los Angeles prior to the 1920's.

[12] J. Max Bond, "The Negro in Los Angeles," (Unpublished Doctoral Dissertation, University of Southern California, 1936), pp. 89-92; *Crisis* (April, 1923), 65; *California Eagle*, February 10, 1923. For information on the Black community in Los Angeles at this time, see Lawrence B. DeGraff, "The City of Black Angels: Emergence of the Los Angeles Ghetto, 1890-1930," *Pacific Northwest Review*, XXXIX (August, 1970), 323-352.

[13] Lawrence B. DeGraff, "Negro Migration to Los Angeles, 1930-1950," (Unpublished Doctoral Dissertation, University of California, Los Angeles, 1962), *passim.*

[14]Many encouraging letters from citizens' groups in these communities were sent to the Chamber of Commerce; Los Angeles Chamber of Commerce, Miscellaneous Materials, Special Collections Division, University Research Library, University of California, Los Angeles.

[15]U.S. Bureau of the Census, *State Compendium, 1920; California* (Washington, 1922), pp. 34-43; Fogelson, pp. 63-84 and 186-204. This chapter is heavily dependent upon a number of secondary sources, of which Fogelson is the most important. My major criticism of Fogelson's treatment is that the developments he studied were not placed within their cultural context. Fogelson's model for an urban community seems to be the corporate structure of New York or Boston at the turn of the century. He therefore concludes that Los Angelenos were antipathetic to the city. They were, in fact, rather enthusiastic about *their* city and horrified by *other* cities. Fogelson concludes that the way in which Los Angelenos went about things "was not the way to resolve satisfactorily the problems of the late nineteenth- and early twentieth-century American metropolis" (p. 276). The point is that Los Angelenos made a conscious effort to perpetuate an older social order rather than adapt themselves to the new metropolitan structure.

[16]Based on an interphasing of data on each of the annexed communities and Los Angeles from *State Compendium, 1920: California, passim,* which contains historical series from 1900 to 1920.

[17]Los Angeles Chamber of Commerce, *General Commercial Report of Los Angeles County* (Los Angeles, 1910), pp. 13-15.

[18]Los Angeles Chamber of Commerce Industrial Department, *General Industrial Report of Los Angeles County* (Los Angeles, 1929), *passim;* Fogelson, pp. 108-135.

[19]*General Industrial Report of Los Angeles County,* pp. 73-77; U.S. Bureau of the Census, *Fifteenth Census of the United States: Manufactures,* 1929 (Washington, 1933), III, pp. 378-384.

[20]Promotional Clippings, Los Angeles Chamber of Commerce, Miscellaneous Materials. The specific quote is from the New York *Times,* June 16, 1897. Newmark "A Short History of the Los Angeles Chamber of Commerce," 57.

[21]Los Angeles Chamber of Commerce Minutes, 1897-1898, *passim.*

[22]The list of men recruited in this way was obtained from *Ibid.,* and correlated to the list of voluntaristic Protestants from sources discussed in Appendix I.

[23]Determined from Manufacturing Tax Records, Office of the County Assessor, Hall of Records, County of Los Angeles.

[24]*General Industrial Report of Los Angeles County,* p. 183.

[25]Swather sent copies of his many speeches on this theme to Franklin Hichborn, and all are assembled in one file in the Hichborn Papers.

[26]*General Commercial Report of Los Angeles County,* pp. 67-69.

[27]Los Angeles Chamber of Commerce Minutes, May 4, 1907; Los Angeles *Times*, June 12, 1907.

[28]Stanley Katze, "A Report on the Boyle Heights Community," typescript, Los Angeles Jewish Community Council, 1927.

[29]"Address to the Los Angeles Federation of Churches," March 16, 1912, Young Papers.   Los Angeles *Times*, April 7, 1912.

[30]At least this was the stated assumption of Young, in *Ibid.*

[31]See Chapter 6, Section II.

[32]"Report on Religious Membership in Los Angeles," typescript, University of Southern California, Religious Studies Department, 1915.   Miscellaneous Materials Relating to the Los Angeles Federation of Churches, Young Papers.

[33]McCauley to John R. Brollough, October 9, 1918, Archives of the San Francisco Theological Seminary, San Anselmo, California.

[34]See James Weinstein, *The Corporate Ideal in the Liberal State, 1900-1918* (Boston, 1968); Robe H. Wiebe, *The Search for Order, 1877-1920* (New York, 1967); Thomas C. Cochran and William Miller, *The Age of Enterprise: A Social History of Industrial America* (rev. ed.; New York, 1961);   and for the study of a specific development within this context, Sidney Kaplan, "Social Engineers as Saviours: Effects of World War I on Some American Liberals," *The Journal of the History of Ideas*, XVII (June, 1956), 341-359.

[35]From a survey of the literature cited in Note 6 of this chapter.

[36]Mowry, p. 37; Rogin and Shover, pp. 48-49; Codius, p. 3.

[37]Codius, pp. 5-6; Lola Kassell, "A History of the Government of Los Angeles, 1781-1925," (Unpublished Master's Thesis, Occidental College, 1929), pp. 53-54; Los Angeles Chamber of Commerce Minutes, 1890-1894, *passim.*

[38]San Francisco *Chronicle*, November 30, 1889, February 11, 1892, December 6, 1894; Los Angeles *Times*, March 8, 1896.

[39]Hanchette to Willard, April 19, 1896, Charles Dwight Willard Papers, Bancroft Library, University of California, Berkeley.

[40]Los Angeles Chamber of Commerce Minutes, July 21, 1901.

[41]Frisch to Willard, August 17, 1901, Willard Papers.

[42]Los Angeles Chamber of Commerce Minutes, 1900-1915, *passim.*

[43]*Ibid.*, January 4, 1894.

[44]Fogelson, pp. 108-135.

[45]Los Angeles Common Council Files and Los Angeles Chamber of Commerce Minutes, 1894-1906, *passim.*

[46]Joseph K. Ritter to John Randolph Haynes, March 23, 1903, Haynes Papers.

[47]Los Angeles Chamber of Commerce, "A Greater City," (Pamphlet, 1906). Fogelson, pp. 212-237.

[48]Fogelson, *loc. cit.* Minutes of Meeting, June 2, 1916, Los Angeles Common Council Files.

[49]Fogelson, pp. 236-241.

[50]*Ibid.,* p. 242. The membership of the League was obtained from a pamphlet published by that organization in 1931, entitled "The Municipal Light and Power Defense League," found in the Los Angeles—Miscellaneous Collection, Special Collections Division, University Research Library, University of California, Los Angeles.

[51]Los Angeles Chamber of Commerce Minutes, January 13, 1902.

[52]Corporations were located and identified by the Manufacturing Tax Records, Office of the County Assessor, Hall of Records, County of Los Angeles. Corporate members of the Chamber were identified by the Los Angeles Chamber of Commerce, *Members Annual,* 1905, pp. 11-18.

[53]Minutes of Meeting, October 4, 1907, Los Angeles Common Council Files.

[54]Los Angeless Stock Exchange, *1917 Report* (Los Angeles, 1917), pp. 74-79.

[55]Minutes of Meeting, March 27, 1911, Los Angeles Common Council Files.

[56]James Findley, "The Economic Boom of the Twenties in Los Angeles," (Unpublished Doctoral Dissertation, Claremont Graduate School, 1958), pp. 137-146.

[57]Minutes of Meeting, August 2, 1911, Los Angeles Common Council Files.

[58]Findley, pp. 41-43.

[59]*Ibid.,* pp. 107-111.

[60]Davis McEntire, *The Labor Force in California: A Study of Characteristics and Trends in Labor Force, Employment and Occupations in California 1900-1950* (Berkeley and Los Angeles, 1952), pp. 331-342; Findley, pp. 289-303.

[61]Minutes of Meeting, August 23, 1921, Los Angeles Common Council Files.

[62]Los Angeles *Times,* June 9, 1927.

[63]Mowry, p. 232.

[64]Dickson to Frank Kimball, September 24, 1907, Edward A. Dickson Papers, Special Collections Division, University Research Library, University of California, Los Angeles.

[65]Findley, pp. 76-78.

[66]Frederick R. Hamilton, "The Los Angeles *Times* Emergence from Parochialism," (Unpublished Master's Thesis, University of California, Berkeley, 1958), *passim*.

[67]U.S. Bureau of the Census, *Fifteenth Census of the United States: 1930; Metropolitan Districts Population and Area* (Washington, 1932), *passim*.

[68]David Farrely and Ivan Hinderaker (eds.), *The Politics of California* (New York, 1951), pp. 17-22.

[69]*Ibid.*, p. 25.

[70]*Ibid.*, p. 29; Mowry, p. 73..

[71]Mowry, pp. 223-224.

[72]Los Angeles *Times*, August 8, 1904.

[73]Mowry, p. 209.

[74]Los Angeles *Times*, July 25, 1906.

[75]See Appendix IV.

[76]Findley, pp. 266-267.

[77]*Ibid.*, p. 263.

[78]Kassell, p. 138.

[79]Mowry, pp. 205-213.

[80]The Los Angeles *Times* carried many supportive editorials and articles on the organization of new Republican clubs throughout the 1920's.

[81]Determined from a survey of local election results as reported in the Los Angeles *Times.*

[82]Perry and Perry, pp. 183-190.

[83]Rogin and Shover, p. 78.

[84]Determined from a survey of the announcement of support in the Los Angeles *Times.* The non-membership of labor-supported candidates is tenuous, but is based on a correlation with the sources listed in Appendix I.

[85]Rogin and Shover, p. 81.

[86]Mexican communities were determined by Spanish surname from the *Los Angeles City Directory*; labor areas were determined by occupational listings in *Ibid.* The determination of Jewish areas is more tenuous, using the Distinctive Jewish Name method (see Vorspan and Gartner, p. 298). For the application of these areas to voting analyses, see Note to Table 28 in this Chapter.

[87]Roger Daniels, *The Politics of Prejudice: The Anti-Japanese Movement in California and the Struggle for Japanese Exclusion* (Berkeley and Los Angeles, 1962), p. 48.

[88]*Ibid.*, p. 84.

[89]See Chapter 4, Section V. This would seem to be a contradiction of the argument in the previous chapter. The men involved, with the exception of Earl, did not continue their broader interests after the crisis had passed. Earl was involved earlier in state and national politics, and continued to do so. See J. Gregg Layne, "The Lincoln-Roosevelt League: Its Origin and Accomplishments," HSSCQ XXV (September, 1943), 79-101.

[90]Based on a survey of campaign statements in the Los Angeles *Times*.

[91]Fogelson, p. 222.

[92]*Ibid.*, pp. 233-234.

[93]Frances Cahn and Valeska Bary, *Welfare Activities of Federal, State, and Local Governments in California, 1850-1934* (Berkeley, 1936), pp. 349-355.

[94]There were over sixty voluntaristic charitable organizations in Los Angeles at this time, and only twenty-three ten years later.

[95]California Department of Social Welfare, *Report* (Sacramento, 1922), p. 3.

[96]*Ibid.*, (Sacramento, 1923), pp. 33-56.

[97]Based on sermons and other materials listed in Appendix II.

[98]"Sermon delivered to the First Congregational Church, July 1921," (minister's name not given), Los Angeles Churches Collection, Special Collections Division, University Research Library, University of California, Los Angeles. Sources referred to in Note 97.

[99]These accounted for over half of the sermons that remain from this period on this topic.

[100]Determined from a survey of campaign statements in the Los Angeles *Times*.

[101]Determined by a correlation of councilmen for 1921, found in *A Chronological Record of Los Angeles City Officials, 1850-1928*, and the master list of voluntaristic

Protestants. For possible relations between the local economy and political changes, see Jacqueline Rorabeck Kasum, *Some Social Aspects of Business Cycles in the Los Angeles Area, 1920-1950* (Los Angeles, 1954), pp. 82-90.

[102] California Department of Social Welfare, *Report* (Sacramento, 1923), p. 67.

[103] Roger and Shover, pp. 115.

[104] Determined from a survey of announcements of contracts in the Los Angeles *Times* and *Examiner*, 1900-1930, and applied against parish reconstructions and reconstructions of denominational and interdenominational agencies from sources listed in Appendices I and II using a multicoordinant repeating program. The trend was linear after 1917, and the two dates reported are not anomalous.

[105] Based on a reconstruction of lay leadership from sources discussed in Appendices I and III.

[106] Based on a tracing of careers using *A Chronological Record of Los Angeles City Officials, 1850-1938* and the *Men of California, 1920-1940.*

[107] Wiebe, p. viii.

[108] See Kuznets and Swain, *passim*, and the works referred to in Note 34 of this chapter.

[109] See, e.g., Arthur Mann, *Yankee Reformers in the Urban Age* (Cambridge, 1954); Roy Lubove, *The Progressives and the Slums: Tenement House Reform in New York City, 1890-1917* (Pittsburgh, 1962); Zane L. Miller, *Boss Cox's Cincinnati: Urban Politics in the Progressive Era* (New York, 1968); Charles N. Glaab, *Kansas City and the Railroads: Community Policy in the Growth of a Regional Metropolis* (Madison, 1962); William H. Wilson, *The City Beautiful Movement in Kansas City* (Columbia, 1964); Stanley Buder, *Pullman: An Experiment in Industrial Order and Community Planning, 1880-1930* (New York, 1967).

[110] Servin and Wilson, p. 261.

[111] Young, *William Stewart Young*, p. 183.

[112] On the secularist implications of the founding of the University, see Governors Commission on the location of the Southern Branch of the University of California, *Papers on the Choice of Los Angeles for the Southern Branch Campus* (Berkeley, 1930), *passim.*

[113] Arnold T. Anderson, "The Motion Picture Industry," in Department of Research Service, Security Trust and Savings Bank, *Industrial Summary of Los Angeles for Year 1927* (Los Angeles, 1928), p. 16.

[114] *Ibid.*, p. 18.

[115] Vorspan and Gartner, pp. 129-131.

CHAPTER 6

THE OUTWARD DRIVE AND THE INWARD LIFE

I

The image of Los Angeles changed no less radically than did the social base between the turn of the century and 1930. The small, bland, and respectable "ideal Protestant city" became known as "Tinsel Town," a place of picturesque characters, and above all, of exotic cults. "God once took the country by Maine as the handle, gave it a good shake, and all the loose nuts and bolts rolled down to Southern California," wrote Carl Sandburg in the late 1920's.[1] One visitor and temporary resident of Los Angeles recalled sermons on such topics as "What would Jesus Do if He were a Great Movie Director Like Cecil de Mille."[2] On another occasion he heard an announcement that the Second Coming would take place in Southern California in the near future, "because here the climate is just like that in the Holy Land."[3] "There are in Los Angeles," claimed a learned sociologist of religion in 1927, "more sects, cults, and denominations than in any other city in the world."[4]

It is curious that such a statement should be made in that year. The 1926 census of religious bodies indicated that New York City contained twenty-three more denominational units than the City of the Angels.[5] If denominational families are used as the measure, Los Angeles was a very weak third, behind Chicago and New York.[6] Indeed, there is a very high correlation between the size of a city and the number of religious organizations represented, and the proportion of esoteric cults among Los Angeles denominations was lower than the proportions in New York or Chicago.[7] There were in Los Angeles, as some commentators have noted, many religions with strange sounding names: Nuptual Feast Ecclesia, Firebrands for Jesus, Agabeg Occult Church, First Assembly of the First Born of the United Sons of the Almighty, and Nothing Impossible.[8] Similar cults, and more, however, were found in New York and Chicago.[9]

There were two reasons why Los Angeles has been perceived as the city of religious oddities. The first is the physical structure of the area. The population, business, and civic services of Los Angeles today are spread over a vast area in comparison with most cities, and in the 1920's the distribution was greater still.[10] The predominance of single-function buildings, and the great amount of space between them, called the attention of the visitor to phenomena that were present in other

TABLE 31

RELIGIOUS ORGANIZATIONS IN SELECTED CITIES
1906-1926

	1906	1916	1926
New York	66	74	80
Chicago	52	58	63
Los Angeles	24	31	57
San Francisco	32	39	41

Source: *Religious Bodies*, 1906-1926.

cities, but not as visibly. One is impressed today, for example, by the number of schools in the Los Angeles area. Playgrounds and the distinctive "neo-penal" architecture of schools highlight their presence. The same was true of ecclesiastical buildings in the 1920's. Neither Angeles Temple nor the World Church are obscured by more imposing buildings, and both are more visible than Chicago's more impressive Moody Memorial Church. Cults that would have been housed in "store fronts" in other cities worshipped in distinctive ecclesiastical buildings in Los Angeles. Furthermore, those who created the image of Los Angeles as a haven for cults were primarily Easterners who were not used to seeing either Protestantism or cultic religion practiced so openly. Apparently, a group of Irish Catholics participating in a ritual in which bread and wine were changed into flesh and blood appeared much less strange to writers from New York than a congregation of peripheral Protestants speaking in tongues.[11]

The second reason for the image is that there is some truth to it. There is no way to measure the intensity of religious activity, but there are reasons to assume that the activity of cults in Los Angeles may have been more intense than in other cities.[12] The peripheral religious organizations were a small, but important, part of the reaction of Los Angelenos to their rapidly changing environment. The reaction was complex and varied. To some extent, the religious community became fragmented into "locals" and "cosmopolitans," but that was in the context of an existing division into congregational, denominational, associational, and municipal levels of activity. The new social order further diversified the population. There was a general pattern that emerged, however, which subsumed the complexities. Los Angeles Protestants and their institutions tended either to accept the new social order in which the voluntaristic churches were no longer at the center, but only one of many functions in a corporate structure, or they rejected the social role of the church and concentrated on the internal religious life. The cleavage was best stated by Aimee Semple McPherson, who beckoned to her flock:

> Oh, my brothers and sisters, I know the agony of your lives. Your city is torn, your families are torn, and you are torn. You don't know how you can get through another day, and you look to City Hall, to Hill Street, to the world for help. Only the Love of Jesus can carry you on. You must choose between the outward drive and the inward life; between the world and Jesus.[13]

II

Before World War I, Los Angeles was notorious among ecclesiastical bureaucrats at the national level for the insular nature of the local denominational affiliates. "We have made every effort to engage your Christian city in our broader work," wrote the Stated Clerk of the Presbyterian Church in 1915. "Certainly you have a good deal to offer us in leadership."[14] At that time, Los Angeles Protestants did not feel a part of the broader society and its attendant problems, to which the programs of the national denominations gave the greatest attention. In the next decade, local denominational agencies became more a part of national church life. Indeed, one prominent churchman complained in 1927, "The Presbytery of Los Angeles might as well be anyplace else. You people seem to be more concerned with the General Assembly than churches in Los Angeles."[15]

The "nationalizing" of the local agencies affected all six voluntaristic denominations in the city, but it was most pronounced in the Protestant Episcopal Church. In 1915 the Province of the Pacific was canonized, which created, in theory, an authority higher than the diocese.[16] In practice, however, the Province was simply a cooperative agency of dioceses in California, Oregon, and Washington. The creation of the new institution was fought vigorously by the Diocese of Los Angeles. Bishop Johnson sought support in his objection to the Province from the Bishop of California, but found no solace.[17] An emergency Diocesan Synod voted twenty-three to four to petition the General Convention to reconsider the establishment of the Province, but to no avail.[18]

By 1925 the Diocese of Los Angeles was a leader in the movement of the national church to increase the power of the provinces in order to create greater cooperation between the dioceses. Part of the explanation of the radical change in diocesan policy was a change in leadership. In 1919 Bishop Johnson requested the Diocesan Synod to secure a Bishop Coadjutor as the first phase in his retirement plans. After an extensive search for an efficient administrator, William Bertrand Stevens was chosen. Stevens, a New Englander, had served as Rector to churches in New York City and San Antonio, Texas. In addition, he had gained a national reputation through the chairmanship of several committees of the General Convention.[19] In the diocesan discussion of the selection of a bishop, the local and national requirements of the candidates were never mentioned, in contrast to the selection of the first Bishop of Los Angeles.[20] The Los Angeles *Times*, however, noted the absence of any Californians among the candidates mentioned. "Is there a possibility that, in spite of the splendid ecclesiastical 'timber' in California for the making of a coadjutor Bishop for the Diocese of Los Angeles, an eastern clergyman will be chosen?"[21]

An Easterner was indeed chosen, but he was careful to establish a local identity as soon as possible. Stevens was consecrated in 1920, and by 1922 he was a member of the Municipal League, the Central Los Angeles Kiwanis, the Westlake Masonic Lodge, and a trustee of Occidental College.[22] He delighted a Diocesan Convention in 1924 by joking about himself and other eastern clergymen who sought pleasant pastoral duties in Los Angeles. "Every man has a right to enjoy the blessings of Southern California and to bask in its sunshine, but it is not fair to the Diocese to expect to enjoy the privilege at its expense."[23]

Stevens was just as careful to make certain that his new Diocese entered more effectively into the structure of the national church. In order to gain popular support for the Institutional Church League, Stevens made personal appearances in at least thirty parishes. "It doesn't take much imagination," he told St. John's parish, "to see that we will soon face the same problems. We can serve the Lord and learn something useful at the same time."[24] Within five years, the Diocese of Los Angeles was one of the major contributors to the League.[25] At his urging, parish guilds affiliated themselves with organizations within the national church. Prominent Los Angeles laymen, absent from national committees until 1919, became noticeably by their presence in large numbers at meetings of the General Convention.[26]

The experience of the Episcopal Church in Los Angeles was unique only in the vigorous leadership provided by one man. Between 1920 and 1930 the Presbytery of Los Angeles doubled the proportion of its budget to finance programs under the auspices of the Synod of California and the General Assembly.[27] William Stewart Young, long the advocate of localist concerns, spoke very favorably in 1926 in support of a motion to engage in cooperative action with other Presbyteries in order to extend the social ministry of the Presbytery of Los Angeles.[28]

In 1923, the Baptist Association of Los Angeles sent, for the first time, delegates and funds to the annual meeting of the Social Service Commission of the Baptist Church, Northern Convention.[29] The Congregationalists of Los Angeles began serving on national boards at the end of World War I, and the local Epworth League of the Methodist Church provided national leaders for the movement in the 1920's.[30] Even the more quietistic Disciples of Christ demonstrated a move toward national structures. In 1920, the Christian Ministers Association of Los Angeles, in the first act of that organization which was not specifically local in its implications, requested guidance and aid from the national denominational organization in establishing a seminary.[31] The following year, the Association pledged $1,000,000 to the national general seminary fund.[32]

Interdenominational activity, which had been limited to churches in Los Angeles before the 1920's, took on national and even international perspectives. The National Federation of Churches, for example, was never mentioned in the sermon literature that remains from the earlier twentieth century, but was frequently discussed in rather favorable terms in the 1920's.[33] To support charitable work in war-torn Europe, the Interchurch World Movement collected $2,700,000 from Los Angeles churches, primarily voluntaristic congregations, in 1920.[34]

There were, of course, new lay leaders in the 1920's who had not been present earlier in the century. Over half of those who had served at the denominational level before 1919, however, were serving similar functions in 1930.[35] Most of these had risen to denominational leadership at the same time they gained positions of importance in the business community. Of those who served on denominational boards at the local and national levels in the 1920's, the vast majority were in occupations which would likely include them in a broader economic framework.

At a time when the function of stewardship in Los Angeles was passing, it may be that the denominational lay leaders were searching for a new framework for the direction of their energies. National institutions with established programs presented an attractive alternative to becoming passive witnesses to the decline of power in the city. Certainly, it was the service function of the national denominations that interested Los Angeles lay leaders. Over seventy percent of the expenditures of local denominational budgets, which were controlled by the local agencies, went to national and local social action funds, such as the ministry to migrant farm workers.[36] Other considerations of the national assemblies, for the most part, did not gain the attention of Los Angeles Protestants.

TABLE 32

DENOMINATIONAL LAY LEADERSHIP, LOS ANGELES
1920-1930
(IN PERCENTAGES)

Corporate Manager	36.4
Entrepreneur	28.7
Professional	12.6
Merchant	12.3
Other[a]	10.0

Source: See Appendix III. Occupations from *Los Angeles City Directory*, 1920-1930;
and *Men of California*, 1920-1930. The implied stability is correct.

a   Independently wealthy, retired, or housewife.

　　　In the response, or rather lack of response, of Los Angeles
voluntaristic Protestants to the "Fundamentalist Controversy," the desire
to avoid conflict and find a stable base of effective action through
national agencies is most clearly seen.   During the 1920's, the
voluntaristic denominations all experienced national debates over the
theological issues of fundamentalism and modernism.   The
fundamentalists insisted on a literal interpretation of scripture and an end
to "higher criticism." The modernists were much less unified in their
ideology, but generally argued for an allegorical interpretation of
scripture in order to reduce the contradiction between biblical and
modern cosmologies.[37] In each of the local denominational affiliates, Los
Angeles Protestants demonstrated a disdain for the debate.
　　　The Presbyterian Church was most identified with the
controversy at the national level.   In 1923, the General Assembly was
presented with an Overture (a proposal from a presbytery) from the
Presbytery of Philadelphia to force Harry Emerson Fosdick into
submission to the doctrinal standards of the Presbyterian tradition.
Fosdick, an ordained Baptist minister, was employed as an Assistant
Pastor at Brick Presbyterian Church in New York. In 1922, he preached
a sermon entitled, "Shall the Fundamentalists Win?" in which he
questioned the doctrine of the Virgin Birth. If Fosdick could be forced
to accept Presbyterian ordination, he would have been open to charges of
heresy.[38]   After the issue had subsided, the General Assembly again
found itself the arena of a fundamentalist-modernist debate.   Between
1926 and 1929, a theological battle at Princeton Theological Seminary

over the control of the administration of the school became an issue for the national church. The immediate issue was the promotion of J. Gresham Machen, an eminent fundamentalist theologian, to a full professorship. The fundamentalist forces were defeated, and Machen withdrew from Princeton, founded his own seminary in Pennsylvania, and soon after formed the Orthodox Presbyterian Church.[39]

In both cases, the Presbytery of Los Angeles was fairly unresponsive. Two Overtures were proposed in the Presbytery of Los Angeles relating to the Fosdick affair: one in support of the Presbytery of Philadelphia, and the other in support of Fosdick. Both were defeated by a margin of more than two to one.[40] Said one prominent laymen, "This is an issue that does not really concern the work of the church. We are called to serve, not to cast aspersions on one another."[41] According to William Stewart Young, the speech brought great applause, and "was a fair statement of the feelings of this Presbytery."[42] The only mention of the Machen debate in the meetings of the Presbytery between 1926 and 1929 was the recognition of the receipt of briefs filed by the two factions from Princeton.[43]

If the participation of the Presbytery of Los Angeles in the fundamentalist controversy was not exciting, the activities of the other voluntaristic denominations were even less so. The general debate in the Baptist Church (Northern Conference) took place in 1921 and 1922. In the former year, a faction of theological conservatives proposed to the General Conference that Baptist colleges be purged of modernists. In the following year, W. B. Hinson, a minister from Oregon, suggested that the General Conference adopt a statement of faith in conformity to *The Fundamentals*.[44] Both proposals were defeated. Los Angeles Baptists were less than enthusiastic about either proposal. The Baptist Association of Los Angeles sent a memorial to the General Conference which recognized the need for "ridding our colleges of infidels and heretics," but questioned whether modernists really could be so classified and pleaded for moderation.[45] Two congregations, with memberships of less than 150 each, sent petitions in favor of the purge, and one, with a membership of four hundred, sent a petition in opposition to the purge. One petition, which suggested that the national church should ask "the Lord to lead us to peace and harmony," was sent by Baptists from the Los Angeles area in response to the Hinson proposal.[46]

The Congregationalists, Disciples, Methodists, and Episcopalians all experienced national conflicts, and the response from Los Angeles was fairly uniform. Four Congregational parishes sent petitions to the National Council asking for harmony in the church, and the Los Angeles Council, as a unit, decided to ignore the "Fundamentalist Controversy."[47] Los Angeles Disciples, whose national church experienced a brief schism over the issue, demonstrated very little interest. Only three of the seventeen congregations in Los Angeles supported the schismatic national organization, and they were three of the smallest Disciples churches.[48] With the exception of Robert Shuler of Trinity Methodist Church, Los Angeles Wesleyans ignored the national conflict. Shuler's congregation sent a petition to the General Conference of 1924 supporting a proposal to purge the seminaries. In response, the University Methodist Church sent a petition in opposition.[49] The Episcopal Church in Los Angeles demonstrated, if possible, even less enthusiasm for the controversy than the other voluntaristic denominations. On the issues of attacks on modernist Bishops Charles Fiske and William Brown, Bishop Johnson stated, in a Pastoral Letter, that the issues in the controversy were so "bizarre" that it would be best for the clergy of his diocese to concern themselves with the work of the church in service to the city and nation.[50] Clergy and laity tended to agree.[51]

In some ways it seems odd that a city so identified with Fundamentalists in the 1920's should have been so unresponsive to the national controversy. It was from Los Angeles that Lyman Stewart financed and directed *The Fundamentals*, which gave the movement its name. Fundamentalism as a movement, however, must be understood on two levels. Most attention has been given to the debate that affected the national voluntaristic denominations. The major strength of the movement, however, was in the World's Christian Fundamentals Alliance, and the small peripheral denominations associated with it.[52] Fundamentalism caused dissension in the major denominations specifically because it was not a general sentiment among voluntaristic Protestants. In each of the larger denominations, the movement was defeated by 1930.[53] There were Fundamentalist sects in Los Angeles in the 1920's, but they were on the periphery of the Protestant community, and were never a part of the voluntaristic culture.

The major denominations did not enter the controversy because the concept of theological division was foreign to them and because they were seeking ways to adjust to the new social reality in which division would have been disastrous. The City of the Angels for over two decades had experienced a relatively harmonious, cohesive community. Until the turn of the century, the First Baptist Church had been theologically conservative, and the First Congregational Church had been liberal, yet both existed in fellowship under the voluntaristic system.[54] In the early twentieth century, their theologies became less distinct.[55] If the potential for controversy existed, it was usually eliminated by a peaceful withdrawal, such as the Nazarene secession from the Methodist church, or by broadening the structure to include, for example, the Bible

Institute of Los Angeles. When the fundamentalist controversy rocked the national assemblies, the Institute and the voluntaristic churches went their separate ways in peace.[56]

It should not be assumed that Los Angeles Protestants were, therefore, modernists. Indeed, there is very little in the denominational records from the 1920's to suggest a theological stance of any type.[57] Voluntaristic Protestantism in Los Angeles had become a civic religion. Earlier in the century, this culture had assumed a role of stewardship, and under the new social system was removed from a central position to a supportive role.   Once the innovators of social programs, the voluntaristic denominations in the 1920's became functionaries of a corporate society. They no longer specified the needs of Los Angeles society, but responded to problems defined by social workers and social scientists.   At the denominational level, this, rather than the fundamentalist controversy, was the logical extension of the role of Protestantism in the City of the Angels.

This shift in function was facilitated by the new clergy in the city.   By 1930, almost two-thirds of the voluntaristic ministers in Los Angeles were graduates of large denominational and interdenominational seminaries which had instituted courses in sociology and social ethics at the turn of the century. In 1910, only five percent of the clergy had received this kind of education.[58] The new clergy were catalytic rather than causative, however. As early as 1914 a few Congregational lay leaders urged the Los Angeles Council to respond to the perceived needs of society rather than formulate those needs from the basis of middle-class Protestant values.[59] In 1917, the churches of Los Angeles were mobilized to aid in the war effort, and the Los Angeles Ministerial Association formed an Information Bureau to provide sermon material relating to the war.[60] Various congregations submitted to the direction of a non-voluntaristic organization, the Salvation Army, in activities to provide for injured soldiers.[61] All voluntaristic denominations in the city gave moral support.   The Los Angeles Conference of the Methodist Episcopal Church, South, declared, "We encourage no soft expression of pacifism in the face of the approach of autocracy, militarism and cruelty. We are fighting to make the world safe for democracy."[62] After the war, all six denominations supported the League of Nations.[63]

It was during the war that the Methodist Church, North, initiated urban services in Los Angeles which had become commonplace in other cities. Recognizing the needs of a small group of laboring-class Methodists who had recently migrated to the city, the Los Angeles Conference founded the City Methodist Church in 1917. G. Bromley Oxnam, a young minister who had participated in the administration of industry parishes while a seminarian in Chicago, was made first pastor of the congregation. Under his direction the parish, while he renamed the Church of All Nations, initiated a series of courses, ranging from cooking to mechanics, and provided a meeting place for small labor organizations.[64] Oxnam was an extreme example of the new clergyman in Los Angeles. His interests were broad, both in subject matter and scope. In 1926, he organized a small group of Los Angeles ministers to draft a petition to the President of the United States urging the recognition of the Soviet Union.[65] He rose rapidly in the Methodist Church, and became one of the leaders of the World Council of Churches in the 1950's.[66]

Few institutional churches were established in Los Angeles, but all six denominations began supporting national agencies which promoted specialized parishes in the early 1920's.[67] Each denomination did establish a system of agencies which were engaged in some form of social work. These were different in kind from the custodial institutions of the earlier twentieth century. They were staffed by clerics with training in social service, or by professional social scientists and social workers. In an effort to revive parishes that were in decline in the central city, Bishop Johnson in 1923, at the request of the Coadjutor, hired six social workers from Chicago to work with the indigent population.[68] In 1924, the Southern California Baptist Convention, which had subsumed the Los Angeles Association, created a Social Service Commission.[69] Other denominations established similar agencies, including the Disciples of Christ, which had been founded in the early nineteenth century as a reaction against the social concerns of the voluntaristic tradition.[70] Each of these agencies made periodic requests to the California Department of Social Welfare for guidance in their activities. In 1926, the Southern California Council of Congregational Churches went so far as to suggest that their denomination offer its services as an auxiliary of the state agency.[71]

The interdenominational life of the voluntaristic churches in Los Angeles experienced similar changes. Social scientists with experience in specific areas were freely loaned across denominational lines.[72] The Ministerial Association of Los Angeles telegraphed Congress in 1924 to protest the immigration act passed that year which excluded Japanese.[73] This was simply an extension of the changes in the function of the various denominations, but the most significant change in interdenominational life was its constituency. In the late 1920's, all Lutheran churches in the city were invited to join the heretofore voluntaristic Los Angeles Federation of Churches. By 1936, the Federation also included Unitarians, Eastern Orthodox, and Jewish congregations.[74] The city was no longer a voluntaristic culture by extension. Each denomination recognized the changes in Los Angeles society and adjusted to it. It was at this level that the Protestants in Los Angeles chose the "Outward Drive." At the level of the congregation, however, both the "Outward Drive" and the "Inward Life" characterized the practice of voluntaristic religion.

III

During the period of Protestant control in Los Angeles, few churchmen concerned themselves with periodic religious surveys. The report in the Los Angeles *Times* that three-quarters of the city's population was unchurched in 1927, however, supplied the material for at least two hundred sermons over the following months.[75] "We have forgotten our Gospel charge," preached Jonathan Richardson of the Wilshire Christian Church. "Great organizations have been created to minister to the needs of society, but only the local congregation, each Christian acting as a missionary, can minister to individual souls."[76] There had been general concern over the relatively small size of the Protestant community since 1920, when the Presbyterian, Baptist, Christian, and Methodist Churches on Wilshire Boulevard combined to take a religious census of the area they served. "The tide of new families moving into the district is tremendous," said the Presbyterian pastor, John A. Ely, "and every effort must be made to offer the services of our churches to them"[77] Canvasses and membership drives were unknown in the City of the Angels prior to 1920, and a survey conducted by the University of Southern California in the prior decade had been less than enthusiastically received by the local religious structure.[78] The general concern about the state of the religious population was expressed exclusively through congregational sources. There is no evidence that the local denominational agencies either took notice or action. Their concerns with the wider world of social problems and national denominational administration were of primary importance.[79] It was at the congregational level that the changing function of the voluntaristic churches was most sharply felt. No longer the center of a cohesive community, the congregations were also losing their neighborhood integrity. By 1930, fewer than two persons in five lived within two miles of the church they attended, and one in five lived more than ten miles away.[80] It is dubious that by 1930 residential clustering would have had the same meaning as it did earlier in the decade, but the cohesive voluntaristic neighborhood was becoming more scarce in the City of the Angels. In addition, the voluntaristic churches, which had enjoyed the greatest rate of growth in Los Angeles since 1890, increased in membership far more slowly than the Catholic, Jewish and small sect and cult population.

Just as the denominational agencies adapted to the new social order by accepting a supportive functionary role, the congregations presented programs which were more clearly responsive to a larger society than had been the case earlier in the century. On those rare occasions when a minister preached on social issues prior to the 1920's, the focus was local.[81]   Not only were a wider variety of subjects

TABLE 33

RESIDENTIAL CLUSTERING FOR VOLUNTARISTIC PROTESTANTS IN LOS ANGELES, 1910-1930 (IN PERCENTAGES)

Cohesion Factor	1910	1920	1930
In Neighborhood with Other Members of Same Congregation[a]	71.7	68.9	41.3
In Neighborhood with Members of Other Voluntaristic Congregations[a]	81.4	81.1	47.6

Source: See Table 18

[a] Living in a neighborhood with 50.1% or greater in this classification.

covered after World War I, but laymen were frequently asked to occupy the pulpit and speak on current affairs. Occasionally, visitors from other nations were asked to address congregations on international concerns.[82]

This general pattern began during World War I. High ranking officers and government officials were given the use of the pulpit to stimulate church participation in the war effort.[83] Immediately following the war, the use of lay speakers continued, and the subject was usually patriotism. In January of 1920, the Wilshire Presbyterian Church announced a program of sermons by California politicians as part of their Better America Campaign against "all forms of un-Americanism."[84] In the following month, the Society of the Sons of the Revolution requested pulpit time for selected members to deliver a patriotic Washington's Birthday sermon, and 198 churches, all but seven of them voluntaristic, cooperated.[85]

TABLE 34

RATE OF GROWTH FOR SELECTED DENOMINATIONS IN LOS ANGELES, 1920-1930

Voluntaristic Denominations	64%
Roman Catholic	102%
Jewish	632%
Small Sects and Cults[a]	381%

Source: Straightline interpolations from *Religious Bodies*, 1916-1936, verified by data listed in Appendix I.

[a]   Determined by the size and nature of each organization in consultation with A. Leland Jamison, "Religions on the Christian Perimeter," in *The Shaping of American Religion*, Vol. I of *Religion in American Life*, eds. James Ward Smith and A. Leland Jamison (Princeton, 1961), pp. 162-231, and Elmer T. Clark, *The Small Sects in America* (rev. ed.; New York, 1949).

The patriotic frenzy in the aftermath of the war ended by mid-1920, but the concern with social issues continued.   Robert M. Barralough of the Calvary Baptist Church took note of the changing emphasis of religious discourses and concluded that the people of Los Angeles, and America in general, were beginning to learn "a truth which the horrors of war helped to impress upon them—that theoretical religion . . . means little or nothing, but that practical Christianity means everything."[86]   Most of the sermons given between 1900 and 1919 were Biblical exegeses.   "Since the War the number of topics that may be covered by a preacher prohibits classification," wrote a compiler of sermons in 1924.[87]   Even when a sermon was exegetical or doctrinal in the 1920's, the opportunity was taken to diminish the importance of divisive issues.   Hunter Hall, pastor of the Knox Presbyterian Church, for example, swept aside such standard Calvinistic tenets of faith as predestination and infant damnation.   "We do not want anyone to put aside Christian fellowship because he thinks our church practices obscure beliefs."[88]

The sermon topics that were used with greatest regularity were morality and success.   The two were interrelated because the morality sermons in the 1920's were guides to the good life and early forms of situational ethics.[89]   Success was perhaps the most popular topic   On almost any Sunday, Los Angelenos could attend various churches in the city and hear such discourses as "Health and Happiness," "Strong in

Mind, Body, and Spirit," or "The Ten Commandments Pay Big Dividends."[90] They resembled nothing so much as the writings of Bruce Barton and Norman Vincent Peale.

Fairly frequently, the sermon in church services would be replaced by a motion picture or play. *Ben Hur* and *King of Kings* were shown at least 263 times in Los Angeles churches. Dramatic clubs were formed in some of the larger churches, and the worship service was often built around a pageant. In 1925, for example, Immanuel Presbyterian Church presented "False Idols of the Modern World," by Mrs. Howard L. Watts, wife of an Elder-osteopath. The dramatis personae included New Thought, Mormon, Socialist, and World-Wise Woman. It concluded with a plea for Christians to become more a part of the world, before the world became corrupted by the false idols.[91]

The message of Sunday morning sermons had changed a great deal since the earlier two decades of the century, when the standard selection of sermons included "Getting Ready for the Other World," "Man a Sinner," and "The Forgotten Lesson of Judas."[92] The changes in the nature of preaching and the alternatives to preaching indicate a greater concern for the things of this world, or at least an attempt to appeal to a greater number of people who were of the world. The order of worship, church buildings, congregational organizations, and expenditures also changed, but in such a way that suggests that the "Inward Life" was a factor of congregational life as much as the "Outward Drive" indicated by the sermons.

The "Inward Life" in the congregations was not so much a choice of Jesus over the world as it was an internalization of institutional practices. The civic functions had long since been relocated in other levels of the voluntaristic community. With the decline of the neighborhood integrity of the congregation, the individual parish church faced a greater crisis than the denominational agencies (which became parts of large bureaucracies). Only the largest congregations, such as First Methodist and Immanuel Presbyterian, could institute large social service programs, such as citizenship classes for immigrants.[93] These churches, like their denominational agencies, were becoming bureaucratized. A system of Associate and Assistant Pastorates in the larger churches assigned specific functions to the clergy. By 1930, St. John's Episcopal parish and First Baptist Church both had five ministers on the staff.[94] In some ways, the large parishes resembled small denominations rather than big congregations. The membership of these churches was distributed over a wider area than the smaller ones.[95] The structure of lay leadership also followed the pattern of denominational agencies, where influential and wealthy men served long terms of office. In the medium and small congregations, the leadership was less prestigious and of shorter tenure. In matters of ecclesiastical policy, the congregational leadership usually accepted the decisions of the denominational agencies without question. Two decades before, local congregations had been influential in the drafting and implementation of denominational policy.[96]

The crisis for the local congregation was one of function. The community as they had understood it was no longer in existence, and the power in the city was more diffuse. The larger ministry of the church was executed in such a way that the local congregation was reduced to the role of financial supporters. In 1900, Los Angeles voluntaristic churches had benevolence programs and funds of their own. By 1930, only seven congregations in the city had separate funds, and the rest simply sent that portion of their income to the local denominational agency.[97] The larger congregations were able to extend their influence by providing social services, but aside from their size, dispersions, and supportive function, they shared a similar experience with most other parishes. Lacking any real function in either the denominational or civic structure, the congregations were simultaneously concerned about their appeal to those outside the church and the internal structure of the peculiarities of the local congregational life. The former concern was met primarily by the "secularization" of the sermons.[98] The latter took many forms, the most visible of which were the order of worship and ecclesiastical architecture.

Protestant worship in Los Angeles, even among Episcopalians, had been of the "plain style." A Scots Presbyterian commented after having been to a number of services in the city in 1909, "I went to Immanuel to hear a good sermon and participate in a Reformed liturgy. The sermon was good, but nothing put me in mind of liturgy. I then went to the Anglican Cathedral, and found the barest bones of corporate worship. I was damned if I would go to a Papist service."[99] Ten years later, a new fashion in liturgical practice began in the Episcopal Church, and spread rapidly through the voluntaristic tradition. In 1919, a small group of writers and actors associated with the film industry, and recently arrived in Hollywood from New York, purchased a lot and financed the construction of a church building. When Bishop Johnson received a mortgage-free deed to the new parish building, he was delighted and consented to consecrate the new parish as rapidly as possible.[100] On December 12, 1919, the Bishop arrived at the corner of Vermont and Hilldale, in a fashionable residential district, vested in surplice and stole. The congregation was horrified. They had all been associated with the Church of St. Mary's in New York, which practiced a strict Anglo-Catholic liturgy. In honor of their former parish and new city, the parishioners named the church in Hollywood, St. Mary's of the Angels. The sight of a Bishop arriving for the consecration of a church without cope, mitre, and crozier, recalls one of the founding communicants, "made me think that someone, as a joke, sent us a Presbyterian or Baptist."[101] The Bishop was also horrified. He was from the broad Anglican tradition, but some practices were too far beyond the pale of acceptability. "When asked to put on papish vestments, I held my tongue," recalled Johnson, "and I did not flinch when I was asked to hold the consecrated host up for their heathenish adoration. But when at the conclusion of the Lord's Supper (which they called a *mass*) they asked me to lead them in the Angelus, I could not oblige."[102]

Through the efforts of the new Bishop Coadjutor, St. Mary's was able to obtain an Anglo-Catholic priest, and high-church practices gained wide acceptance in Episcopal parishes over the next five years. Vestries and congregations spent months investigating new forms of worship and new ways to adapt the *Book of Common Prayer* to their particular desires.[103] Similar interest in more formal and structured worship services began to be evidenced in Baptist, Methodist, Congregational, and Presbyterian churches. Many simply used a modified form of the basic Anglican rite, and others availed themselves of the new orders of worship emanating from courses in liturgics in Eastern seminaries. In each case, the choice of a specific form took months, and in a few cases, over a year.[104] Even the larger Disciples of Christ congregations were eventually involved in the liturgical interest. In 1927, Wilshire Christian Church abandoned its simple Memorial Feast and instituted a structured Lord's Supper, which included some form of the Kyrie, Gloria, Credo, Sanctus, and Agnus Dei.[105] The specifics of Sunday morning worship had never been a subject of discussion in the voluntaristic community before the 1920's. By then, however, they had little else to devote their energy to as congregations.

Coincident with and related to liturgical innovation was an ecclesiastical building boom. In the early part of the century in Los Angeles, the church in the voluntaristic tradition was identified with a concept of community rather than with a building. The older term, "meeting house" better defined the structure used for worship and congregational gatherings. By the 1920's, the broader sense of religious community was no longer supported with the specifics of those elements that were peculiar to the life of the church. In architecture, a more distinctive monumental style was needed. "We desire a structure which will remind us of the timeless nature of the Church and the power of God," wrote the Vestry of St. James Episcopal Church to a prospective architect.[106]

Over 150 new church buildings of the voluntaristic denominations were built in Los Angeles in the 1920's, and only thirty-four of these were new congregations. The relatively simple wood frame building gave way to psuedo-Gothic and Romanesque giants. A few of these were rather successful recreations, such as St. Paul's Cathedral and St. John's Episcopal Church. Most, however, were caricatures. First Methodist constructed a new building in 1922-1923 which included the sanctuary, social hall, offices and recreational facilities all in one structure, which faintly resembled a medieval prison. Just behind the tall spire, the arched roof of the gymnasium provided a curious relief.[107] Hollywood First Methodist Church, constructed in 1927, was typical of many of the anachronistic structures. In an effort to capture the subtle blend of sculpture and architecture that is the glory of the gothic style, the facade contained niches for statues of saints, but as a staunchly Protestant edifice, the statues were omitted.[108] On seeing the new First Baptist Church in 1929, the architect-scholar Ralph Adams Cram commented on the un-Protestant interior, "the 'Communion table' is an altar, and by simply adding sanctuary candles, a crucifix, and a tabernacle, it would be suitable for a celebration of a solemn high mass."[109]

It is a testimony to the desire for a new physical representation for the concept of church in the face of the collapse of the voluntaristic tradition that over $60,000,000 were spent by American Protestant congregations in Los Angeles on the construction and remodeling of churches. Some individual buildings represented investments of hundreds of thousands of dollars each, and the new sanctuary of Immanuel Presbyterian Church was built at a cost of over $2,000,000.[110] The proportionate amount of money spent on buildings is an excellent indication of the internalization of congregational life in Los Angeles. Funds for charity and missionary activity once administered by the congregation gradually became consolidated in denominational agencies, which ultimately collected the funds from the individual parishes, which no longer participated in the decisions concerning the expenditure of these funds. The city and state government, and a handful of civic organizations that became less clearly identified with the voluntaristic denominations, provided adequate welfare programs which diminished the need for charitable activity at the congregational level. Los Angeles Protestants by the 1920's found it necessary to internalize and localize their concept of the church, and as a result of the dynamics that led to this need, had the funds to build the appropriate structures.

TABLE 35

EXPENDITURES OF VOLUNTARISTIC CONGREGATIONS IN LOS ANGELES, 1900-1930 (IN PERCENTAGES)

	Missions	Benevolence & Charities	Education	Denomination Agencies	Building	Other
1900-1910	35.8	29.3	11.6	5.7	9.1	8.5
1911-1920	34.6	25.1	10.3	10.3	8.3	9.4
1921-1930	17.6	11.4	8.9	24.7	28.1	10.3

Source: See Appendix I.

The placement of the new edifices was indicative of another trend.   By 1930, less than one-half of all churches in the voluntaristic tradition in Los Angeles were located in residential neighborhoods. Most of them were built along the route of middle-class migration north and west on or near the major boulevards; Adams, Wilshire, Hollywood, and Franklin.[111]   Lacking a neighborhood base either geographically or by constituency, the Protestant churches created a variety of organizations (which served three functions) within the congregation. First, they made these churches more attractive to the people they wished to appeal to, or at least that was the justification for implementing the organizations in most cases.[112]   Second, and more important, they provided a surrogate for neighborhood cohesion.[113]   Third, these organizations provided some sense of identity with the Protestant community beyond the Sunday services. This had been unnecessary before the 1920's. To participate in any aspect of Los Angeles civic culture was to have an identity with the Protestant community.   After World War I, this was no longer true. Ancillary organizations, which were virtually unknown to most voluntaristic denominations earlier in the century, appeared in every congregation between 1919 and 1930.   Some of these were huge and general, such as the Wesley Brotherhood with a membership of over two hundred at Trinity Methodist Church in 1926.[113]   Others were small and specific, such as the Chess Club of Silver Lake Presbyterian Church.[114]

Most of the new organizations were designed to appeal to the youth.   Some of these were fairly transitory movements,, such as the Moral America Club of Westlake Presbyterian Church, which sponsored speaking contests with prizes provided by the WCTU.[115]   Most were general and more permanent.   The Methodist Church already had the structure of the Epworth League, which became a model for congregations of other denominations.   In 1920, the Pico Heights Christian Church, for example, created a Young People's Fellowship.   At the first meeting, Dr. Sarah J. Wise of the University of California, addressed the squirming and embarrassed youngsters on "Sex Problems."[116]   More often than not, dinners, picnics, or athletic events were held rather than meetings or lectures.   Indeed, sports became the major interdenominational contact made through the youth movement. Only seven of the three hundred and twelve voluntaristic congregations in 1930 did not have a basketball team.[117]   In the following year, a breakthrough in interdenominational relations was made when the totally voluntaristic Protestant Church Basketball League invited Lutherans, Unitarians, United Brethren, Churches of God, and others to participate.[118]

There were good reasons for the churches, especially the smaller ones, to concentrate on youth programs.   The decline in the cohesive membership patterns for the nuclear family begun in the nineteen-teens continued and accelerated in the 1920's. A greater proportion of teenage children of the members of smaller congregations began to join the large churches.   More significantly, there was a rapid rise in the proportion of children who had been on the Sunday school rolls of the voluntaristic churches in the nineteen-teens who were not to be found as members of any of the congregations for which records remain from the 1920's, and who were still residents of the city. Of course, they may have joined one of the few congregations for which records do not remain, or a non-voluntaristic religious organization.   A movement out of church life altogether, however, has been suggested by Los Angelenos who were active in church work in the 1920's.   One recalls, "I met so many young people on the street I hadn't seen in church for some time. They had this to do and that to do, and didn't have time for church any more."[119]

There were a few exceptions to the general internalization of congregational life, and a handful of parishes made a conscious effort to regain the central position of the voluntaristic churches in Los Angeles society.   The most active was Trinity Methodist Church led by Robert

"Fighting Bob" Shuler, whose image of the City of the Angels as an "Ideal Christian Community" had been formed earlier in the century.[120] "What has happened to this city?" he asked after his first month in his new pastorate.[121] "What does it say about our community," he asked on another occasion, "that the Prince of Laughter, Charlie Chaplin, is paid more than the President of the United States, and the unhealthy element he represents is more important than the churches to most of our citizens?" In order to "regain the leadership the churches have abandoned," Shuler and his congregation organized a meeting in front of the California Institute of Technology to launch a campaign for an anti-evolution law.[122] The movement did not receive the support of other congregations and came to a rather abrupt end.[123] In the next year, Shuler was able to gain greater support for a bill which would require daily reading from the King James version of the Bible in public schools. The measure went to the electorate in 1924, and was defeated.[124] His weekly radio programs and magazine constantly called for vigorous leadership from the Protestant community. Shuler's campaign for a seat in the United States Senate in 1932 was a logical extension of his attempt to place the church back in the center of society. His defeat was the logical extension of the quiet resignation to the new social order that denominations and congregations had accepted.

All of this outlines the basic configuration of congregational life in the 1920's, but it reveals very little about the religious life of the individual members. A number of studies conducted by sociologists at the University of Southern California in the late 1920's indicated that the response of Los Angelenos to questions on religion were similar to those of the residents of "Middletown."[125] Most of those interviewed expressed a personal religion, based on the individual's relationship with God or Jesus, rather than an organic concept of the church as a community. In Los Angeles there was one important difference. Many of those interviewed remembered a time in the recent past when neighborhoods and the city in general experienced a more communal religion. "I remember when we prayed and thought everybody in the city was praying with us," recalled one respondent. "Now it seems like we all have personal prayers."[126]

By concentrating on the life of the congregation in this discussion, a misleading assumption may arise that Protestants in Los Angeles, once the wielders of power, were now reduced to a pitiful remnant huddled together in internalized parishes in order to avoid contact with the new secular society. While this pattern may have been true for a few, it can hardly be applied to the majority. Many Los Angeles Protestants were still actively engaged in local politics, business, civic organizations, and social clubs.[127]   The difference between the earlier decades and the 1920's was that non-ecclesiastical activities had been an extension of a voluntaristic concept of community and became diversified functions in a corporate society, of which the churches were only a part. In their daily lives most churchmen probably gave evidence of the "Outward Drive." It was at the level of the congregation that Los Angeles Protestants concentrated on the "Inward Life," which meant for the individual member that his church association was no longer an organizing principle for the rest of his activities.[128]

This pattern cannot be proven for the whole Protestant community, but it can be demonstrated in the life of one prominent Los Angeles family. George Bell moved to Los Angeles with his wife in 1872 and immediately became involved in the Presbyterian church. He had been a Sunday school teacher in Indianapolis and assumed similar duties at the First Church in Los Angeles. By 1895, Bell had became a prosperous merchant and Elder of the church. He was one of the founders of Occidental College, and enrolled his son, Alphonzo, in the first class. Alphonzo inherited his father's interest in the Protestant community, and decided to become a minister and serve in a Los Angeles pastorate. His speech at his graduation from Occidental demonstrated his belief that the church could provide social leadership. "On what does the fate of this nation depend more than its religious training?" he asked. As an example of the kind of leadership that could be provided he proclaimed, "Crush the Saloon and you crush the tap root of evil."[129]

Alphonzo entered the San Francisco Theological Seminar in 1899, but withdrew after two years of study. He wrote to his father, "I am called to the Christian life, but not the ministry. . . The active layman can be a religious force in the community."[130] He returned to Los Angeles in 1901 as a real estate agent and became an active layman at the denominational and congregational levels. In 1916, Alphonzo was hired as an agent for Standard Oil. He rose quickly in the corporation and was able to continue his real estate activities. During the 1920's he maintained his membership in the First Presbyterian Church, but held no offices in the congregation or denominational agencies.[131] With the most effective leaders of the Protestant community turning their attention to denominational, civic, or business activities, the internalization of the congregations was perhaps the only way in which they could maintain their identities as institutions.

IV

The rise of peripheral religious organizations in Los Angeles during the 1920's was one example of the diversification that accompanied urbanization. It also represented another way in which Los Angeles Protestants reacted to the decline of the cohesive community and the rise of the corporate life. It was in the sects and cults that the "Inward Life" was most stressed. Common to all of these diverse groups, ranging from the oriental mysticism of the Vedanta Society to the biblical literalism of the Adventists, was one common message: forsake the world and its problems and look inward for your strength and identity.[132] This message took various forms. Swami Yojandi of the Vedanta Society instructed his students to "Rid your mind of the streets and newspapers and tensions outside yourself. Concentrate on the inner being."[133] The Pentecostal Assembly preached the "Glorious rapture of the Holy Ghost. He will make you whole and remove you from the cares of this world. Open yourself to His gracious being."[134] The most exaggerated form of the message was announced by The Mighty I Am: "Only you exist—you in union with the Godhead."[135]

The rise in the proportion of the population in peripheral organizations from 1920 to 1930 does not give an adequate indication of their diversity. In 1920 there were only two Adventist congregations and no Pentecostal Assemblies in the city. By 1930, there were eleven Adventist and six Pentecostal congregations. Some organizations, such as the Vedanta Society, existed in the City of the Angels since as early as 1904, but with only a handful of members, then grew rapidly in the 1920's. Between 1916 and 1925, thirty-two religious organizations which had not been represented previously in the city made their appearances. Of these, twelve were indigenous to Los Angeles.[136]

It is impossible to reconstruct these organizations with the same degree of accuracy as the voluntaristic congregations. Only a handful of records remain, but enough information exists to suggest that some Protestants in Los Angeles left their more established denominations, which no longer provided a sense of a cohesive community, and joined individualistic sects. From the eleven organizations that can be reconstructed, it is clear that a large portion, at least thirty-six percent, of their membership was composed of former members of voluntaristic congregations. The social base of these ex-voluntarists was not random. They tended to come from either the highest or lowest ranks of the Protestant community. Those of the upper and middle class became members of one of the mystic or New Thought organizations, and those from the lower classes became fundamentalists, Adventists, or Pentecostalists.[137]

The social division is compatible with the specific form of the individualistic message. Vedanta, the Liberal Catholic Church, and Christian Science all taught a fairly sophisticated ideology which included a plea to ignore the physical conditions of daily life and concentrate on the inward self. The conservative and enthusiastic Protestant cults taught the saving grace of Jesus and the promise of a better world to come.[138] It is hardly strange that those living in comfort would be able to ignore the squalor of daily life, and it is not surprising that the laboring class would respond to the message of a better life.

There is one tantalizing handful of evidence which indicates that the lack of cohesive community in Los Angeles, which was evidenced by the rise of the peripheral organizations, may have had a serious effect on the Protestant family. Sixty-four Protestants requested letters of transfer to Christian Science churches from eight voluntaristic congregations in the 1920's. Only six such requests had been made before 1919.[139] Of those made between 1919 and 1930, all but two were married women, and of these, fifty-one filed divorce actions within two years of their change in religious affiliation.[140] A general pattern emerges from their divorce proceedings. They were "widows to the company."[141] Their husbands were "married to the job."[142] These women had lost their functions as wives, and the church no longer gave them a feeling of participation in the broader community. It was quite reasonable that they should seek solace in a religion which taught the integrity and self-sufficiency of the individual. It is also reasonable that they should join an organization that was founded by a woman and addressed the deity as "Our Father-Mother."[143]

These bits of evidence are not conclusive, but do suggest that a retreat from the world, rather than an extension of a religious concept to the entire community, came to be the religious expression of a few Protestants. This is further supported by the location of the new cults. As the larger congregations moved their church buildings west, their abandoned structures were purchased or rented by peripheral religious organizations.[144] There was a thirty percent loss of membership in those neighborhoods from which the voluntaristic churches moved which cannot be accounted for by relocation in other voluntaristic parishes.[145] It is possible that some of these churchmen, who tended to be in the lower social ranks, felt abandoned and alienated from the established Protestant community, and joined the "Inward Life."

It was within this context that Aimee Semple McPherson founded the Four Square Gospel and built Angeles Temple, that the Liberal Catholic Church combined the Roman Mass and Theosophy, and that the World Church exhorted converts to drive the demons from their souls.[146]   These sects were not, as some casual commentators have suggested, the results of Mid-Westerners' rejection of their old culture and search for a new avenue for the religious impulse.[147] If any primary cause can be isolated, it is the decline of a cohesive concept of community imported from the Mid-West and beyond, that can best explain the rise of religious movements dedicated to the "Inward Life."

V

In 1931, Los Angeles celebrated its one hundred and fiftieth anniversary. Unlike the ceremonies of the Fourth of July in 1876, the Centennial of the city in 1881, and the first *La Fiesta de Los Angeles* in 1894, the glories of the future were not proclaimed. In speeches and pageants, Don Abel Stearns, James Woods, William Stewart Young, and Lyman Stewart were all recalled as great moving spirits in the past of the City of the Angels. Constant references were made to the "unique sense of community that led this small village to a great city."[148]   Los Angelenos congratulated each other for living in a city where the "general spirit of civic responsibility created a purity of local government that was an example to the rest of the state and nation."[149]   When the future of Los Angeles was mentioned it was within the context of the nation.[150]

By the end of the 1920's, Los Angeles was a major metropolis. As was the case in other large cities, the majority of its citizens did not belong to religious organizations. The cohesive voluntaristic community no longer exercised its influence through the other elements of the local society. Indeed, the voluntaristic community no longer existed. The changes between 1850 and 1930 were great. The first efforts to establish a Protestant sense of community in Los Angeles had failed, but with a change in the social structure, the voluntaristic principle flourished. The city became too large to support the cohesive sense of community, however. In response to this growth, the voluntaristic community became a corporate structure, and the economic and political life of the city became more diverse and was included in a broader framework of activity. By 1930, the City of the Angels had joined the larger American society. If it became a "fragmented metropolis," it was not entirely a result of the geographical spread of the city, not the lack of strong central governmental agencies. Los Angeles became a part of an American society which was fragmented. The social changes that the early Protestant migrants left behind finally caught up with them. In the new corporate nation, there was no place left to migrate to and perpetuate the voluntaristic system.

The changes in Los Angeles over the past fifty years have also been great, but the place of religion in the City of the Angels has remained stable.[150] The churches are supportive at the denominational level and internalized at the congregational level.[151] The city has become even more fragmented, and has seen its share of mass violence.[152] Voluntaristic Protestantism, not as a theological system but as a concept of social organization, made such overt displays of urban factionalism impossible. It had provided a center of community life. After its decline, nothing emerged to replace it. In this sense Los Angeles, although atypical, was a microcosm of one important aspect of the history of American society.

NOTES

[1] Quoted in the New York *Times*, August 14, 1928.

[2] Louis Adamic, *Laughing in the Jungle: The Autobiography of an Immigrant in America* (New York, 1932), p. 207.

[3] *Ibid.*, p. 208.

[4] H. Paul Douglass quoted in the New York *Times*, May 5, 1927.

[5] *Religious Bodies, 1926*, I, *passim.*

[6] Ibid. Denominations are listed in family units (e.g., Methodist, Lutheran, etc.) with specific denominations as subcategories.

[7] Determined from a computerized rank order correlation of these variables from data obtained in the religious censuses of 1906-1936. For an extension of the implications of this correlation (173), see William Fielding Ogburn and Ottis Dudley Duncan, "City Size as a Sociological Variable," in Ernest W. Burgess and Donald J. Bogue (eds.), *Contributions to Urban Sociology* (Chicago, 1964), pp. 124-153.

[8] *Religious Bodies*, I, pp. 457-459. This data is supported by the listing of local religious bodies in the *Los Angeles City Directory* for that year. For an example of the commentary on the "numerous" cults of Los Angeles, see Robert Glass Cleland, *California in Our Time, 1900-1940* (New York, 1947), pp. 212-213.

[9] *Religious Bodies*, I, *passim.* Directories for these cities also indicate that the census material was accurate in the listing of religious organizations.

[10] See Fogelson, pp. 247-272, and Shevsky and Williams, *passim.*

[11] This assumption is based on a rather crude survey of the backgrounds of commentators in the 1920's who had written on eastern cities as well as Los Angeles.

[12] Cultic publications such as *The Word is Calling* recognized Los Angeles as a place of "a great outpouring of the Spirit."

[13] A sermon given in 1928, quoted in Lawrence Leland Lacour, "A Study of the Revival Method in America, 1920-1955; With Special Reference to Billy Sunday, Aimee Semple McPherson and Billy Graham," (Unpublished Doctoral Dissertation, Northwestern University, Evanston, Illinois, 1956), p. 238.

[14] Lewis L. Mudge to William Stewart Young, June 17, 1915, Young Papers.

[15] James R. Sloan to the Committee on Planning, November 21, 1927, Archives of the Presbytery of Los Angeles.

[16] Sanford, p. 72.

[17] *Ibid.* p. 91.

[18]"Minutes of the Diocesan Synod of July, 1915," Archives of the Diocese of Los Angeles.

[19]Sanford, pp. 114-123; Stephen C. Clark, *The Diocese of Los Angeles: A Brief History* (Los Angeles, 1945).

[20]Based on a systematic reading of the File on the Selection of a Bishop Coadjutor, 1919-1920, Archives of the Diocese of Los Angeles.

[21]Los Angeles *Times*, January 24, 1920.

[22]Summary Files on His Excellency, Bishop William B. Stevens, Archives of the Diocese of Los Angeles.

[23]Address to the Diocesan Convention of 1924, *Ibid.*

[24]Sermon given at St. John's Church, February 2, 1921, *Ibid.*

[25]Institutional Church League, *Annual Report*, (Detroit, 1926), p. 12.

[26]Determined from a survey of listings in the *Journal of the General Convention* (New York, 1900-1930).

[27]Determined from a survey of the *Report of the Presbytery of Los Angeles* (Los Angeles, 1920-1930).

[28]"Minutes of the Meeting of the Presbytery, May 19, 1926," Archives of the Presbytery of Los Angeles.

[29]Baptist Association of Los Angeles, *Report, 1923*, p. 34.

[30]Determined from a survey of the various records of these denominations discussed in Appendix III.

[31]Los Angeles *Times*, January 10, 1920.

[32]Christian Ministers Association, *Bulletin*, March 11, 1921.

[33]Based on a survey of the sermon material listed in Appendix II.

[34]Los Angeles *Times*, May 15, 1920.

[35]Determined from a reconstruction of lay leadership in the denominations based on sources discussed in Appendix III.

[36]Determined from a survey of denominational budgets from sources listed in Appendix II.

[37]See Furniss; Stewart G. Cole, *The History of Fundamentalism* (New York, 1931); Robert T. Handy, "Fundamentalism and Modernism in Perspective," *Religion in Life*, XXIV (Summer, 1955), 381-394; and Carter.

[38]Furniss, pp. 71-87.

[39]*Ibid.*, pp. 94-95.

[40]"Minutes of a Meeting of Presbytery, April 8, 1923," Archives of the Presbytery of Los Angeles.

[41]*Ibid.*

[42]Young to Joseph Silman, May 3, 1923, Young Papers.

[43]Based on a systematic reading of minutes of meetings of the Presbytery, 1926-1929, Archives of the Presbytery of Los Angeles.

[44]Furniss, pp. 33-35.

[45]Baptist Association of Los Angeles, *Report, 1923*, p. 67.

[46]Baptist Church, Northern Conference, *Journal of the General Conference* (New York, 1922), IV, pp. 386-388; *Ibid.* (New York, 1924), IV, p. 174.

[47]National Council of the Congregational Churches, *Proceedings: Memorials and Petitions* (New York, 1924), pp. 289-297.

[48]Furniss, pp. 207-211; Carl Douglas Wells, "A Changing Institution in an Urban Environment: A Study of the Changing Behavior Patters of the Disciples of Christ in Los Angles," (Unpublished Doctoral Dissertation, University of Southern California, 1931), p. 137-141.

[49]Jervey, pp. 174-179.

[50]Pastoral Letter of the Bishop of Los Angeles, June 23, 1923, Archives of the Diocese of Los Angeles.

[51]Of the fifty-three letters that were received in response to the Pastoral Letter, only one was not supportive.

[52]Furniss, *passim*; Sandeen, *passim*.

[53]Furniss, *passim*.

[54]See Chapters 3 and 4.

[55]Based on a survey of the sermon materials discussed in Appendix III.

[56]After 1921, there was very little evident contact between BIOLA and the voluntaristic churches, and there is no evidence to suggest that any "confrontation" occurred, or that any hard feelings were expressed: based on a survey of pertinent materials mentioned in Appendices I and III.

[57]Based on a survey of the pertinent materials in Appendices I and II.

[58] Determined from a survey of seminary catalogues from archival sources listed in Appendix IV, and the biographical information obtained on the ministers of these denominations in the Los Angeles area from sources mentioned in Appendix III. Also see Abell, pp. 224-245.

[59] "Petition of the Lay Members of the Council, August 14, 1914," in Report of the Los Angeles Council of Congregational Churches (Los Angeles, 1914), pp. 317-318.

[60] Los Angeles *Times*, January 7, 1918.

[61] *Ibid.*, March 22, 1918.

[62] *Minutes of the Los Angeles Conference of the Methodist Episcopal Church, South, 1917* (Los Angeles, 1917), p. 52.

[63] Based on a survey of the pertinent materials described in Appendix III.

[64] Jervey, pp. 96-99.

[65] Ralph Lord Roy, *Apostles of Discord* (Boston, 1953), p. 19.

[66] Ronald Eugene Ossmann, "Some Aspects of the American Contribution to the Ecumenical Movement," (Unpublished Doctoral Dissertation, Princeton Theological Seminary, 1955), pp. 47-53; George Kennedy Allen Bell, *The Kingship of Christ: The Story of the World Council of Churches* (Baltimore, 1954), p. 106.

[67] Determined from a review of budgetary reports from sources listed in Appendix II. Also see D. Charles Gardner, "Service to the Social Order," in Pacific School of Religion (ed.), *Religious Progress on the Pacific Slope* (Boston, 1917), pp. 294-306, for the background of the "Social Gospel" in the Far West.

[68] Diocese of Los Angeles, *Annual Report* (Los Angeles, 1924), pp. 213-217.

[69] *Annual of the Southern California Baptist Convention* (Los Angeles, 1924), p. 46.

[70] See A. F. Bunney, "A Study of the Social Work Program of the Disciples of Christ in Los Angeles County," (Unpublished Master's Thesis, University of Southern California, 1933).

[71] *Report of the Los Angeles Council of Congregational Churches* (Los Angeles, 1926), p. 32.

[72] Based on a survey of the pertinent materials listed in Appendix II.

[73] Robert Moats Miller, p. 292.

[74] Los Angeles *Times*, September 30, 1927, February 9, 1936.

[75] Los Angeles *Times*, August 8, 1927. Based on a survey of the sermon materials discussed in Appendix II.

[76] *Fuller Notes*, XI, p. 481.

[77]Los Angeles *Times,* January 10, 1920.

[78]See Chapter 4, Section III.

[79]Based on a survey of the pertinent materials mentioned in Appendix III.

[80]Determined from congregational reconstructions based on sources listed in Appendix I.

[81]Based on a survey of sermon materials mentioned in Appendix III.

[82]This trend was first noted in the Los Angeles *Times,* January 24, 1920.

[83]*Ibid.,* January 14, 1918 - March 21 1918.

[84]*Ibid.,* January 24, 1920.

[85]*Ibid.,* February 19, 1920 - February 24, 1920. For a broader national perspective on this activity, see Stanley Coben, "A Study in Nativism: The American Red Scare of 1919-1920," *Political Science Quarterly,* LXXIX (March, 1964), 52-75.

[86]Sermon of Robert M. Barraclough, delivered to the Calvary Baptist Church, Los Angeles, August 11, 1920, Sermon Collection, Southern California School of Theology, Claremont Graduate School and University Center, Claremont, California.

[87]*Fuller Notes,* XV, Appendix.

[88]Los Angeles *Times,* November 17, 1922. I have been aided in my analysis of the sermon material by Francis Emmett Cook, "Problems of Authority in Contemporary Preaching with Specific Reference to the Pulpits of Los Angeles," (Unpublished Master's Thesis, University of Southern California, 1928).

[89]See, e.g., the sermon series reprinted in the Los Angeles *Times,* October 27, 1928; also see Cook, pp. 83-85.

[90]Determined from a survey of the sermon material cited in Appendix II.

[91]*Ibid.,* and the Los Angeles *Times,* November 20, 1920.

[92]*Ibid.* See also Hine, p. 122.

[93]Determined from a survey of the congregational problems from church records cited in Appendix I.

[94]In both of these churches, the specific instructions to the auxiliary clergymen indicated specialized labor functions.

[95]Determined from parish reconstructions based on sources listed in Appendix I.

[96]See Chapter 4, Section III.

[97]Determined from a reconstruction of church budgets based on sources discussed in Appendices I and III.

[98]"Secularization" here means a growing concern for non-ecclesiastical or non-biblical topics.

[99]James T. McTagget to William Stewart Young, December 2, 1909, Stewart Papers. This discussion is based on a survey of orders of 1909, Stewart Papers. This discussion is based on a survey of orders of worship from sources discussed in Appendix I.

[100]File on Founding of New Parishes, St. Mary's of the Angels, Archives of the Diocese of Los Angeles.

[101]Interview with Ralph G. Harrison, Hollywood Chamber of Commerce, Los Angeles, California, January 16, 1970.

[102]"Personal Reflections," (typescript), p. 137, Archives of the Diocese of Los Angeles.

[103]"Report of the Committee on Liturgical Practices, 1924," Archives of the Diocese of Los Angeles.

[104]Determined from a survey of the church records discussed in Appendix I.

[105]Based on a survey of service bulletins in the files of Wilshire Christian Church, Los Angeles. I was aided in this general discussion by Von Ogden Vogt, *Modern Worship* (New Haven, 1927); Horton Davies, *Christian Worship, Its Making and Meaning* (New York, 1957); and Evelyn Underhill, *Worship* (New York, 1957).

[106]"Specification of the Sanctuary, by the Vestry," (n.d.), Files of St. James Episcopal Church, Los Angeles.

[107]From pictures and floor plans for the church building, Files of Los Angeles First Methodist Church.

[108]From a visual investigation of Hollywood First Methodist Church.

[109]Cram quoted in the Los Angeles *Times*, August 30, 1928. Cram later applied similar statement to the chapel of Princeton University in *My Life in Architecture* (Boston, 1936), p. 255. On earlier Gothic revivals in American history, see Cram, *The Gothic Quest* (New York, 1907, and Phoebe B. Stanton, *The Gothic Revival and American Church Architecture: An Episode in Taste, 1840-1856* (Baltimore, 1968). I have been aided in my investigation of ecclesiastical architecture by A. L. Drummond, *Church Architecture of Protestantism* (Edinburgh, 1934), and drawings and photographs of Los Angeles church buildings from 1886 to 1927 collected by the Security Trust Company, Los Angeles.

[110]Determined from a reconstruction of parish budgets from sources mentioned in Appendix I.

[111]Based on site locations from the *Los Angeles City Directory*, 1900-1930, and parish and residential reconstructions based on sources listed in Appendices I and V. Also

see Duke, xvii, and William May, "A Study of the Factors Influencing the Geographical Movement of Churches in a Metropolitan Area," (Unpublished Doctoral Dissertation, University of Pittsburgh, 1956).

[112]The conscious motivation is indicated in all of the remaining records from this period.

[113]See Bessie Averne McClenahan, *The Changing Urban Neighborhood: From Neighbor to Nigh Dweller* (Los Angeles, 1929), pp. 93-94 and Wells, *passim.*

[114]Based on a reconstruction of auxiliary organizations from sources mentioned in Appendix I.

[115]Los Angeles *Times*, May 5, 1920.

[116]*Ibid.*, May 22, 1920. The Disciples of Christ had long reacted against the institution of social organizations within the congregation, but the trend reversed rapidly in Los Angeles after 1919. See M. E. Fish, "A Study of the Christian Youth Fellowship of the Wilshire Christian Church," (Unpublished Master's Thesis, University of Southern California, 1942), pp. 12-16.

[117]See Note 114.

[118]Los Angeles *Times*, March 21, 1931.

[119]Interview with J. Stull Pearson, Glendale Presbyterian Home, Glendale, California, February 9, 1970. This discussion is based on a reconstruction of parishes and family structures within parishes, based on sources mentioned in Appendix I.

[120]*Supra*, pp. 3-5.

[121]Los Angeles *Times*, February 3, 1921.

[122]*Bob Shuler's Magazine* (October, 1922), 34; Los Angeles *Times*, September 21, 1922.

[123]For reactions of other Methodist Churches, South, to Shuler's crusade, see *Minutes of the Los Angeles Conference of the Methodist Episcopal Church, South, 1921*, (Los Angeles, 1922), pp. 52ff.

[124]Jervey, p. 37; McWilliams, pp. 343-344.

[125]These are summarized in McClenahan. These studies were rather self-conscious attempts to apply the methods of Robert S. and Helen Merrill Lynd, which had received wide circulation among sociologists prior to the publication of *Middletown, A Study in Contemporary American Culture* (New York, 1930).

[126]McClenahan, p. 97.

[127]Based on reconstructions of these correlate activities from sources in Appendixes I, III and IV.

[128]This, at least, is hinted at by interviewees who had been active in church work in the 1920's: see M. I. Berneman, "A Study of the Social Program and the Social Welfare

Service of the First Methodist Episcopal Church of Los Angeles," (Unpublished Doctoral Dissertation, University of Southern California, 1939), pp. 51-58; and D. D. Eitzen, "A Quantitative Approach to Parish Problems," (Unpublished Doctoral Dissertation, University of Southern California, 1939), pp. 291-306.

[129] John O. Pohlmann, "Alphonzo E. Bell: A Biography," HSSCQ XLVI (September, 1964), 197-222.

[130] Reported in a letter from James G. Bell to William Stewart Young, January 9, 1901, Stewart Papers.

[131] Determined from an examination of the reports and records of the Los Angeles First Presbyterian Church.

[132] I was aided in the following discussion by Elmer T. Clark, *The Small Sects in America* (Rev. ed.; New York, 1949); Gaius Glenn Atkins, *Modern Religious Cults and Movements* (New York, 1923); Louis Richard Binder, *Modern Religious Cults and Society: A Sociological Interpretation of Modern Religious Phenomenon* (Boston, 1933); Charles S. Braden, *These Also Believe: A Study of Modern American Cults and Minority Religious Movements* (New York, 1949); and Charles W. Ferguson, *The Confusion of Tongues: A Review of Modern Isms* (Grand Rapids, Michigan, 1936). In conjunction with the works of Bryan Wilson, already cited, and the rather unsystematic collection of materials in the "Los Angeles Religion" Files, Special Collections Division, University Research Library, University of California, Los Angeles, a fair estimation of the surface ideologies of the small religious organizations listed in *Religious Bodies* and the city Directory, was able to be made.

[133] Vedanta Society Pamphlet, 1924, "Los Angeles Religion" Files.

[134] Los Angeles *Times*, May 28, 1926.

[135] *Ibid.*, March 4, 1925.

[136] Based on a programmed survey of data presented in *Religious Bodies*, 1906-1936.

[137] From a reconstruction and linkage with the Master List of voluntaristic Protestants, from sources mentioned in Appendix I.

[138] The diverse ideology was determined from local ephemeral sources, and the literature cited in Note 132 of this chapter.

[139] Determined from a survey of letters of transfer, from sources mentioned in Appendix I.

[140] Determined from a programmed survey of the *Abstract of Divorce Actions*, Hall of Records, County of Los Angeles, correlated with the list determined from the survey cited in Note 139 of this chapter.

[141] Determined from a systematic reading of the specific cases isolated by the surveys in the previous two notes in "Transcripts of Divorce Actions," Hall of Records, County of Los Angeles.

[142]*Ibid.*

[143]In addition to Meyer, *The Positive Thinkers*, see Norman Beasley, *The Cross and the Crown: The History of Christian Science* (New York, 1952); Robert Peel, *Christian Science: Its Encounter with American Culture* (New York, 1958); Charles S. Braden, *Christian Science Today: Power, Policy, Practice* (Dallas, 1958).

[144]Duke, pp. 157-163.

[145]Based on residential and parish reconstructions from sources discussed in Appendices I and IV.

[146]See William Bloongren, "Aimee Semple McPherson and the Four-Square Gospel, 1921-1944.:" (Unpublished Master's Thesis, Stanford University, Palo Alto, California, 1952); Charles W. Leadbeater, *The Science of the Sacraments* (Los Angeles, 1920); Edmund Sheehan, *Teaching and Worship of the Liberal Catholic Church* (Los Angeles, 1925); and Geoffrey W. Warburton, "The World Church and Sectarian Typologies," (Unpublished Doctoral Dissertation, University of Southern California, 1927).

These organizations are often associated by scholars with earlier communitarian experiments in Southern California in an attempt to create a "tradition" for religious enthusiasm. A difference between the solipsism of the 1920's movements with the communal perfectionism of the earlier movements, such as the Point Loma Community, can be seen by comparing the above cited treatments with Robert V. Hine, *California's Utopian Colonies* (New Haven, 1953).

[147]See, e.g., Cleland, *California in Our Time*, p. 214.

[148]Laurence L. Hill, "A Great City Celebrates Its 150th Anniversary," HSSCQ XV (1931), 7-55.

[149]Los Angeles *Times*, July 14, 1931.

[150]For an outline of the dynamics in Los Angeles history over the past forty years, see Thernstrom, "The Growth of Los Angeles in Historical Perspective," *passim*. Also see Winston W. Crouch and Beatrice Dinesman, *Southern California Metropolis; A Study in Development of Government for a Metropolitan Area (Berkeley and Los Angeles, 1963).*

[151]See, e. g., M. E. Fish, "The Adjustment of Large Downtown and Boulevard Churches to Socio-Culture Factors in the Community." (Unpublished Doctoral Dissertation, University of Southern California, 1959), and James E. Davis, "A Study of the Official Attitudes of Local Denominational Affiliates," (Mimeograph report of the Los Angeles Ministerial Association, 1967).

[152]Although the Watts Riot of 1965 was perhaps the most publicized, and the Century City incident involving the visit of President Lyndon B. Johnson was the most notorious, these occurrences were hardly isolated; see "Violence Indicators for Los Angeles in the 1960's" (Mimeograph report of the University of Southern California School of Social Welfare, 1969).

EPILOGUE

LOS ANGELES AND OUR PROTESTANT HERITAGE

"Our Protestant Heritage" is most often discussed by historians—advocates and critics alike—at the useful, but limited and vague plane of values and attitudes. It is credited with such tendencies as the reformist impulse and such concepts as individual liberty, and blamed for a host of national sins ranging from sexual repression to American imperialism. The dramatis personae of the tale usually include such august figures as John Winthrop, Jonathan Edwards, Lyman Beecher, and Horace Bushnell. Occasionally, the anonymous members of various reform groups within the voluntary system are given honorary mention. Studies of the tradition usually locate it all but exclusively in New England, the Mid-Atlantic states, and the Mid-West. Certainly Los Angeles in the late nineteenth and early twentieth centuries has not been considered an important site for such studies. To the extent that the City of the Angels has received the attention of scholars of American religion, it has been as the haven of the exotic and the hotbed of Fundamentalism—as an example of the post-Protestant era.[1]

When I first began this study, I was interested in the social origins of the exotic cults and Fundamentalist sects. To my surprise, my research indicated that the bizarre image of post-Protestant Los Angeles had as much to do with the Protestant past as with impersonal external forces. Furthermore, I discovered that Protestantism in that city was an important element in the dynamics which ultimately led to a post-Protestant culture. I decided that the perpetuity of voluntaristic Protestantism in Los Angeles was more important, more in need of explanation, and more interesting than the later development of peripheral organizations. The fact that Los Angeles was dominated by a Protestant culture well into the twentieth century means that the city is a chronological anomaly—but one which sheds light on an important relationship between Protestantism and American social change, and brings that relationship into sharper focus than in other areas where it is obscured by greater religious, ethnic, and economic diversity.

Having said that Los Angeles is something of an anomaly, how can I now extend my remarks beyond that city? I would argue that the chronological irregularity is not of great importance when one considers the high degree to which the objective data relating to urbanization and religion in the City of the Angels conforms to national trends (see Appendix V). That is to say, the statistical patterns for the nation as a whole may have preceded the configuration of the Los Angeles data by a few decades, but the changing patterns are remarkably similar.

Furthermore, Los Angeles entered the post-Protestant era in generally the same way that other urban areas had earlier.[2] In spite of the bizzare image of the city in the 1920's and thereafter, there is no evidence to support the notion that Los Angeles had more than its fair share of religious curiosities commensurate with the rise of social and economic diversity. Qualitatively, the response of Los Angelenos in normative Protestant denominations seems very much like the resigned, quietistic, internalized posture of their fellow churchmen in a variety of other cities in the 1920's and 1930's.[3] In style, the church buildings they erected in the 1920's seem not unlike George F. Babbitt's Presbyterian church which was "gracefully Episcopalian" and "contained everything but a bar."[4] Finally, the evidence presented in Chapters 1-3 indicate that the establishment of Protestant culture in Los Angeles was directly related to more general structural and religious changes in nineteenth-century America.

What then may be inferred from this study of religion in the City of the Angels? Obviously, the structure of American society changed remarkably in the years between the close of the Civil War and the 1920's, but we cannot explain this change entirely by reference to impersonal forces. In the theological *angst* of the turn of the century and in the continual search for "relevance" since that time, the spokesmen of the Protestant community often invoked that vague process called "secularization." In their cosmology the concept had validity, and after all, delivering jeremiads was part of their job. The historian's job is quite something else, however, and although twentieth-century Protestant rhetoric is important for understanding how one segment of society perceived its situation in modern America, we must look beyond the articulated causes of social change into the dynamics of change itself. Urbanization is a more definable process, but it is too often introduced as an immediate explanation for change rather than as a starting point for understanding change. In Los Angeles, Protestantism was an active agent in urbanization. While this cannot be said for other large cities at the same time, Protestantism was an important element in social change (of which secularization and urbanization were a part) throughout the nineteenth century.

The changes that led to post-Protestant America must be understood, to an extent, as the result of the social dynamics prevalent during the period of Protestant dominance. The voluntary system itself was born of structural change. Accommodation to new social realities allowed a form of ecclesiocentric culture to maintain itself during a period of rapid change. Indeed, the system lived on into the twentieth century in the most rapidly expanding metropolis in the nation. American Protantism, as a centristic and initiative social force, was too much a part of structural change and continual accommodation to die easily. It was too much rooted in pre-industrial culture to exist in anything but a peripheral supportive role of the world of Andrew Carnegie and Henry Ford. The rulers of the new America were (and are), for the most part, the children of voluntaristic Protestants, and indeed, have themselves been Protestants;[5] but they are part of an industrial world where the church is *an* organization. Their parents were part of a pre-industrial world where the church was the prototype of organization

This study of Los Angeles does not prove this line of interpretation, but the experience of Protestants in the City of the Angels suggests that it may be a fruitful direction of inquiry. To place these considerations in a slightly different context, based on my study of religion and social change in one setting, I would argue that: 1) nineteenth-century American Protestantism needs to be understood more fully in a social context, beyond the obvious "social implication" of Protestant rhetoric; 2) American society needs to be understood developmentally more fully in a Protestant context; and 3) the twentieth century condition of the Protestant churches (both denomination and sect) needs to be understood—sympathetically—within the context of the implications of the de-churching of American Protestantism. This last proposition probably requires a brief additional comment. Scholars of modern American Protestantism criticize this cluster of denominations for erecting barriers, serving specific class and ethnic interests, and refusing to adhere to the ultimate social and ethical implications of the teachings of Christ. American Catholicism and Judaism, coversely, are praised for providing institutions which facilitate the continuance of cultural integrity within specific ethnic, and often class, neighborhoods. I am a full member of the secular order and I would not care to be a part of the religious world I have studied. I have, in short, no brief to present on behalf of Protestantism. I am simply arguing that scholars have generally studied Catholicism and Judaism in the United States, quite properly, primarily as part of the social structure. Protestantism, however, has been studied as a system of beliefs. Functionally, Protestants have not been understood as a set of social groups responding to certain historical and existential conditions, which I would argue is the only valid scholarly starting point.

"Our Protestant Heritage," therefore, has left its imprint not only on our national institutions, literature, and values, but also on the history of our social development. I am mindful of the importance of the transportation revolution, the development of regional economic markets, and the many gross and subtle effects of industrial development during this period. It would be foolhardy to attempt a systematic analysis of the development of modern American society which ignored these factors or attempted to subordinate them to a "religious" interpretation. It would be ridiculous to suggest that the dynamics of Protestant organizations *caused* the rise of the corporate state. The position taken here is simply that it is impossible to understand the specifically American development of the general modern social structure apart from the dynamics of pre-industrial society, clear examples of which can be found in voluntary denominations and associations. That is one of the most important aspects of "Our Protestant Heritage," and that aspect can be seen clearly in the emergence of secular Los Angeles.

NOTES

[1]The phrase "post-Protestant era" has become popular among Protestant thinkers over the last decade. Conceptually, it has its origins in Dietrich Bonhoeffer's formulation of "religionless Christianity" and his specific remarks on the state of Protestantism in the United States; see Bonhoeffer's *No Rusty Swords: Letters, Lectures and Notes, 1928-1936, from the Collected Works of Dietrich Bonhoeffer*, vol. 1, ed. Edwin H. Robinson (New York, 1965), pp. 94ff. In theology, the phrase is used in a positive way. The church, the argument goes, is no longer responsible for maintaining the secular order, but is free to operate within that order as a prophetic agent. I am using the phrase to define the recognition on the part of Protestant thinkers of cultural and religious pluralism and the realities of a secular society; see Ahlstrom, *A Religious History of the American People*, pp. 1-13. According to Ahlstrom's categories, this study of religion in the City of the Angels would have to be considered a post-Protestant interpretation of the Protestant era.

[2]See Huggins, *Protestants Against Poverty* and the "Introduction" to Cross, *The Church and the City.*

[3]See Robert S. and Helen Merrell Lynd, *Middletown: A Study in Modern American Culture* (New York, 1929), pp. 315-409, and *Middletown in Transition: A Study in Cultural Conflicts* (New York, 1937), pp. 295-318; H. Paul Dougless and Edmund deS. Brunner, *The Protestant Church as a Social Institution* (New York, 1935), pp. 82-205. The Douglass and Brunner book is a summary of forty-eight separate microcosmic studies conducted between 1922 and 1934 by the Institute of Social and Religious Research.

[4]Sinclair Lewis, *Babbitt* (New York, 1922), p. 168.

[5]The Bell family is the most obvious example in Los Angeles, but the general trend has been studied more fully in E. Digby Baltzell, *Philadelphia Gentlemen: The Making of a National Upper Class* (New York, 1958), pp. 223-261, and *The Protestant Establishment.*

APPENDIX I

SOCIAL ANALYSIS OF LOS ANGELES PROTESTANTS: SOURCES AND METHODS

The basic sources for the identification of the members of voluntaristic denominations are church rolls and directories, from which a random sample of 7,014 were drawn for the period from 1890 to 1930. Smaller samples were first chosen at ten year intervals for exploratory analysis and to establish patterns of persistence, which were assumed to be highly related to occupation and participation in local organizations. After establishing the patterns of persistence (which was done by denomination rather than for the voluntaristic congregations as an undifferentiated whole), it was then possible to determine what proportion of the 1890 sample could be maintained for the 1900, 1919, etc., samples without skewing the resulting analysis. Therefore, the 1900-1930 samples contain only the proportion from the samples of the previous ten, twenty, thirty or forty years indicated by the earlier analysis. Obviously, the resulting sample provided only names, and social information had to be supplied from other sources, but this was the most crucial step.

Fortunately, Los Angeles Protestants have preserved a great many materials that are useful to the historian. As a result, the membership of entire congregations can easily be re-created, and this was done for a few parishes in order to test the validity of patterns suggested by the more general random sample. There were no discrepancies, so I have depended most heavily upon my basic list of Protestant church members in Los Angeles, which represents a listing from available sources of over eighty percent of the voluntaristic Protestants in the city during this time. A name listing was made of all 94,183 persons who appear on church rolls.[1] These names have been stored on tape under general denominational and specific congregational groupings, with retrieval function capabilities in the name field. This provided a base of identification for local civic, social and business personalities.

The documents for this portion of the study are literally located all over Los Angeles. A few congregations have placed their records in archival depositories, and these are listed in the bibliography. Most, however, have not. Directories for the majority of the churches were obtained at the various denominational headquarters: the Los Angeles Association of the American Baptist Convention; the Los Angeles Area Office of the Southern California-Arizona Conference of the Methodist Church; the Presbytery of Los Angeles of the United Presbyterian Church, U.S.A.; the Protestant Episcopal Diocese of Los Angeles; the

Los Angeles Christian Association (Disciples of Christ); and the Los Angeles Association of the United Church of Christ (Congregational) in Pasadena. These records from denominational headquarters account for approximately three-quarters of my name list and sample. Aside from archival sources mentioned earlier, the balance of the sample was obtained from sources loaned to me by individual churches and churchmen. Eight series of congregational directories not available at the specific church office or at the denominational headquarters were loaned to me by retired laymen. Copies have now been deposited with the denominational agencies and the parishes. Those congregations in Los Angeles which have chosen to retain their own records—often remarkably well intact—are: First Baptist Church, Hoover Street Baptist Church, Wilshire Baptist Church, First Congregational Church, Trinity Congregational Church, Pilgrim Congregational Church, Grace Congregational Church, Central Christian Church (Disciples of Christ), Figueroa Boulevard Christian Church, Griffith Park Christian Church, University Christian Church, Wilshire Boulevard Christian Church, the Church of All Nations (Methodist), the First Methodist Church of Los Angeles, Trinity Methodist Church, Hollywood Presbyterian Church, Immanuel Presbyterian Church, Knox Presbyterian Church, Wilshire Presbyterian Church, St. John's Protestant Episcopal Church, and St. Matthias' Protestant Episcopal Church.

The directories are of uneven quality. Most list the address of members, and a few list the occupation. A handful list the age, and a larger number give the date of membership in the congregation. In order to include as much social information as possible for the individuals in the sample, data from city, county, and civic associations records were included for each entry, as well as information from city directories.[2] Data for the most mutable variables (e.g., occupation and address) were obtained for each year, which provided a fairly accurate estimate of time of migration to Los Angeles as well as giving a somewhat more flowing profile than the ten-year sample would initially indicate. The basic information listed for each person is: name, age, sex, address, occupation, relation to head of household, denomination, specific congregation, and valuation of taxable land. This last variable was included in order to determine socio-economic ranking in cases where the occupation was not sufficient, and as a check against a simplistic occupational ranking. The sources for the data are listed in the bibliography. Care was taken to make certain that the sample chosen for greater scrutiny from the master list was representative for each year, for each denomination and congregation, and for persistence, using the number of years names appear on the master list as a rough estimate. The data collected for the random sample were also collected for all congregational and denominational officers. These data were stored in such a way that these individuals were not included in the retrieval functions for general social configurations unless they were a part of the random sample.[3]

Aside from the identification of church members through directories, there is a wealth of information in these church records: minutes of church meetings, ministerial correspondence, social announcements, congregational newsletters, worship bulletins, budgets, and letters of transfer. The latter were of great importance in determining the flow of membership from the major Protestant denominations discussed in Chapter 6. This material was surveyed systematically, although most of it is presented in rather narrative style in the text. Furthermore, these data have enriched my understanding of church life in Los Angeles immeasurably.

The social analysis of the peripheral religious organizations in Chapter 6 was based on a collection of membership directories that is much less complete than the master list for the six major denominations and represents the fragmentary material available rather than anything approaching a random sample. Directories for the following organizations were found in the Los Angeles Churches Collection, Special Collections, University Research Library, University of California, Los Angeles: Grace Fundamental Church, Aquarian Fellowship Church of Chirothesia, Second Brethren Church of Los Angeles, Spiritual Temple of Immortality, the William T. Stead Church of Eternal Light, Agabeg Occult Church, Westlake Calvary Church, and Shoredale Chapel. The Los Angeles Public Library contains the directories of the following: Avalon Boulevard Four Square Church, Glassell Park Church of the Nazarene, Church of God in Christ (Wilmington Avenue), Church of God in Christ (Central Avenue), The Gospel Tabernacle, Inc., Plymouth Brethren, Seventh Day Baptist Church of Los Angeles, Pentecostal Church (Pico Street), and the West Washington Community Church. The Small Religious Organizations Collection in the Library of Southern California School of Theology, Claremont, California, contains directories for the following churches: First Full Gospel Church, Berean Chapel, Full Gospel Assembly, Temple of Ananda Ashrana (Vedanta), Theosophy Hall, Voice of Prayer Church, the Church in the Name of Jesus Christ of the First Born, and the Scientific Truth Center. Directories for the Church of the Open Door are in the files of that church, and the directories for the Cathedral Church of St. Alban, Liberal Catholic Church, were examined at the Cathedral Church, located until recently in Hollywood. The church has since been sold to a Russian Orthodox congregation, and the records of St. Alban's are now in the personal possession of Archbishop Lawrence Mathews, Primate of

the Church Universal, and Metropolitan of North America. Archbishop
Mathews has retired to Arizona, and there are no active clergy in the Los
Angeles area.

The following tables (with the exception of I-A which is
primarily descriptive) are summaries of some of the more useful
statistical analyses of the data from the random sample of voluntaristic
Protestants.

TABLE I-A

VOLUNTARISTIC PROTESTANTS AS
PERCENTAGE OF LOS ANGELES POPULATION
AND NUMBER OF ENTRIES ON BASIC AND SAMPLE LISTS

	Percentage of L.A. Population	Total Voluntaristic Membership[a]	Number of Name Entries[b]	Sample Size
1890	12.5	6,300	5,712	937
1900	17.6	17,387	14,585	1,476
1910	11.2	36,198	31,607	2,137
1920	10.6	60,993	51,831	3,218
1930	6.6	83,691	69,984	4,986

a. Based on Yearbooks and Religious Censuses.

b. From available denomination and congregational files.

TABLE I-B

OCCUPATIONAL STRUCTURE OF
VOLUNTARISTIC PROTESTANTS IN LOS ANGELES

	1890	1900	1910	1920	1930
Manager (Corp.)	----	----	7.6	9.3	8.5
Merchant-Proprietor[a]	38.1	42.6	33.7	24.9	36.0
Professional	17.0	18.7	11.8	6.9	6.7
Agriculturalist	23.0	13.8	----	----	----
Supervisor-Clerical[b]	13.6	17.1	31.9	37.1	39.2
Labor[c]	8.3	7.8	15.0	11.4	9.6

a.   Including minor industrialists until 1910.

b.   After 1910, a significant proportion who had formerly been in the merchant-proprietor category are included in the "Supervisor" category.

c.   Primarily skilled.

TABLE I-C

PATTERNS OF FAMILY COHESION BY CONGREGATIONAL AND DENOMINATIONAL MEMBERSHIP
(IN PERCENTAGES)

	Children Age 12-18				Children over 18				Spouse			
	In same congregation as spouse	Same denomination as spouse, but different cong.	In different denomination within the six voluntaristic denominations	Member of one of twelve largest congs., spouse membership elsewhere	In same congregation as spouse	Same denomination as spouse, but different cong.	In different denomination within the six voluntaristic denominations	Member of one of twelve largest congs., spouse membership elsewhere	In same congregation as spouse	Same denomination as spouse, but different cong.	In different denomination within the six voluntaristic denominations	Member of one of twelve largest congs., spouse membership elsewhere
1890	97.4	2.6	*	----	73.9	18.5	5.6	----	98.2	----	1.1	----
1900	91.6	7.5	*	2.1	52.3	23.7	10.4	7.4	91.6	----	3.2	*
1910	72.8	12.4	11.7	9.6	32.7	21.4	22.1	12.9	84.0	----	3.7	2.8
1920	54.2	17.3	19.4	18.3	19.8	23.2	28.3	19.6	79.1	----	4.8	3.1

* Less than .1%

NOTE: The basis for this analysis is 1,709 household families. The sample was taken from the original sample. Data on member of the family of the sample group was obtained by a name search of the scanograph list and comparison of addresses.

TABLE I-D

DISTANCE OF RESIDENCE OF MEMBERS
FROM CHURCH BUILDING
(IN PERCENTAGES)

	1890	1900	1910	1920	1930
Within 1 mile	74.7	69.8	51.6	32.1	20.9
Within 2 miles	89.2	87.5	79.4	46.4	31.6
Within 5 miles	98.1	98.3	96.3	78.6	62.3
More than 5 miles	1.9	1.7	3.7	21.4	37.7

NOTE: While it is true that increased transportation technology undoubtedly was a large factor in the greater average distance between residences and church buildings over time, there is a possibility that a proportion of the large membership beyond five miles from the church building had moved away from the immediate neighborhood and had become inactive members. These most likely would not bother to change congregational affiliation.

TABLE I-E

GEOGRAPHICAL MOBILITY AND DENOMINATIONAL INTEGRITY
(IN PERCENTAGES)

	No Change of Address					Change of Address in Los Angeles				
	Denominational change with resultant membership in 1 of 12 largest churches	Change to another denomination within 6 major denominations	Change congregation within denomination	No change of congregation--lapsed membership	No change of congregation	Denominational change with resultant membership in 1 of 12 largest churches	Change to another denomination within 6 major denominations	Change congregation within denomination	No change of congregation--lapsed membership	No change of congregation
1890-1899	----	5.4	4.7	.3	89.6	----	3.7	61.4	.7	34.2
1900-1909	1.7	3.0	6.5	.4	90.1	5.3	17.2	58.7	.5	23.6
1910-1919	6.2	10.5	2.8	.3	86.4	12.9	44.7	35.6	.9	18.8
1920-1929	11.6	15.8	2.3	.2	81.7	26.3	54.6	28.9	2.4	14.1

NOTE: The following percentages of the voluntaristic population changed addresses within the city: 1890-1899, 12.7; 1900-1909, 14.6; 1910-1919, 28.4; 1920-1929, 32.4

TABLE I-F

OCCUPATIONAL STRUCTURE OF
LAY LEADERSHIP IN CONGREGATIONS
(IN PERCENTAGES)

	1890	1900	1910	1920	1930
Manager (Corp.)	----	----	11.4	14.7	9.6
Merchant-Proprietor[a]	71.7	57.1	44.4	38.4	42.1
Professional	18.6	24.1	25.3	24.9	25.3
Agriculturalist	7.4	3.2	----	----	----
Supervisor-Clerical[b]	12.3	15.6	18.9	20.4	19.6
Labor	----	----	*	1.6	3.4

*   Less than .1 percent.

a.   See Notes a and b, Table I-B.

NOTE: "Lay Leadership" is specified as members of Boards of Sessions, Vestries, Deacons, Stewards, Trustees, etc.

NOTES

[1] This was done by using the rapid scanograph process then being developed by TRW Systems Group, Inc. I am grateful to Harold Ellis of the Systems Development Division of the Management Systems Office for making it possible for me to use the process during its experimental phase.

[2] These sources are listed in the Bibliography, but a detailed description of the city and county records can be found in The Southern California Historical Records Survey, Inventory of the *County Archives of California*, (Mimeograph, n.d.) No. 20, Vols. 1, 2 and 4.

[3] I have used a sub-routine similar to that described in M. H. Skolnick, "A Computer Program for Linking Records," *Historical Methods Newsletter* (September, 1971), pp. 114-125.

APPENDIX II

HOMOGENEITY OF VOLUNTARISTIC DENOMINATIONS IN LOS ANGELES

In the text and in the tables of the previous appendix the data on the six denominations are presented collectively and compared with the general population of Los Angeles. The case for treating these denominations as one unit has already been made in the introduction and throughout the text. As was mentioned in Appendix I, the random sample was collected on the basis of a denominational breakdown—as if denominational affiliation might be a significant variable in social analysis. If the scanty data from other denominations is included in the analysis, religious identification is indeed a significant factor; but *within* the six voluntaristic denominations in Los Angeles, specific affiliation was found to be of no significance for any of the variables studied. This was determined using a number of measures. I originally used Pearson's C, a contingency coefficient automatically included in the processing of my data. The values that result, however, are difficult to use with any degree of accuracy when tables with different numbers of cells are being compared. Furthermore, 1.00 (perfect correlation, or in this context absolute differentiation and lack of homogeneity) can never be achieved. I next attempted to adapt the index of dissimilarity most often associated with Taeuber and Taeuber's *Negroes in Cities.*[1] I could not use their index in its original form, because only two groups could be compared at a time.

After many trials (and almost as many errors) I was able to use an index of dissimilarity capable of making a comparative analysis of an infinite number of groups. I have further perfected the measure so that one formula provides both an index of dissimilarity comparable to, but with greater versatility than, the Taeuber and Taeuber measure, and a contingency coefficient (with a realized range from 0 to 1) which can be used to compare tables with different number of cells. Obviously, homogeneity (or lack of dissimilarity) yields a small value which is in fact a statement of weak contingency, just as a statement of high contingency suggested dissimilarity and heterogeneity. The problem is that we have been forced to use different measures for what is really the same spectrum. The measure that follows has the added advantage of ease. It is no more difficult to compute than measures of dissimilarity, and is much more simple than the computation of expected values and the other steps required to generate the chisquare statistic, which must then be reduced to a coefficient.

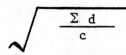

$$\sqrt{\frac{\Sigma\ d}{c}}$$

The formula for the measure, which I will call delta, for differentiation, is the square root of the sum of the differences between the largest and smallest percentages of each row (d), divided by the number of columns (c). This establishes the parameters of 1 and 0. If the value is used as a correlation coefficient, it is interpreted in the way that any other measurement of association would be interpreted. If it is being used as a measure of dissimilarity, then 1 would indicate that the categories in the columns are absolutely dissimilar and share none of the categories in the rows at all. 0 would indicate that the column categories are absolutely similar, and share the categories in the rows in exactly the same proportion.

If the six denominations in this study, for example, were tested for differentiation by income level, and we found that all of the members of the Baptist Church were in one income category, all Congregationalists in another, and so on, we would have a d value of 1.0 (100%, expressed as 1.00, minus 0). The sum of the d values would be 6.00, divided by c (number of columns) would be 1.00, and the square root of 1.00 is 1.00: a statement of perfect contingency and dissimilarity. If on the other hand, each denomination was represented in exactly the same percentages in each of the rows, then each row would have a d value of 0, at which point calculation can cease. The square root of zero is zero: a statement of absolutely no contingency and absolute similarity.

Of course, 1 and 0 are very rarely realized in most social research. Two examples of what is more likely to be the case should clarify the usefulness of this measure. We know from Table 23 in Chapter 3 that in 1900 the occupational division of the voluntaristic community in Los Angeles was: 42.6% merchants, 13.8% agriculturalists, 18.7% professionals, 17.1% clerical, and 7.8% laborers. The following table indicates a hypothetical occupational distribution in the six voluntaristic denominations which could have yielded the percentages given for 1900 for all six denominations as a group. It is obvious from a brief glance that the six denominations in this hypothetical table seem to have very little in common in their occupational distributions. A precise statement of how little they have in common is delta. The d values for each of the rows are .95, .51, .51, .27, and .27. The sum of the d values is 2.51, which divided by 6 is .41, the square root of which is .65 - a very strong statement of contingency and dissimilarity. The actual occupational distribution of the six voluntaristic denominations in 1900 is found in Table II-B.

TABLE II-A

HYPOTHETICAL OCCUPATIONAL DISTRIBUTION OF VOLUNTARISTIC PROTESTANTS IN LOS ANGELES
1900
(IN PERCENTAGES)

	Baptist	Congre-gational	Disciples of Christ	Epis-copal	Method-ist	Presby-terian
Merchant	2	80	12	34	50	97
Agriculture	43	7	52	2	36	1
Professional	1	5	3	52	4	2
Clerical	27	8	21	11	8	0
Labor	27	0	12	1	2	0

Table II-B

ACTUAL OCCUPATIONAL DISTRIBUTION OF VOLUNTARISTIC PROTESTANTS IN LOS ANGELES
1900
(IN PERCENTAGES)

	Baptist	Congre-gational	Disciples of Christ	Epis-copal	Method-ist	Presby-terian
Merchant	41.2	43.7	39.6	40.7	40.8	43.1
Agriculture	18.3	11.2	17.3	13.4	15.3	12.6
Professional	18.0	19.8	15.1	20.6	18.7	20.3
Clerical	20.5	18.4	15.8	15.9	16.9	16.5
Labor	2.0	6.9	12.2	9.4	8.3	7.5

While we do not find here the absolute similarity which would result in a measure of 0, the similarity is striking, and again, delta is a precise measurement of that similarity. The d values are .04, .07, and .06, .05

and .15. The sum of the d values is .37, which divided by 6 is .06, the square root of which is .08—a very weak statement of contingency and dissimilarity, but a very strong statement of homogeneity. The tables that follow contain the delta values for the variables reported in Appendix I, all of which indicated a high and sustained homogeneity among the voluntaristic Protestants throughout the time studied.

TABLE II-C

SIGNIFICANCE OF DENOMINATIONAL AFFILIATION FOR PROPORTIONAL REPRESENTATION ON MASTER TAPE DETERMINED BY COMPARISON WITH YEARBOOKS AND RELIGIOUS CENSUSES

Year

1890	.14
1900	.13
1910	.10
1920	.07
1930	.13

NOTE: No denomination is consistently over- or under-represented from 1890-1930.

TABLE II-D

SIGNIFICANCE OF DENOMINATIONAL AFFILIATION FOR DIFFERENTIATION BY OCCUPATIONAL STRUCTURE

Year

1890	.19
1900	.08
1910	.09
1920	.07
1930	.09

NOTE: From 1900 to 1920, differentiation from year to year was random. Between 1920 and 1930, the Protestant Episcopal and Methodist Churches were advantageously differentiated.

TABLE II-E

SIGNIFICANCE OF DENOMINATIONAL AFFILIATION FOR DIFFERENTIATION BY PATTERNS OF FAMILY COHESION BY CONGREGATIONAL AND DENOMINATIONAL MEMBERSHIP

Year	
1890	.03
1900	.05
1910	.04
1920	.11
1930	.16

NOTE: Until 1920, no denomination was consistently differentiated. After that period, members of the Disciples of Christ demonstrate a slightly higher degree of family cohesion than the other five denominations.

TABLE II-F

SIGNIFICANCE OF DENOMINATIONAL AFFILIATION FOR AVERAGE DISTANCE OF MEMBERSHIP FROM CHURCH BUILDING

Year	
1890	.06
1900	.07
1910	.14
1920	.16
1930	.15

NOTE: Until 1910, no denomination is consistently differentiated. After that period, members of the Disciples of Christ demonstrate a slightly higher degree of membership residence within the two and five mile areas. The Episcopalians, who theoretically had residentially determined parishes, had a slightly higher proportion of the membership living beyond five miles from the church building than the other five denominations.

TABLE II-G

SIGNIFICANCE OF DENOMINATIONAL AFFILIATION FOR GEOGRAPHICAL MOBILITY AND DENOMINATIONAL INTEGRITY

Year

1890	.13
1900	.10
1910	.13
1920	.09
1930	.11

NOTE: Until 1920, no denomination was consistently differentiated from the others. After that time, the Episcopalians and Disciples of Christ demonstrate a slightly higher degree of denominational integrity than the other four denominations.

TABLE II-H

SIGNIFICANCE OF DENOMINATIONAL AFFILIATION FOR OCCUPATIONAL STRUCTURE OF LAY LEADERSHIP IN CONGREGATIONS

Year

1890	.09
1900	.15
1910	.17
1920	.11
1930	.14

NOTE: No denomination is consistently differentiated.

The implications of these tables require some comment. Many books and articles on the relationship between class and denominational affiliation suggest that there exists in American society a status ranking among major Protestant denominations which includes the Episcopalians at the top and the Baptists and Disciples of Christ at the bottom. Most of this literature is based on impressionistic sources and national samples with no controls for proportional loading by region.[2] The majority of Baptists, for example, are in the South. If Baptists from this region are compared with Episcopalians in the South, social and economic distinctions are not as readily apparent.[3] Furthermore, by using denominational *families* rather than denominations themselves, many scholars have made some serious errors of judgment. In the data for Los Angeles, I have limited my "Baptist" sample to the American Baptist Convention. Other organizations which carry the name "Baptist" conform more to sect than denominational typologies. The churches of the American Baptist Convention in Los Angeles were involved in many interdenominational activities with the other voluntaristic denominations, but there is no evidence that they ever had contact with the smaller sects, from which they were socially differentiated, and which shared the name "Baptist" and little more. It may be that the amount of homogeneity in Los Angeles among the major Protestant denominations is atypical, but this study is better specified and the data more closely scrutinized than in any of the more general works on the subject. The relationship between denominational affiliation and class is still an open question which needs careful and rigorous study.

The categorization of these denominations as one cohesive unit, although supported by the data from Los Angeles, and the historical development of denominational activity in the United States, also requires some comment. Readers familiar with H. Richard Niebuhr, Sidney Mead, and others, will recognize the integrity of the denominational grouping I have used. More recently, however, Paul Kleppner and Richard Jensen have used another form of categorization.[4] Kleppner's "Traditionalist" and "Pietist" typologies and Jensen's "Liturgical" and "Pietist" categories are interesting, but involve many conceptual and empirical problems. Kleppner's categories are not well specified and lack anything approaching a real empirical base, in spite of his seemingly scientific approach. Jensen's categories are much better specified and are measured with greater accuracy. The major problems with Jensen's treatment, however, involve an "either/or" fallacy and an erroneous assumption that denominationalism and theological style are similar, if not the same. Even if we assume that the latter proposition is true, denominations such as the Lutherans and Presbyterians must certainly be considered both "Liturgical" and "Pietist." My research, however, suggests that theological style might be identified at the congregational level, but that it is dangerous to do so at the denominational level. That being the case, we cannot be certain what is being measured in the Jensen analysis. Are we measuring denominations which have official statements which would place them in one category or another, or are we measuring denominations who have a majority of congregations in one of the two categories? If the latter is true, is there significant variation from county to county? Although my categorization of "voluntaristic Protestants" is less precise, it has more historical and empirical justification, and there is less confusion about how it relates to the individual and the congregation.

NOTES

[1]Karl E. and Alma F. Taeuber, *Negroes in Cities* (Chicago, 1965), 203-4, 223-238. Pearson's C is explained in any basic statistics handbook; the treatment in Charles M. Dollar and Richard J. Jensen, *Historian Guide to Statistics: Quantitative Analysis and Historical Research* (New York, 1971), 80-81, is as good as any.

[2]For examples of this literature, see H. Richard Niebuhr, *The Social Sources of Denominationalism*, and Herbert Schneider, *Religion in Twentieth-Century America* (Cambridge, Massachusetts, 1952), pp. 228ff. The literature in general is summarized and criticized in Demarath, *Social Class in American Protestantism*.

[3]See Demarath, Chapter 1.

[4]Pal Kleppner, *The Cross of Culture: A Social Analysis of Midwestern Politics, 1850-1900* (New York, 1970), and Richard J. Jensen, *The Winning of the Midwest: Social and Political Conflict, 1888-1896* (Chicago, 1971).

SOURCES FOR LOCAL
DENOMINATIONAL HISTORY

The major sources for this material are the local denominational headquarters mentioned in Appendix I. Although the printed and mimeographed reports and the manuscript files of these agencies are listed in the bibliography, a word should be said about the rich variety of materials. In addition to information about individual congregations, these archives contain minutes of meetings of various committees, rather extensive files of correspondence about local denominational activities, and detailed budgetary reports. In addition, all of these headquarters contain complete sets of national and California regional denominational reports of general conventions and specialized committees. It was from these sources that the lay leadership at the denominational level was obtained. The following is a summary of the findings of that analysis.

TABLE III-A

OCCUPATIONAL STRUCTURE OF
LAY LEADERSHIP IN DENOMINATIONS
(IN PERCENTAGES)

	1890	1900	1910	1920	1930
Manager (Corp.)	----	----	2.4	9.5	17.4
Merchant-Proprietor[a]	83.2	84.7	69.9	65.8	63.1
Professional	6.1	8.4	18.9	21.6	16.2
Agriculturalist	5.7	----	----	----	----
Supervisor-Clerical[a]	6.0	6.9	8.8	3.3	2.6
Labor	----	----	----	*	.7

*   Less than .1 percent.

a.   See Notes a and b, Table I-B.

NOTE: "Lay Leadership" is specified as members of local, regional and national denominational committees and delegates to meetings at these levels.

APPENDIX

TABLE III-B

PROPORTION OF EACH CATEGORY
OF DENOMINATIONAL LAY LEADERS ALSO
INVOLVED IN CONGREGATIONAL LEADERSHIP
(IN PERCENTAGES)

	1890	1900	1910	1920	1930
Manager (Corp.)	----	----	89.7	68.2	65.8
Merchant-Proprietor	93.2	93.5	84.3	74.1	70.6
Professional	84.6	87.1	85.6	76.5	74.9
Agriculturalist	95.3	----	----	----	----
Supervisor-Clerical	91.8	94.2	87.3	91.9	92.1
Labor--	----	----	----	89.8	93.7

NOTE: The data on denominational leadership was interfaced with the data from the sources mentioned in Appendix I for this analysis.

Information on sermons delivered in the Los Angeles area were obtained from three basic sources. Newspaper reports, the Sermon Collection at the Southern California School of Theology, Claremont, California, and the *Fuller Notes*, at Fuller Theological Seminary, Pasadena, California. The latter source is a series of loosely bound abstracts of sermons prepared by students at the Seminary. The project was begun by students at Occidental College in 1889, continued by students at the University of Southern California, and taken over by Fuller in the mid-twenties. The abstracts are from one-half to one page in length and contain the Biblical text, a summary of the sermon, date, minister, and church.

APPENDIX IV

SELECTED SOCIAL PATTERNS:
LOS ANGELES, 1850-1930

The following tables are summaries of a selected portion of more detailed analyses of social patterns in Los Angeles. I was aided in my research and interpretation by three of my fellow graduate students at the University of California, Los Angeles: Michael Hanson, Stephan Erie, and Charles Slosser.

TABLE IV-A

RESIDENTIAL PERSISTENCE IN LOS ANGELES
(IN PERCENTAGES)

	1880-1890	1890-1900	1900-1910	1910-1920	1920-1930
Total Population	54.2	50.1	57.4	50.2	48.7
Voluntaristic Protestants	83.7	86.9	86.3	85.2	68.3

SOURCE: For total population, *Los Angeles City Directory*, 1880-1930; for voluntaristic Protestants, the sample described in Appendix I.

NOTE: A random sample of approximately 200 names was chosen from the city directories of 1880, 1890, 1900, 1910, 1920, and 1930 respectively. The data presented here, therefore, is limited to the proportion of the same at the beginning of each decade who were present at the end of that decade. The 1880, 1890, 1900 and 1910 samples were traced for twenty, thirty, and forty year persistence rates also, which indicated that voluntaristic Protestants were twice as likely to be long-term residents of the city as the population in general.

The problems inherent in using city directories for this sort of analysis have been discussed in Peter R. Knight's, "City Directories as Aids to Ante-Bellum Urban Studies: A Research Note," *Historical Methods Newsletter*, II (September, 1969), 1-10, and *The Plain People of Boston, 1830-1860: A Study in City Growth* (New York, 1971). Nevertheless, the data are indicative. From the material presented here and in the text, it would seem that in Los Angeles the categories of migrants and continuous residents established by Sidney Goldstein "Migration: Dynamics of the American City," *American Quarterly*, VI (Winter, 1964), 337-348, have definite correlates along a Protestant (voluntaristic) and non-Protestant axis.

TABLE IV-B

SELECTED PATTERNS OF INTERMARRIAGE
(IN PERCENTAGES)

	1850-1860	1861-1970	1871-1880	1881-1890	1891-1900	1901-1910	1911-1920	1921-1930
Voluntary Protestant-Voluntary Protestant[a]	----	----	----	87.3	89.6	82.5	76.1	59.8
Voluntary Protestant-Non-Voluntary Protestant[b]	----	----	----	12.7	10.4	17.5	23.9	40.2
Gringo-Mexican[c]	15.6	11.3	4.1	----	----	----	----	----
N=	37	76	148	157	153	187	241	318

SOURCE: Random samples for each cohort from: Libro primero de Matrimonios, 1850-1857, Marriage License Division, County Clerk's Office, County of Los Angeles; Certificate of Marriage Contracts (various 1850's), Ibid.; Applications for license to marry, 1862-1930, Ibid.

a. Voluntaristic Protestant marrying voluntaristic Protestant (proportion of voluntaristic Protestant marriages).

b. Voluntaristic Protestant marrying individual not identified as voluntaristic Protestant (proportion of voluntaristic Protestant marriages).

c. Native-born American marrying individual of Mexican ancestry (proportion of total marriages).

TABLE IV-C

LAND USAGE IN LOS ANGELES
(ESTIMATED)
(IN PERCENTAGES)

	1850	1860	1870	1880	1890	1900	1910	1920	1930
Farm	26	25	20	31	34	8	2	3	1
Orchards	--	--	6	18	21	11	9	12	8
Commercial	12	7	8	14	16	26	34	30	33
Industrial	--	--	2	7	11	13	31	34	36
Residential	--	--	--	16	18	21	24	21	22
Ranching	62	68	64	14	--	--	--	--	--

SOURCES FOR ESTIMATION: List of Real Property Owners, 1850-1851, Archives of the County of Los Angeles; County Assessor's Map Books, 1895-1930, Office of the Assessor, County of Los Angeles; *Report of the State Surveyor General of the State of California* (Sacramento, 1869); Los Angeles Chamber of Commerce Industrial Department, *General Industrial Report of Los Angeles County* (Los Angeles, 1930); appropriate census volumes listed in the Bibliography.

TABLE IV-D

PROPORTION OF CIVIC, SOCIAL, COMMERCIAL AND CULTURAL ORGANIZATIONS AS VOLUNTARISTIC PROTESTANTS

Organizations	1890	1900	1910	1920	1930
Civic	84.6	86.1	81.3	80.7	49.4
Commercial	81.2	84.5	84.7	72.8	47.1
Cultural	88.4	91.3	89.4	85.6	62.9
Social	84.7	84.5	87.2	75.8	53.2
Total	83.9	88.7	85.7	83.2	51.6

TABLE IV-D (Cont)

NOTE: The organizations chosen for this analysis were identified by city directories and the annual summary of social and civic organizations in the Los Angeles *Times* each January, and membership was identified through the "Organizational Records: Non-Ecclesiastical" listed in the Bibliography. This summary excludes specifically religious or ethnic organizations, such as the Knights of Columbus and the Armenian Patriotic League. This obviously creates a bias favoring the inclusion of Protestant citizens, but the major criterion for organizations included in this analysis was the absence of restrictions which would limit membership on the basis of religion or ethnicity. Organizations such as the Mason and Elks, therefore, are also not included, even though they are logical extensions of the Protestants community in Los Angeles. The table was derived by adding the information from these sources with the basic list explained in Appendix I.

TABLE IV-E

SELECTED NON-PROTESTANT (VOLUNTARISTIC) INSTITUTIONS IN LOS ANGELES, 1890-1930

	Eastern Orthodox Parishes	Foreign Language Lutheran Parishes	Synagogues	Ethnic Social Organizations	Foreign Language Newspapers
1890	--	--	1	2	1
1900	--	1	1	4	3
1910	3	4	2	6	4
1920	7	12	2	7	4
1930	13	23	21	33	12

SOURCE: *Los Angeles City Directory*, 1890-1930; Religious Censuses listed in the Bibliography.

APPENDIX V

URBAN GROWTH AND RELIGIOUS MEMBERSHIP

The indices associated with the decline of voluntaristic power in Los Angeles—a rapid increase in size and diversity, a declining proportion of the population formally affiliated with religious organizations, and an increasing number of religious organizations competing for a declining proportion of the population—deserve a brief investigation based on general national data. The sources for the following analysis are the Federal population and religious censuses and the yearbooks of churches listed in the Bibliography, interpolated for decennial estimates. The data base for urban places is a random ten percent sample (alphabetical, weighted for regional representation) of urban areas within each size cohort up to 25,000, and all cities larger than that. All rural counties (here defined as counties with populations of greater than fifty percent living outside of urban places) were included for the analysis.[1]

On the most superficial level, the growth of urban America and the proportion of the population in religious organizations have been colinear.

TABLE V-A

AMERICAN URBAN AND RELIGIOUS GROWTH

	Percentage of population in urban areas	religious organizations
1890	35.1	34.6
1900	39.8	39.9
1910	45.7	41.2
1920	51.3	44.3
1930	56.1	44.9
1940	56.5	49.1
1950	59.0	57.6

NOTE: Data base for urban areas in this table is *all* urban areas.

Dividing the data into rural and urban areas, it is clear that the greatest increase in religious categories were in urban areas (see Table V-B). A significant urban-rural differentiation is in the number of

TABLE V-B

URBAN-RURAL DIFFERENTIALS

	URBAN				RURAL			
	percentage of population in religious organizations	rate of growth of religious membership	rate of growth of number of denominations	rate of growth of number of congregations	percentage of population in religious organizations	rate of growth of religious membership	rate of growth of number of denominations	rate of growth of number of congregations
1890	24.9				39.7			
1890-1900	31.3	49.2	21.9	21.3	41.4	9.8	2.3	16.7
1900-1910	38.9	47.8	13.2	14.6	46.2	22.5	1.6	9.1
1910-1920	43.3	28.9	8.5	11.9	47.1	6.3	.7	1.4
1920-1930	46.5	25.6	12.9	23.3	42.3	10.2	.2	6.5

NOTE: The data base for urban areas in this table is all urban areas.

denominations and congregations. In general, it is easier to found any organization in an urban area. There is greater diversity and a concentrated population from which to draw membership. Rural areas in the twentieth century have depended on national denominational structures for economic and organizational support.[2] Although small sects can be found in the most isolated areas of the deep South and South-West, they are much more common in urban areas.

This does not mean the rural America was less religious. The summary above is an average for the nation. The study of individual rural counties, however, indicates that from 1890 to 1930 these areas tended to have either a much higher proportion of the population in churches than the urban areas or a religious population of less than ten percent. In 1920, for example, ten percent or less of the total population of forty-three percent of the rural counties in the nation were members of religious organizations. In thirty-seven percent of all rural counties, the religious population constituted eighty percent or more of the total. There are some slight regional variations, but the most convincing categories are: isolated rural counties having contiguous boundaries with other rural counties, those that share a boundary with an urban county, and the presence in the county of an urban area.[3]

TABLE V-C

RELIGIOUS MEMBERSHIP IN RURAL COUNTIES
(PERCENTAGE OF TOTAL POPULATION IN EACH CATEGORY)

	Isolated rural county	Contiguous boundary with urban county	Urban area in county[a]
1890	11.7	24.3	76.1
1900	12.1	28.9	76.4
1910	10.2	29.1	77.3
1920	9.8	33.2	79.5
1930	10.4	31.4	81.3

[a]Not including the urban area.

The urban areas must further be divided by size (which is also to say diversity, as will be argued in Appendix VI). The relationship between this elementary variable and religious membership is immediately visible by reference to the following tables.

The proportion of the population in religious organizations is inversely related to size, but the number of denominations is directly related. There are individual variations, of course. St. Louis and Minneapolis, for example, are in the same size cohort for 1930, but seventy-five percent of the Missouri community were members of religious organizations and only forty percent of the population of Minneapolis appears in the religious index. There are some regional variations. The Far West until 1940 had a smaller proportion of religious membership than the nation, but the basic configuration is the same. Whether the norm is the region or the nation, cities that experience growth in size (and, of course, diversity) take on the characteristics of similar urban areas at the same point in time rather than retaining the religious configuration of their former size and function.

There are a few conclusions that can be drawn from these indices that are important extensions of the general argument of this study. Rural folk during this period had either very little access to religious organizations or lived in counties where religious affiliation was the norm. In those counties with a high religious index, there was even greater cohesion than in small towns. Religious affiliation in urban areas was a function of size and was generally not the norm in larger cities. The metropolitan regions experienced an increase in denominational organizations, including new and peripheral sects. Smaller towns were more cohesive in religious structures, with a large proportion of the population in fewer denominations. The data from the national sources in many ways seem like the Los Angeles experience writ large.

Unfortunately, religious data for the period prior to 1890 are notoriously unreliable, but a survey of the Federal census data relating to urban growth indicate that New York, Ohio, Illinois, Missouri, Iowa, Pennsylvania and Indiana—the states of heaviest voluntaristic migration to Los Angeles between 1880 and 1900—were among the states experiencing the most rapid urban growth in the late nineteenth century. My research in the reports and archives of the six denominations studied (listed in the Bibliography) indicate a pattern in these areas of tension within the voluntaristic community during a time of rapid urban growth and, presumably, the decline of the proportion of the population in religious organizations generally and the strength of the voluntary denominations specifically.

TABLE V-D

URBAN POPULATION AND RELIGIOUS MEMBERSHIP BY SIZE
1890

	%of Total Population in Size Cohort	% of Urban Population in Size Cohort	Average Number of Denominations	Proportion of Population in Religious Or-ganizations
2,500-5,000	3.6	10.3	12	47.4
5,000-10,000	3.8	10.8	19	44.3
10,000-25,000	5.5	15.6	27	38.3
25,000-50,000	3.6	10.2	39	35.9
50,000-100,000	3.2	9.2	62	35.9
100,000-250,000	4.4	12.6	74	26.4
250,000-500,000	3.9	11.1	93	17.7
500,000-1,000,000	1.3	3.6	97	18.3
1,000,000	5.8	16.6	101	16.6

TABLE V-E

URBAN POPULATION AND RELIGIOUS MEMBERSHIP BY SIZE
1900

	% of Total Population in Size Cohort	% of Urban Population in Size Cohort	Average Number of Denominations	Proportion of Population in Religious Organizations
2,500-5,000	3.8	9.6	11	46.8
5,000-10,000	4.2	10.6	22	45.1
10,000-25,000	5.7	14.4	26	37.4
25,000-50,000	3.7	9.3	37	35.2
50,000-100,000	3.6	9.0	64	34.3
100,000-250,000	4.3	10.9	71	31.6
250,000-500,000	3.8	9.4	95	23.7
500,000-1,000,000	2.2	5.5	97	21.5
1,000,000	8.5	21.3	106	17.1

TABLE V-F

URBAN POPULATION AND RELIGIOUS MEMBERSHIP BY SIZE
1910

	% of Total Population in Size Cohort	% of Urban Population in Size Cohort	Average Number of Denominations	Proportion of Population in Religious Organizations
2,500-5,000	4.1	8.9	14	47.3
5,000-10,000	4.6	10.0	21	46.5
10,000-25,000	6.0	13.2	27	38.1
25,000-50,000	4.4	9.6	31	37.6
50,000-100,000	4.5	10.0	35	35.4
100,000-250,000	5.3	10.5	37	38.7
250,000-500,000	4.3	9.4	43	24.7
500,000-1,000,000	3.3	7.2	48	22.9
1,000,000	9.2	21.2	53	19.4

TABLE V-G

URBAN POPULATION AND RELIGIOUS MEMBERSHIP BY SIZE
1920

	% of Total Population in Size Cohort	% of Urban Population in Size Cohort	Average Number of Denominations	Proportion of Population in Religious Organizations
2,500-5,000	4.1	8.1	15	48.2
5,000-10,000	4.7	9.2	23	47.1
10,000-25,000	6.7	13.0	24	40.6
25,000-50,000	4.8	9.4	39	45.5
50,000-100,000	5.0	9.7	52	44.6
100,000-250,000	6.2	12.0	50	43.7
250,000-500,000	4.3	8.4	47	38.3
500,000-1,000,000	5.9	11.5	53	31.4
1,000,000	9.6	18.7	64	21.6

TABLE V-H

URBAN POPULATION AND RELIGIOUS MEMBERSHIP BY SIZE
1930

	% of Total Popu- lation in Size Cohort	% of Urban Popu- lation in Size Cohort	Average Number of Denominations	Proportion of Population in Religious Or- ganizations
2,500-5,000	3.8	6.8	14	51.0
5,000-10,000	4.8	8.7	23	49.8
10,000-25,000	7.4	13.3	22	43.4
25,000-50,000	5.2	9.3	38	45.6
50,000-100,000	5.3	9.4	47	46.7
100,000-250,000	6.1	11.9	53	46.3
250,000-500,000	6.5	11.7	52	43.1
500,000-1,000,000	4.7	8.1	59	37.5
1,000,000	12.3	21.8	71	26.9

The following table consolidates the number of incidents involving denomination litigation in deciding an issue of authority between local congregations and denominational agencies between 1870 and 1890. Unfortunately, adequate data does not exist which would allow for greater sophistication of this data by factoring. Nevertheless, the amount of such activity in the states of New York, Ohio, Illinois, Missouri, Iowa, Pennsylvania, and Indiana is not only much greater than the rest of the states, but it is proportionately greater than can be accounted for by a simple size factoring.

TABLE V-I

ORGANIZATIONAL TENSION IN
VOLUNTARISTIC DENOMINATIONS, 1870-1890

| | Level of Litigation[a] | | |
	Local	Regional	National
New York	672	478	43
Ohio	547	483	2
Illinois	594	406	14
Missouri	611	326	27
Iowa	387	463	18
Pennsylvania	407	275	36
Indiana	295	221	9
All Other States	1244	909	78

[a]Includes only the highest level of litigation involved. "Local" implies units such as Presbyterians, "Regional" implies units such as Synods, and "National" implies units such as a General Assembly.

NOTES

[1]There are many fascinating variables to be studied in urban religious population statistics, such as age distribution and sex ratios. For a discussion of these see C. Luther Fry, *The U.S. Looks at Its Churches* (New York, 1930), pp. 7-22.

[2]See Elizabeth R. Hooker, *Hinterlands of the Church* (New York, 1931); John W. Meyers and Edwin E. Sundt, *The Country Church as It Is: A Case Study of Rural Churches and Leaders* (New York, 1930); and John Williams Jent, *Rural Church Problems* (Shawnee, Oklahoma, 1935).

[3]Geographic areas and concentration was determined by a multi-coordinant repeating program, interfacing data from population and religious censuses.

URBAN GROWTH AND INDICES OF DIVERSITY

It is by now a commonplace that the simple increase in the population of a city is not an adequate expression of the complexities of urbanization. The diversity of the population and the complexity of the social structure also must be taken into account. The following two tables attempt to present the urban growth of Los Angeles in such a framework by comparing the diversity of Los Angeles at various stages of its growth and comparing Los Angeles with the norm for its same cohort, using the census classification of urban areas, at these various stages. No measure is really adequate to give evidence of the subtleties involved in urban diversity, and no formula, no matter how complex, is as complex as the society it proports to measure. Nevertheless, some comparative analysis is possible.

I have attempted to indicate the diversity of the urban population by using three variables: ethnic identification, religious affiliation, and economic activity, or occupation. The specifications of these variables are: the proportion of the total population in each ethnic group (including nationality for the foreign-born) given in the printed census data; the proportion of the total religious population in each denomination as reported in the 1890, 1906, 1916, 1926 and 1936 religious censuses, and interpolated for 1900, 1910, 1920, and 1930; and the proportion of the total work force in each occupational grouping as reported in the printed census data. One can make a case for including the non-affiliated as a category in the religious index, but this raises serious conceptual questions about whether non-affiliation meant the same sort of thing as affiliation. Was there a decision-making model for the individual who did not join a religious organization comparable to that for one who did join? The index of diversity, therefore, is comparable only within a variable. One can compare the economic diversity of Los Angeles with that of other cities, for example, but one cannot compare the economic, ethnic, or religious indices for Los Angeles in the same year.

The formula used for the index is $1 - \Sigma x^2$, when x is the percentage of the total in each category (expressed as a fraction). This is an adaptation of indices of market monopoly that have been used for some time by economists (See, e.g., F. A. Fetter, "The Economic Law of Market Areas," *Quarterly Journal of Economics*, XXXVIII (June, 1923), 187-196; W. Goldner, "Spatial and Locational Aspects of Metropolitan Labour Markets," *American Economic Review*, XLV (December, 1955), 217-224; and C. D. Harris, "The Market as a Factor in the Localisation of Industry in the United States," *Annals of the Association of American Geographers*, XLIV (June, 1954), 29-41. The formula measures diversity as a factor of both the number of categories and the proportional representation, and has a range from 0 to 1. 0 indicates absolutely no diversity—only one category accounting for one hundred percent of the total (the sum of x^2 would then be 1.00, subtracted from 1 yields an index of 0). 1 is a theoretical value that is achieved absolutely only when there are an infinite number of categories with equitable distribution of the total. It is never achieved in fact, but may be achieved when the value is rounded to the nearest hundredth. If a city contained two hundred different occupational groups, for example, and each category contained exactly the same proportion of the total (.005), then each $x^2 = .000025$, and $\Sigma x^2 = .005$, subtracted from 1 yields an index of .995, rounded to 1.00.

It must be kept in mind that the index measures *both* the equality or inequality of distribution *and* the total number of categories. Thus, an absolutely equitable distribution in four categories would result in a lower index of diversity than an absolutely equitable distribution in ten categories. In the former case, each category would contain .25 of the total, each x^2 would be .0625, $\Sigma x^2 = .25$, subtracted from 1 yields an index of .75. If the equitable distribution involves ten categories, each category contains .10 of the total, each $x^2 = .01$, the $\Sigma x^2 = .10$, subtracted from 1 yields an index of .90. If we introduce another hypothetical case involving ten categories in which the proportions are inequitable, the generation of the x^2 values would be as follows:

% of Total	x^2
.50	.2500
.18	.0324
.06	.0036
.17	.0298
.04	.0016
.17	.0289
.02	.0004
.03	.0009
.02	.0004
.01	.0001

$$\Sigma x^2 = .3472$$

Then, $1 - \Sigma x^2 = .65$, which is a lower value than the case with an equitable distribution in only four categories (.75).

The index used throughout the text for an analysis of Los Angeles is derived from printed census data and the estimates of the religious population prior to 1890, and the religious censuses after that time. Table VI-A summarizes this material for the period from 1890 to 1930 so that Los Angeles can be compared with the norms for cities of similar size using the religious as well as population censuses. The base for the analysis in Table VI-B was drawn from the same used in Appendix V. The implication of theses data is that size, while not a sufficient measure of urban growth, is highly related to diversity.

TABLE VI-A

URBAN GROWTH AND SOCIAL CHANGE
LOS ANGELES, 1890-1930

		Diversity Index		
	Size	Ethnic	Religious	Economic
1890	50,393	.48	.23	.35
1900	102,479	.46	.25	.47
1910	319,198	.57	.31	.52
1920	576,673	.59	.43	.56
1930	1,283,000	.65	.55	.68

TABLE VI-B

NORMS OF DIVERSITY IN AMERICAN CITIES
IN SAME SIZE COHORT AS LOS ANGELES, 1890-1930

		Diversity Index		
	Size	Ethnic	Religious	Economic
1890	50,000-100,000	.71	.35	.42
1900	100,000-250,000	.65	.43	.51
1910	250,000-500,000	.69	.46	.60
1920	500,000-1,000,000	.72	.58	.67
1930	1,000,000	.73	.61	.69

BIBLIOGRAPHY

PRIMARY SOURCES

Archival Sources: General

Fremont Ackerman Papers, Special Collections Division, University Library, University of California, Los Angeles.

Archives of Occidental College, Los Angeles.

Archives of the University of Southern California, Los Angeles, California.

Brier, James W.; Dairy.   Henry E. Huntington Library, San Marino, California.

California Club Papers, Special Collections Division, University Research Library, University of California, Los Angeles.

California Genealogical Society Library, San Francisco, California.

Cole Family Papers, Special Collections Division, University Library, University of California, Los Angeles.

Collection of the Security Trust Company, Los Angeles.

Robert E. Cowan Collection, Special Collections, University of California Library, Los Angeles.

"Declaration of a Convention to Divide the State of California, Los Angeles, November 10, 1851," Henry E. Huntington Library, San Marino, California.

Edward A. Dickson Papers, Special Collections Division, University Research Library, University of California, Los Angeles.

Early Los Angeles History Collection, Special Collections Division, University Library, University of California, Los Angeles.

Files of the Friday Morning Club, Special Collections Division, University Research Library, University of California, Los Angeles.

Files of the Armenian Patriotic League, Los Angeles, California.

Files of the Civic Association of Los Angeles, Special Collections Division, University Research Library, University of California, Los Angeles.

Theodore Percival Gerson Papers, Special Collections Division, University Research Library, University of California, Los Angeles.

Haynes Foundation, Los Angeles.

John Randolph Haynes Papers, Special Collections Division, University Research Library, University of California, Los Angeles.

Franklin Hichborn Papers, Special Collections Division, University Research Library, University of California, Los Angeles.

Hunt, Timothy Dwight. "Diary," Library of San Francisco Theological Seminary, San Anselmo, California

Indiana Colony Papers (Pasadena), Henry E. Huntington Library and Art Gallery, San Marino, California

Leo B. Lesperance Papers, Special Collections Division, University Research Library, University of California, Los Angeles.

Los Angeles Chamber of Commerce Minutes, Los Angeles Chamber of Commerce.

Los Angeles Chamber of Commerce, Miscellaneous Materials, Special Collections Division, University Research Library, University of California, Los Angeles.

Los Angeles Churches Collection, Special Collections Division, University Research Library, University of California, Los Angeles.

Los Angeles—Miscellaneous Collection, Special Collections Division, University Research Library, University of California, Los Angeles.

"Los Angeles Religion" Files, Special Collections Division, University Research Library, University of California, Los Angeles.

"Miscellaneous Records: Los Angeles County Almshouse," Special Collections, University of California, Los Angeles.

Papers of the Historical Society of Southern California, Los Angeles County Museum Library.

Records of the California Women's Christian Temperance Union, Bancroft Library, University of California, Berkeley.

William Andrew, Spalding Papers, Henry E. Huntington Library and Art Gallery, San Marino, California.

Shuler: Sermons and Broadcasts, Doheney Library, University of Southern California, Los Angeles, California.

Stearns Manuscripts.   Henry E. Huntington Library, San Marino, California.

Lyman Stewart Papers, Bible Institute of Los Angeles.

Charles Dwight Willard Papers, Bancroft Library, University of California, Berkeley.

Woods, James. Dairy.   Henry E. Huntington Library, San Marino, California.

William Stewart Young Papers, San Francisco Theological Seminary, San Anselmo, California.

Archival Sources: Religious Institutions

Archives of the Bible Institute of Los Angeles.

Archives of the Los Angeles Baptist Conference, Los Angeles.

Archives of the Methodist Church, Historical Society of the California-Nevada Annual Conference of the Methodist Church, Berkeley, California.

Archives of the Presbytery of Los Angeles.

Archives of the Protestant Episcopal Diocese of California, San Francisco.

Archives of the Protestant Episcopal Diocese of Los Angeles.

Archives of the San Francisco Theological Seminary, San Anselmo, California.

Archives of the United Presbyterian Church, U.S.A., San Francisco Theological Seminary Library, San Anselmo, California.

Congregational and Methodist Collections, Pacific School of Religion Library, Berkeley, California.

Files of the Union Rescue Mission, Los Angeles.

First Congregational Church Collection, Special Collections Division, University Research Library, University of California, Los Angeles.

First Methodist Church Collection, Special Collections Division, University Research Library, University of California, Los Angeles.

First Protestant Society of Los Angeles Papers, Henry E. Huntington Library and Art Gallery, San Marino, California.

First Unitarian Church, Files, Special Collections Division, University Research Library, University of California, Los Angeles.

Files of the United Church of Christ, Los Angeles District.

Manuscript Reports of the Los Angeles YMCA, 1882-1900, Los Angeles Young Men's Christian Association.

Records of the First Congregational Church of Los Angeles, to 1900, Henry E. Huntington Library, San Marino, California.

Records of the First Methodist Church of Los Angeles, Special Collections Division, University Research Library, University of California, Los Angeles.

Records of the Immanuel Presbyterian Church, Special Collections Division, University Research Library, University of California, Los Angeles.

Records of St. Athanasius Protestant Episcopal Church of Los Angeles, to 1900, Henry E. Huntington Library, San Marino, California.

Sermon Collection, Southern California School of Theology, Claremont Graduate School and University Center, Claremont, California.

Westminster Church Papers, 1871-1890, Library, San Francisco Theological Seminary, San Anselmo, California.

Interviews

Interview with Diantha Harper, United Christian Home, Los Angeles, California, January 17, 1970.

Interview with Ralph G. Harrison, Hollywood Chamber of Commerce, Los Angeles, California, January 16, 1970.

Interview with Jack Kincaid, United Christian Home, Los Angeles, January 17, 1970.

Interview with J. Stull Pearson, Glendale Presbyterian Home, Glendale, California, February 9, 1970.

Interview with George Postam, Presbyterian Home, Los Angeles, February 23, 1970.

Interview with Eugene Simpkins, Glendale Presbyterian Retirement Home, Glendale, California, February 6, 1970.

Printed Reports: Religious Institutions

American Home Missionary Society Report.

Annual of the Southern California Baptist Convention. Los Angeles: 1924.

Annual Report of the American Board of Commissioners for Foreign Missions.

Annual Report of the Women's Christian Temperance Union of California. San Francisco: 1882.

Associated Baptist Missions Boards: *Report.* New York: 1853.

Christian Ministers' Association. *Bulletin.* March 11, 1921.

Congregational Church, *Minutes of the Association of Southern California.* Los Angeles.

Diocese of California, *Diocesan Report on Charitable Works.* San Francisco; 1885.

Diocese of Los Angeles. *Annual Report.* Los Angeles: 1924.

Institutional Church League. *Annual Report.* Detroit: 1926.

Journal of the General Convention. New York: 1900-1930.

Journal of the General Convention of the Protestant Episcopal Church. New York.

Journal of the Protestant Episcopal Diocese of California. San Francisco.

Los Angeles Baptist Association, *Report.* 1906.

Methodist Episcopal Church, North, Southern California Conference *Report.*

Minutes of the General Assembly of the Presbyterian Church in the U.S.A. Philadelphia.

Minutes of the Los Angeles Baptist Association, 1869-1880.

Minutes of the Los Angeles Conference of the Methodist Episcopal Church, South, 1917. Los Angeles: 1917.

Minutes of the Los Angeles Conference of the Methodist Episcopal Church, South, 1922. Los Angeles: 1922.

Minutes of the Synod of the Pacific of the Presbyterian Church in the United States of America. San Francisco.

National Council of the Congregational Churches. *Proceedings: Memorials and Petitions.* New York: 1924.

The Northern Baptist Association, *Report of the General Association, 1891.*

Northern Baptist Convention, *Annual Report.* New York: 1916.

Baptist Church, Northern Conference, *Journal of the General Conference* (New York, 1922), IV, pp. 386-388.

Presbyterian Board of Home Missions. *Report.* Philadelphia: 1851.

Protestant Episcopal Convention, Diocese of California, *Proceedings.* 1870.

Report of the American Tract Society. 1850-1870.

Report of the Diocese of New York. New York: 1852.

Report of the Los Angeles Baptist Association.

Report of the Los Angeles Council of Congregational Churches. Los Angeles: 1914,1926.

Report of the Presbytery of Los Angeles. Los Angeles: 1920-1930.

Southern California Conference Minutes. Los Angeles: 1909.

Thirty-Seventh Annual Report of the Missionary Society of the Methodist Episcopal Church. New York: 1866.

Twenty-First Annual Report of the Missionary Society of the Methodist Episcopal Church. New York: 1850.

Twenty-Fourth Annual Report of the Missionary Society of the Methodist Episcopal Church. New York: 1853.

Twenty-Third Annual Report of the Missionary Society of the Methodist Episcopal Church. New York: 1852.

Union Rescue Mission. *Report.* 1906.

Printed Reports: General

Abstract of Divorce Actions. Hall of Records, County of Los Angeles.

California Department of Social Welfare. *Report.* Sacramento: 1922.

"Farm and Orchard Lands, 1850," Archives of the Common Council, City of Los Angeles, Office of the City Clerk, City Hall, Los Angeles, California.

The Los Angeles City School Board. *Report.*

Los Angeles Common Council Files, City Hall, Los Angeles.

Manufacturing Tax Records, Office of the County Assessor, Hall of Records, County of Los Angeles.

Municipal Reference Department. *A Chronological Record of Los Angeles City Officials, 1850-1938.* Los Angeles: 1938.

Office of the Tax Assessor, Hall of Records, County of Los Angeles.

"Transcripts of Divorce Actions," Hall of Records, County of Los Angeles.

U.S. Bureau of the Census. *Fifteenth Census of the United States: Manufacturers, 1929.* Washington: 1933.

U.S. Bureau of the Census. *Fifteenth Census of the United States: 1930; Metropolitan Districts.* Washington: 1932.

U.S. Bureau of the Census. *Fifteenth Census of the United States: 1930; Metropolitan Districts Population and Area.* Washington: 1932.

U.S. Bureau of the Census: *Seventh* [through] *Fifteenth Census of the United States: Population.* Washington: 1853-1933.

U.S. Bureau of the Census. *State Compendium, 1920: California.* Washington: 1922.

Newspapers

California   Eagle.

California   Independent.

California   Star.

Daily   Alta   California.

Los   Angeles   *Daily   Herald.*

Los   Angeles   *Daily   News.*

Los   Angeles   *Examiner.*

Los   Angeles   *Express.*

Los   Angeles   *Semi-Weekly   News.*

Los   Angeles   *Socialist.*

Los   Angeles   *Star.*

Sacramento   *Union.*

San   Francisco   *Chronicle.*

Periodicals

Bob   Schuler's   Magazine.

California   Christian   Advocate.

Catholic   World.

Century.

The   Dawn.

Home   Missionary.

Missionary   Herald.

Municipal   Conference   of   Los   Angeles.   *Bulletin.*

North   American   Review.

The   Occident.

Overland Monthly.

The Pacific.

Pacific Banner.

The Word is Calling.

Books

Adamic, Louis. *Dynamite.* New York: 1931.

Adamic, Louis. *Laughing in the Jungle: The Autobiography of an Immigrant in America.* New York: 1932.

Adams, Emma H. *To and Fro in Southern California.* Cincinnati: 1887.

An Historical Sketch of Los Angeles County, California. Los Angeles: 1876.

Autobiography, Correspondence, etc., of Lyman Beecher, C.D. Ed. Charles Beecher. New York: 1871.

Bartlett, Dana W. *The Better City.* Los Angeles: 1907.

Bartlett, Dana W. *The Christian City.* Los Angeles: 1923.

Beecher, Lyman. *A Plea for the West.* New York: 1835.

Bell, Horace. *On the Old West Coast: Being Further Reminiscences of a Ranger.* New York: 1930.

Bell, Horace. *Reminiscences of a Ranger, or, Early Times in Southern California.* Santa Barbara, California: 1881.

Blackstone, William E. *Jesus is Coming.* New York: 1903.

Brace, Charles L. *The Dangerous Classes of New York.* New York: 1872.

Briggs, Charles Augustus. *American Presbyterianism: Its Origin and Early History, Together with an Appendix of Letters and Documents, Many of Which have Recently been Discovered.* New York: 1885.

Brook, Harry Ellington. *The Land of Sunshine: Southern California, an Authentic Description of its Natural Features, Resources, and Prospects. Containing Reliable Information for the Homeseeker, Tourist, and Invalid: Compiled for the Southern California World's Fair Association and Southern California Bureau of Information.* Los Angeles: 1893.

Brown, John H. *Reminiscences and Incidents of the Early Days in San Francisco.* San Francisco: 1886.

Cipriani, Count Leonetto. *California and Overland Diaries, 1853-171.* Trans. and ed. Ernest Falbo, San Francisco: 1962.

Census of the City and County of Los Angeles, California, for the Year 1850. Los Angeles: 1929.

Colton, Walter. *Three Years in California.* New York: 1850.

Edwards, William A., and Beatrice Harraden. *Two Health Seekers in Southern California.* Philadelphia: 1896.

Graves, Jackson A. *My Seventy Years in California, 1857-1927.* Los Angeles: 1927.

Hallenbeck, Wilbur C. *Minneapolis Churches and their Comity Problems.* New York: 1929.

History of Los Angeles County, California. Oakland, 1880.

Kip, William Ingraham. *The Early Days of My Episcopate.* New York: 1892.

Langley, Harold J. *Our Candidate, Fighting Bob.* Los Angeles: 1932.

Leadbeater, Charles W. *The Science of the Sacraments.* Los Angeles: 1920.

Loomis, Samuel Lande. *Modern Cities and Their Religious Problems.* New York: 1887.

Los Angeles Chamber of Commerce. *California Citrus: A Real Opportunity.*

Los Angeles Chamber of Commerce. *General Commercial Report of Los Angeles County.* Los Angeles: 1910.

Los Angeles Chamber of Commerce Industrial Department. *General Industrial Report of Los Angeles County.* Los Angeles: 1929.

Los Angeles Chamber of Commerce. *Members Annual.*

Los Angeles City Directory.

Los Angeles Stock Exchange. *1917 Report.* Los Angeles: 1917.

Los Angeles *Times. The Forty Year War for a Free City: A History of the Open Shop in Los Angeles.* New York: 1929.

Mead, George Herbert. *Modern Methods of Church Work.* New York: 1897.

Men of California: Western Personalities and their Affiliations. San Francisco and Los Angeles: 1924-1930.

Myers, John W., and Edwin E. Sundt. *The Country Church as It Is: A Case Study of Rural Churches and Leaders.* New York: 1930.

Money, William. *Reform of the New Testament Church.* Los Angeles: 1854.

Newmark, Harris. *Sixty Years in Southern California.* New York: 1916.

Niebuhr, Reinhold. *Leaves from the Notebook of a Tamed Cynic.* New York: 1929.

Rauschenbusch, Walter. *Christianity and the Social Crisis.* New York: 1907.

Sheehan, Edmund. *Teaching and Worship of the Liberal Catholic Church.* Los Angeles: 1925.

Stead, William T. *If Christ Came to Chicago!* Chicago: 1894.

Strong, Josiah. *The Challenge of the City.* New York: 1907.

Van Dyke, Theodore S. *Millionaires of a Day: An Inside History of the Great Southern California "Boom." New York: 1890.*

Walker, Williston. *A History of the Congregational Churches in the United States.* New York: 1894.

Widney, R. N. *Los Angeles County Subsidy, Which Subsidy Shall I Vote for—or—Shall I Vote Against Both? Discussed From a Business Standpoint for the Business Community.* Los Angeles: 1872.

Articles and Pamphlets

Adams, O. F., "Aristocratic Drift of American Protestantism," *North American Review* (1886), 194-199.

Anderson, Arnold T., "The Motion Picture Industry," in Department of Research Service, Security Trust and Savings Bank, *Industrial Summary of Los Angeles for Year 1927.* Los Angeles: 1928.

Berneman, M. I., "A Study of the Social Program and the Social Welfare Service of the First Methodist Episcopal Church of Los Angeles," (Unpublished Doctoral Dissertation, University of Southern California, 1939).

Briggs, C. A., "The Alienation of Church and People," *Forum,* (1893-1894), 375-377.

Katzen, Stanley, "A Report on the Boyle Heights Community," typescript, Los Angeles Jewish Community Council, 1927.

Los Angeles Chamber of Commerce, "A Greater City," (Pamphlet, 1906).

McQuaid, B. J. "The Decay of Protestantism," *North American Review,* CXXXVI (1883), 135-152.

Perry, H. F., "The Workingman's Alienation from the Church," *American Journal of Sociology,* (1898-1899), 622.

"Report on Religious Membership in Los Angeles," typescript, University of Southern California, Religious Studies Department, 1915.

"Trends in Beliefs and Concerns," mimeograph report of the United Campus Ministry, October 13, 1957.

Wakeman, T.B., "Our Unchurched Millions," *Arena* (1890), 604-613.

Wright, Willard Hunt, "Los Angeles—The Chemically Pure," *The Smart Set Anthology,* eds. Burton Rasoe and Graff Conkin (New York, 1934), p. 91.

Printed Source Collections

Cross, Robert D. (ed.). *The Church and the City: 1865-1910.* Indianapolis: 1967.

Sweet, William Warren. *Religion on the American Frontier: A Collection of Source Materials: The Baptists, 1793-1830.* New York: 1931.

Sweet, William Warren. *Religion on the American Frontier: A Collection of Source Material: The Congregationalists, 1783-1850.* Chicago: 1939.

Sweet, William Warren. *Religion on the American Frontier: A Collection of Source Material: The Methodists, 1783-1840.* Chicago: 1946.

Sweet, William Warren. *Religion on the American Frontier: A Collection of Source Material: The Presbyterians, 1783-1840.* Chicago: 1936.

SECONDARY WORKS

Books

Abell, Aaron Ignatius. *The Urban Impact on American Protestantism, 1865-1900.* Cambridge: 1943.

Abrecht, Rudy. *The YMCA on the Western Frontier: A Brief History of the California State Young Men's Christian Association.* Los Angeles: 1964.

Anderson, Charles H. *White Protestant Americans: From National Origins to Religious Group.* Englewood Cliffs, New Jersey: 1970.

Atkins, Gaius Glenn. *Modern Religious Cults and Movements.* New York: 1923.

Baltzell, E. Digby. *Philadelphia Gentlemen: The Making of a National Upper Class.* New York: 1958.

Baltzell, E. Digby. *The Protestant Establishment: Aristocracy and Caste in America.* New York: 1964.

Bancroft, Hubert Howe. *California Pastoral, 1769-1848.* San Francisco: 1868.

Bancroft, Hubert Howe. *History of California.* San Francisco: 1884-1890.

Banham, Reyner. *Los Angeles.* New York: 1971.

Barclay, Wade Crawford. *History of Methodist Missions.* 3 vols. New York: 1949-1957.

Battis, Emery. *Saints and Sectaries: Anne Hutchinson and the Antinomian Controversy in Massachusetts Bay Colony.* Chapel Hill: 1962.

Baur, John E. *The Health Seekers of Southern California.* San Marino, California: 1959.

Beasley, Norman. *The Cross and the Crown: The History of Christian Science:* New York: 1952.

Bell, George Kennedy Allen. *The Kingship of Christ: The Story of the World Council of Churches.* Baltimore: 1954.

Berger, Peter. *The Noise of Solemn Assemblies.* Garden City, New York: 1961.

Berthoff, Rowland. *An Unsettled People: Social Order and Disorder in American History.* New York: 1971.

Bestor, Arthur Eugene. *The Sectarian and Owenite Phases of Communitarian Socialism in American, 1663-1829.* Philadelphia, 1950.

Billington, Ray Allen. *The Protestant Crusade, 1800-1860.* New York: 1938.

Binder, Louis Richard. *Modern Religious Cults and Society: A Sociological Interpretation of Modern Religious Phenomenon.* Boston: 1933.

Bogue, Allen G. *From Prairie to Corn Belt.* Chicago: 1963.

Boulard, F. *An Introduction to Religious Sociology.* London: 1960.

Braden, Charles S. *Christian Science Today: Power, Policy, Practice.* Dallas: 1958.

Braden, Charles S. *These Also Believe: A Study of Modern American Cults and Minority Religious Movements.* New York: 1949.

Bremner, Robert H. *American Philanthropy.* Chicago: 1960.

Bruner, Edmund deSantis. *Churches of Distinction in Town and Country.* New York: 1923.

Bruner, Edward deSantis. *Tested Methods in Town and Country Churches.* New York: 1930.

Buder, Stanley. *Pullman: An Experiment in Industrial Order and Community Planning, 1880-1930.* New York: 1967.

Buley, Roscoe Carlyle. *The Old Northwest: Pioneer Period, 1815-1840.* 2 vols. Indianapolis: 1950.

Burr, Nelson R. *A Critical Bibliography of Religion in America.* ("Religion in American Life") Princeton, New Jersey: 1961.

Cahn, Frances, and Valeska Bary. *Welfare Activities of Federal, State, and Local Governments in California, 1850-1934.* Berkeley: 1936.

Carter, Paul A. *The Decline and Revival of the Social Gospel.* Ithaca, New York: 1956.

Clark, Elmer T. *The Small Sects in America.* Rev. ed. New York: 1949.

Clark, Stephen C. *The Diocese of Los Angeles: A Brief History.* Los Angeles: 1945.

Clebsch, William A. *From Sacred to Profane America: The Role of Religion in American History.* New York: 1968.

Cleland, Robert Glass. *California in Our Time, 1900-1940.* New York: 1947.

Cleland, Robert Glass. *The Cattle on a Thousand Hills: Southern California, 1850-1880.* San Marino, California, 1941.

Cochran, Thomas C., and William Miller. *The Age of Enterprise: A Social History of Industrial American.* 2nd ed. revised. New York: 1961.

Cole, Stewart G. *The History of Fundamentalism.* New York: 1931.

Cram, Ralph Adams. *The Gothic Quest.* New York: 1907.

Cram, Ralph Adams. *My Life in Architecture.* Boston: 1936.

Cross, Ira B. *A History of the Labor Movement in California.* Berkeley: 1935.

Cross, Whitney R. *The Burned-Over District: the Social and Intellectual History of Enthusiastic Religion in Western New York, 1800-1850.* Ithaca, New York: 1950.

Crouch, Winston W., and Beatrice Dinerman. *Southern California Metropolis: A Study in Development of Government for a Metropolitan Area.* Berkeley and Los Angeles: 1963.

Curti, Merle. *The Making of an American Community.* Stanford: 1959.

Daniels, Roger. The Politics of Prejudice: The Anti-Japanese Movement in California and the Struggle for Japanese Exclusion. *Berkeley and Los Angeles: 1962.*

Davies, Horton. *Christian Worship, Its Making and Meaning.* New York: 1957.

Demerath, N.J., III. *Social Class in American Protestantism.* Chicago: 1965.

Desmond, Humphrey Joseph. *The A.P.A. Movement, A Sketch.* Washington, D.C.: 1912.

Doherty, Robert W. *The Hicksite Separation: A Sociological Analysis of Religious Schism in Early Nineteenth-Century America.* New Brunswick, New Jersey: 1967.

Dondore, Dorothy Anne. *The Prairie and the Making of Middle America: Four Centuries of Description.* Cedar Rapids, Michigan: 1926.

Douglass, Harlan Paul. *Church Comity: A Study of Cooperation Church Extension in American Cities.* Garden City, New York: 1929.

Douglass, Harlan Paul. *The Church in the Changing City, Case Studies Illustrating Adaptation.* New York: 1927.

Douglass, Harlan Paul. *1000 City Churches: Phrases of Adaptation to Urban Environment.* New York: 1926.

Douglass, Harlan Paul. *Protestant Cooperation in American Cities.* New York: 1930.

Douglass, Harlan Paul. *The St. Louis Church Survey, A Religious Investigation with a Social Background.* New York: 1926.

Drummond, A. L. *Church Architecture of Protestantism.* Edinburgh: 1934.

Duclos, R.P. *Histoire de Protestantism Francais au Canada et aux Etats-Unis.* Lausanne: 1913.

Dumke, Glenn S. *The Boom of the Eighties in Southern California.* San Marino, California: 1944.

Durkheim, Emile. *The Elementary Forms of the Religious Life.* Trans. by Joseph W. Swain. Glencoe: 1947.

Dykstra, Robert. *The Cattle Towns.* New York: 1967.

Ellis, George. *Half-Century of the Unitarian Controversy.* Boston: 1857.

Elsbree, Oliver Wendell. *The Rise of the Missionary Spirit in America, 1790-1815.* Williamsport, Pa.: 1928.

Emery, Julia C. *A Century of Endeavor, 1821-1921, A Record of the Domestic and Foreign Missionary Society of the Protestant Episcopal Church in the United States of America.* New York: 1921.

Ferguson, Charles W. *The Confusion of Tongues: A Review of Modern Isms.* Grand Rapids, Michigan: 1936.

Frisch, Michael H. *Town into City: Springfield, Massachusetts, 1840-1880.* Cambridge, Mass.: 1973.

Fogelson, Robert M. *The Fragmented Metropolis: Los Angeles, 1850-1930.* Cambridge: 1967.

Foster, Charles I. *An Errand of Mercy: The Evangelical United Front.* Chapel Hill: 1954.

Frothingham, Octavious Brooks. *Boston Unitarianism, 1820-1850: A Study of the LIfe and Work of Nathaniel Langdon Frothingham.* New York: 1890.

Furniss, Norman F. *The Fundamentalist Controversy, 1918-1931.* New Haven: 1954.

Garrison, Winfred Ernest. *Religion Follows the Frontier: A History of the Disciples of Christ.* New York: 1931.

Garrison, Winfred Ernest, and Thomas DeGroot. *The Disciples of Christ, A History.* St. Louis: 1948.

Ghent, W. J. *The Early Far West.* New York: 1931.

Gilbert, Richard. *City of the Angeles.* London: 1964.

Glaab, Charles N. *Kansas City and the Railroads: Community Policy in the Growth of a Regional Metropolis.* Madison: 1962.

Glock, Charles Y., and Rodney Stark. *Religion and Society in Transition.* Chicago: 1965.

Goodykoontz, Colin Brummitt. *Home Missions on the American Frontier.* Caldwell, Idaho: 1939.

Gottman, Jean. *Megalopolis: The Urbanized Northeastern Seaboard of the United States.* Cambridge, Massachusetts: 1961.

Hadden, Jeffrey K. *The Gathering Storm in the Churches.* Garden City, New York: 1969.

Hart, Hornell N. *Selective Migration.* Iowa City: 1921.

Hawley, Amos. *The Changing Shape of Metropolitan America: Deconcentration Since 1920.* Glencoe, Illinois: 1956.

Hays, Samuel. *The Response to Industrialism, 1885-1914.* Chicago: 1957.

Henry, Helga Bender. *Mission on Main Street.* Boston: 1955.

Herberg, Will. *Protestant—Catholic—Jew.* Garden City, New York: 1955.

Higham, John. *Strangers in the Land: Patterns of American Nativism, 1865-1925.* New Brunswick, New Jersey: 1955.

Hind, Leland D. *Baptists in Southern California.* Valley Forge, Pennsylvania: 1966.

Hine, Robert V. *California's Utopian Colonies.* New Haven: 1953.

Hofstadter, Richard. *The Age of Reform: From Bryan to F.D.R.* New York: 1955.

Hooker, Elizabeth R. *Hinterlands of the Church.* New York: 1931.

Hopkins, Charles Howard, *History of the Y.M.C.A. in North America.* New York: 1936.

Hopkins, Charles Howard. *The Rise of the Social Gospel in American Protestantism, 1865-1915.* New Haven: 1940.

Howlett, Duncan. *The Fourth American Faith.* New York: 1954.

Hudson, Winthrop. *The Great Tradition of the American Churches.* New York: 1953.

Huggins, Nathan I. *Protestants Against Poverty: Boston's Charities, 1870-1900.* Westport, Connecticut: 1971.

Isambert, F. A. *Christianisme et classe ouviere.* Tournai: 1961.

Jent, John William. *Rural Church Problems.* Shawnee, Oklahoma: 1935.

Jervey, Edward Drewry. *The History of Methodism in Southern California and Arizona.* Nashville: 1960.

Jervey, Edward Drewry. "The Methodist Church and the University of Southern California," HSSCQ, XL (March, 1958).

Kasun, Jacqueline Rorabeck. *Some Social Aspects of Business Cycles in the Los Angeles Area, 1920-1950.* Los Angeles: 1954.

Kincheloe, Samuel C. *Religion in the Depression.* ("SSRC Bulletin") New York: 1937.

Kolko, Gabriel. *The Triumph of Conservatism: A Re-Interpretation of American History, 1900-1916.* New York: 1967.

Kuznets, Simon, and Dorothy Swaine Thomas. *Population Redistribution and Economic Growth: United States, 1870-1950.* 3 vols. Philadelphia: 1957.

LeBras, Gabriel. *Etudes de sociologie religieuse.* Paris: 1955.

Leiffer, Murray H. *City and Church in Transition: A Study of the Medium-Sized City and Its Organized Religious LIfe.* Chicago: 1938.

Lenski, Gerhard. *The Religious Factor.* Garden City, New York: 1961.

Lerner, Daniel. *The Passing of Traditional Society.* New York: 1958.

Littell, Franklin Hamlin. *From State Church to Pluralism: A Protestant Interpretation of Religion in American History.* Chicago: 1962.

Lubove, Roy. *The Progressives and the Slums: Tenement House Reform in New York City, 1890-1917.* Pittsburgh: 1962.

Lynd, Robert S., and Helen Merrill Lynd. *Middletown: A Study in Contemporary American Culture.* New York: 1930.

Malin, James C. *The Grassland of North America.* Lawrence: 1950.

Mann, Arthur. *Yankee Reformers in the Urban Age.* Cambridge: 1954.

Martindale, Don, and R. Galen Hanson. *Small Town and the Nation: The Conflict of Local and Translocal Forces.* Westport, Connecticut: 1969.

Marty, Martin E. *Righteous Empire: The Protestant Experience in America.* New York: 1970.

Marty, Martin, Stuart E. Rosenberg and Andrew M. Greeley. *What Do We Believe?* New York: 1968.

Mascall, E. L. *The Secularization of Christianity.* London: 1965.

Matthews, Lois Kimball. *The Expansion of New England: The Spread of New England Settlement and Institutions to the Mississippi River, 1620-1865.* Boston: 1909.

May, Henry F. *Protestant Churches and Industrial America.* 2nd ed. revised. New York: 1967.

McClenaham, Bessie Averne. *The Changing Urban Neighborhood: From Neighbor to Nigh Dweller.* Los Angeles: 1929.

McEntire, Davis. *The Labor Force in California: A Study of Characteristics and Trends in Labor Force, Employment and Occupations in California, 1900-1950.* Berkeley and Los Angeles: 1952.

McKelvey, Blake. *The Emergence of Metropolitan America, 1915-1966.* New Brunswick: 1968.

McLaughlin, William G. *Modern Revivalism: Charles Grandison Finney to Billy Graham.* New York: 1959.

McLoughlin, William G. *New England Dissent, 1630-1833: The Baptists and the Separation of Church and State.* Cambridge, Massachusetts: 1971. 2 vols.

McQuarie, John (ed.) *Twentieth-Century Religious Thought: The Frontiers of Philosophy and Theology, 1900-1960.* New York: 1963.

McWilliams, Carey. *North From Mexico: The Spanish-Speaking People of the United States.* Philadelphia: 1949.

McWilliams, Carey. *Southern California Country: An Island on the Land.* New York: 1946.

Mead, Sydney. *The Lively Experiment.* New York: 1963.

Meier, Richard L. *A Communications Theory of Urban Growth.* Cambridge, Massachusetts: 1962.

Meland, Bernard E. *The Secularization of Modern Cultures.* New York: 1966.

Meyer, Donald B. *The Positive Thinkers: The American Quest for Health, Wealth and Personal Power From Mary Baker Eddy to Norman Vincent Peale.* Garden City, New York: 1965.

Meyer, Donald B. *The Protestant Search for Political Realism: 1919-1941.* Berkeley: 1960.

Miller, Kenneth Dexter. *Man and God in the City.* New York: 1954.

Miller, Robert Moats. *American Protestantism and Social Issues, 1919-1939.* Chapel Hill: 1958.

Miller, Zane L. *Boss Cox's Cincinnati: Urban Politics in the Progressive Era.* New York: 1968.

Miyakawa, T. Scott. *Protestants and Pioneers: Individualism and Conformity on the American Frontier.* Chicago: 1964.

Morgan, H. Wayne (ed.). *The Gilded Age.* Rev. ed. Syracuse, New York: 1970.

Morse, Hermann Nelson. *From Frontier to Frontier: an Interpretation of 150 Years of Presbyterian National Missions.* Philadelphia: 1952.

Mowry, George E. *The California Progressives.* Berkeley: 1951.

Nadeau, Remi A. *City Makers.* Garden City, New York: 1948.

Nadeau, Remi A. *Los Angeles: From Mission to Modern City.* New York: 1960.

Newcomb, Rexford. *Architecture of the Old Northwest Territory.* Chicago: 1950.

Newman, Henry: *A History of the Baptist Churches in the United States.* New York: 1915.

Neibuhr, H. Richard. *The Social Sources of Denominationalism.* New York: 1929.

Olin, Spencer C., Jr. *California's Prodigal Sons: Hiram Johnson and the Progressives, 1911-1917.* Berkeley and Los Angeles: 1968.

Ostrander, Gilman M. *The Prohibition Movement in California, 1848-1933.* ("University of California Publications in History.") Berkeley and Los Angeles: 1957.

Peel, Robert. *Christian Science: Its Encounter with American Culture.* New York: 1958.

Perry, Louis B. and Richard S. *A History of the Los Angeles Labor Movement, 1911-1941.* Berkeley and Los Angeles: 1963.

Peters, John Leland. *Christian Perfection and American Methodism.* New York: 1956.

Pin, Emile. *Pratique religieuse et classes sociales.* Paris: 1956.

Pitt, Leonard. *The Decline of the Californios: A Social History of the Spanish-Speaking Californians, 1846-1890.* Berkeley and Los Angeles: 1966.

Pope, Liston. *Millhands and Preachers: A Study of Gastonia.* New Haven: 1942.

Pratt, John Webb. *Religion, Politics, and Diversity: The Church-State Theme in New York History.* New York: 1963.

Pred, Alan R. *The Spatial Dynamics of U.S. Urban-Industrial Growth, 1800-1914: Interpretive and Theoretical Essays.* Cambridge, Massachusetts: 1966.

Quiett, Glen Chensey. *They Built the West: An Epic of Rails and Cities.* New York. 1934.

Rand, Christopher. *Los Angeles: The Ultimate City.* New York: 1967.

Rayback, Joseph G. *A History of American Labor.* Rev. ed. New York: 1966.

Redford, M.E. *The Rise of the Church of the Nazarene.* Kansas City: 1951.

Reinarch. S. *Cultes, Mythes, et Religions.* Paris: 1905.

Rice, William B. *The Los Angeles Star, 1851-1864: The Beginnings of Journalism in Southern California.* Ed. John Walton Caughey. New York: 1947.

Rice, William B. *William Money, a Southern California Savant.* Los Angeles: 1943.

Rogin, Michael P., and John R. Shover. *Political Change in California.* Westport, Connecticut: 1970.

Roy, Ralph Lord. *Apostles of Discord.* Boston: 1953.

Sandeen, Ernest R. *The Roots of Fundamentalism: British and American Millenarianism, 1800-1930.* Chicago: 1970.

Sanford, Louis C. *The Province of the Pacific.* Philadelphia: 1949.

Schlesinger, Arthur. *The American as Reformer.* Cambridge, Massachusetts: 1950.

Schlinger, Arthur M. *The Rise of the City.* ("A History of American Life.") New York: 1933.

Schroeder, W. Widick, and Victor Obenhaus. *Religion in American Culture: Unity and Diversity in a Midwestern County.* Glencoe, Illinois: 1964.

Servin, Manuel P., and Iris Higbe Wilson. *Southern California and Its University.* Los Angeles: 1969.

Shapley, Harlow (ed).   *Science Ponders Religion.* New York: 1960.

Shevky, Eshref, and Marilyn Williams. *The Social Areas of Los Angeles: Analysis and Typology.* Berkeley and Los Angeles: 1949.

Smith, Page. *As A City Upon a Hill.* New York: 1966.

Smith, Timothy L. *Called Unto Holiness: The Story of the Nazarenes: The Formative Years.* Kansas City: 1962.

Smith, Timothy L. *Revivalism and Social Reform.* New York: 1957.

Stanton, Phoebe B. *The Gothic Revival and American Church Architecture: An Episode in Taste, 1840-1956.* Baltimore: 1968.

Stark, Rodney, and Charles Y. Clock. *American Piety: The Nature of Religious Commitment.* Berkeley and Los Angeles: 1968.

Stein, Maurice R. *The Eclipse of Community: An Interpretation of American Studies.* Princeton: 1960.

Stimson, Grace Heilman. *Rise of the Labor Movement in Los Angeles.* Berkeley and Los Angeles: 1955.

Strong, William E. *The Story of the American Board.*   Boston: 1910.

Sweet, William Warren. *Methodism in American History.* New York: 1954.

Sweet, William Warren. *The Story of Religion in America.* 2nd ed. revised. New York: 1950.

Tewksbury, Donald G. *The Founding of American Colleges and Universities Before the Civil War.* New York: 1932.

Thernstrom, Stephan. *Proverty and Progress: Social Mobility in a Nineteenth-Century City.* Cambridge, Massachusetts: 1964.

Thompson, Warren S. *The Growth of Metropolitan Districts in the United States, 1900-1940.* Washington: 1947.

Tuveson, Ernest Lee. *Redeemer Nation: The Idea of America's Millennial Role.* Chicago: 1968.

Tyack, David B. *George Ticknor and the Boston Brahmins.* Cambridge, Massachusetts: 1967.

Tyler, Alice Felt. *Freedom's Ferment.*   Minneapolis: 1944.

Underhill, Evelyn. *Worship.* New York: 1957.

Vidich, Arthur J., and Joseph Bensman. *Small Town in Mass Society: Class, Power, and Religion in a Rural Community.* Princeton: 1958.

Vogt, Von Ogden. *Modern Worship.* New Haven: 1927.

Vorspan, Max, and Lloyd P. Gartner. *History of the Jews in Los Angeles.* San Marino, California: 1970.

Wade, Richard. *The Urban Frontier: Pioneer Life in Early Pittsburgh, Cincinnati, Lexington, Louisville, and St. Louis.* Cambridge, Massachusetts: 1959.

Wallace, Anthony F. C. *Religion: An Anthropoligical View.* New York: 1966.

Warner, Sam Bass, Jr. *The Private City: Philadelphia in Three Periods of its Growth.* Philadelphia: 1968.

Weber, Max. *The Sociology of Religion.* Trans, by Ephraim Fischoff. Boston: 1963.

Weinstein, James. *The Corporate Ideal in the Liberal State: 1900-1918.* Boston: 1968.

Weisberger, Bernard. *They Gathered at the River.* Boston: 1958.

White, Charles L. *A Century of Faith: Centenary Volume Published for the American Baptist Home Mission Society.* Philadelphia: 1932.

Wickman, E. R. *Church and People in an Industrial City.* London: 1957.

Wiebe, Robert H. *The Search for Order, 1877-1920.* New York: 1967.

Wicher, Edward Arthur. *The Presbyterian Church in California, 1849-1927.* New York: 1927.

Wilson, Bryan R. *Religion in Secular Society: A Sociological Comment.* London: 1966.

Wilson, Bryan R. *Sects and Society.* Berkeley and Los Angeles: 1961.

Wilson, R. Jackson. *In Quest of Community: Social Philosophy in the United States, 1860-1920.* New York: 1968.

Wilson, William H. *The City Beautiful Movement in Kansas City.* Columbia: 1964.

Winter, Gibson, *The Suburban Captivity of the Churches: An Analysis of Protestant Responsibility in the Expanding Metropolis.* Garden City, New York: 1961.

Wright, Louis B. *Culture on the Moving Frontier.* Bloomington: 1955.

Yinger, J. Milton *Religion, Society and the Individual* New York: 1957.

Young, Nellic May. *William Stewart Young, 1859-1937: Builder of California Institutions.* Glendale, California: 1967.

Articles and Pamphlets

Barrows, H. D., "Early Clericals of Los Angeles," HSSCQ, V (1901), 133.

Begue de Packman, Anna "A Brief Society History," HSSCQ XL (September, 1958), 223.

Berger, Peter, "A Sociological View of the Secularization of Theology," *Journal for the Scientific Study of Religion, VI (Spring, 1967), 3-16.*

Berghorn, Forrest J., and Geoffrey H. Stuse, "Are American Values Changing? The Problem of Inner-or-other Direction," *American Quarterly,* XVIII (Spring, 1966), 52-62.

Billington, Ray Allen, "Anti-Catholic Propaganda and the Home Missionary Movement, 1800-1860," *Mississippi Valley Historical Review,* XXII (December, 1935), 361-384.

Bohome, Frederick G., "Episcopal Beginnings in Southern California: The Centennial of Los Angeles' First Parish," HSSCQ, XLVII (June, 1965), 171-190.

Bowers, William L. "Crawford Township, 1850-1870," *Iowa Journal of History,* LVIII (1960), 1-30.

Breen, Timothy H., "Who Governs: The Town Franchise in Seventeenth-Century Massachusetts," *William and Mary Quarterly, XXVII (July, 1970), 460-474.*

Cherry, Conrad, "Two American Sacred Ceremonies: Their Implications for the Study of Religion in America," *American Quarterly, XXI (Winter, 1969), 739-754.*

Clark, Clifford E., Jr., "The Changing Nature of Protestantism in Mid-Nineteenth Century America: Henry Ward Beecher's *Seven Lectures to Young Men," The Journal of American History,* LVII (March, 1971), 832-846.

Coben, Stanley, "A Study in Nativisim: The American Red Scare of 1919-1920, " *Political Science Quarterly, LXXIX (March, 1964), 52-75.*

Cooley, Laura C., "The Los Angeles Public Library," HSSCQ, XXIII (March, 1941), 5-23.

Cox, Harvey, *The Secular City: Secularization and Urbanization in Theological Perspective.* New York: 1965.

Cunningham, Raymond J., "The Impact of Christian Science on the American Churches, 1880-1910," *American Historical Review,* LXXII (April, 1967), 885-905.

Davis, James E., "A Study of the Official Attitudes of Local Denominational Affiliates," (mimeograph report of the Los Angeles Ministerial Association, 1967).

Davis, Rodney C. "Prairie Emporium: Clarence, Iowa, 1860-1880, A Study of Population Trends," *Mid-America: An Historical Review,* LVI (April, 1969), 130-139.

DeGraff, Lawrence B., "The City of Black Angels: Emergence of the Los Angeles Ghetto, 1890-1930," *Pacific Historical Review*, XXXIX (August, 1970), 323-352.

Dixon, Manes Main, "A Presbyterian Settlement in Southern California," HSSCQ, X (1915-1917).

Drury, Clifford M. "A Chronology of Protestant Beginnings in California," (Pamphlet published by the Centennial Committee of the Northern California—Western Nevada Council of Churches, no date).

Dumont, F., "An Investigation of Religious Practice in an Urban Milieu," *Recherches Sociographiques*, I (November, 1960), 500-520.

Fenn, Richard K., "The Secularization of Values: An Analytical Framework for the Study of Secularization," *Journal for the Scientific Study of Religion*, VIII (Spring, 1969), 112-124.

Friedman, John "Two Concepts of Urbanization: A Comment," *Urban Affairs Quarterly*, I (June, 1966), 78-84.

Gardner, D. Charles, "Service to the Social Order," in Pacific School of Religion (ed.), *Religious Progress on the Pacific Slope* (Boston, 1917), pp. 294-306.

Gay, Leslie F., Jr., "The Founding of the University of Southern California," HSSCQ, VIII (1909-1910), 37-50.

Glaab, Charles N., "Metropolis and Suburb: The Changing American City," in *Change and Continuity in Twentieth-Century America: The 1920's*, eds. John Braeman, Robert H. Bremner, and David Brody. Columbus, Ohio: 1968.

Goist, Park Dixon, "City and 'Community': the Urban Theory of Robert Park," *American Quarterly*. XXIII (Spring, 1971), 46-59.

Griffen, Clude, "The Progressive Ethos," in *The Development of an American Culture*, eds. Stanley Coben and Lorman Ratner. Englewood Cliffs, New Jersey: 1970.

Handy, Robert T., "The American Religious Depression, 1925-1935," *Church History*, XXIX (March, 1960), 3-16.

Handy, Robert T., "Fundamentalism and Modernism in Perspective," *Religion in Life*, XXIV (Summer, 1955), 381-394.

Hays, Samuel P., "The Politics of Reform in Municipal Government in the Progressive Era," *Pacific Northwest Quarterly*, LV (October, 1964), 157-169.

Herberg, Will, "There is a Religious Revival!" *Review of Religous Research*, I (Fall, 1959), 45-50.

Hill, Laurence L., "A Great City Celebrates Its One Hundred and Fiftieth Anniversary," HSSCQ, XV (1931), 7-55.

Hubbell, Thelma Lee, and Gloria R. Lothrop, "The Friday Morning Club: A Los Angeles Legacy," HSSCQ, L (March, 1968), 59-61.

Jamison, A. Leland, "Religions on the Christian Perimeter," in *The Shaping of American Religion*, eds. James Ward Smith and A. Leland Jamison ("Religion in American Life"; Princeton, New Jersey, 1961), 162-231.

Kaplan, Sidney, "Social Engineers as Saviors: Effects of World War I on Some American Liberals," *The Journal of the History of Ideas*, XVII (June, 1956), 341-359.

Kett, Joseph F., "Growing Up in Rural New England, 1800-1940," in *Anonymous Americans: Explorations in Nineteenth-Century Social History*, ed. Tamara K. Hareven (Englewood Cliffs, New Jersey: 1971).

Kincheloe, S. C., "The Sociological Study of Religion in the City," *Review of Religious Research*, VI (June, 1965), 63-76.

Landis, Benson Y., "A Guide to the Literature on Statistics of Religious Affiliation with References to Related Social Studies," *Journal of the American Statistical Association*, LIV (June, 1959), 335-357.

Layne, J. Gregg, "The Lincoln-Roosevelt League: Its Origin and Accomplishments," HSSCQ, XXV (September, 1943), 79-101.

Le Bras, Gabriel, "Dechristianisation: mot fallacieux," *Social Compass*, X (1963), 448-451.

Lipset, Seymour Martin, "Religion in America: What RelIgous Revival?" *Columbia University Forum*, (Winter, 1959).

Lockhard, E. Kidd, "The Influence of New England in Denominational Colleges in the Northwest, 1830-1960," *Ohio State Archaeological and Historical Quarterly*, LIII (1944), 1-13.

Lowman, Charles LeRoy, "The Orthopaedic Medical Center—A Los Angeles Achievement, 1903-1962," HSSCQ, (June, 1962), 133.

Mathews, Donald G., "The Second Great Awakening as an Organizing Process, 1780-1830: An Hypothesis," *American Quarterly*, XXI (Spring, 1969), 23-43.

May, Henry F., "The Recovery of American Religious History," *American Historical Review*, LXX (October, 1964), 79-92.

Nelson, Ronald R., "The Legal Relationship of Church and State in California, Part II," HSSCQ XLVI (June, 1964), 146-154.

Newmark, Marco R., "Calle de los Negros and the Chinese Massacre of 1871," HSSCQ, XXVI (June-September, 1944).

Newmark, Marco R., "*La Fiesta de Los Angeles* of 1894," HSSCQ, XXIX (June, 1947), 107.

Newmark, Marco R., "A Short History of the Los Angeles Chamber of Commerce," HSSCQ, XXVII (June, 1945).

Newmark, Marco R., "The Story of Religion in Los Angeles, 1781-1900," *Historical Society of Southern California Quarterly*, XXVIII (March, 1946), 38.

Nichols, J. H., "American Christianity," in *Religion*, ed. Paul Ramsey (Princeton, New Jersey, 1965), pp. 195-216.

Nichols, J. H., "Church History and Secular History," *Church History*, XIII (1944), 87-99.

Ogburn, William Fielding, and Ottis Dudley Duncan, "City Size as a Sociological Variable," in Ernest W. Burgess and Donald J. Bogue (eds.), *Contributions to Urban Sociology* (Chicago, 1964).

Parsons, Talcott, "Christianity and Modern Industrial Society," in *Sociological Theory, Values, and Sociological Change*, ed. Edward Tiryakian. Glencoe, Illinois: 1963.

Petersen, William, "Religious Statistics in the United States," *Journal for the Scientific Study of the Religion*, I (April, 1962), 165-173.

Pfautz, Harold W., "A Case Study of an Urban Religious Movement: Christian Science," in *Contributions to Urban Sociology*, eds. Ernest W. Burgess and David J. Bogue. Chicago: 1964.

Pohlman, John O., "Alphonzo E. Bell: A Biography," HSSCQ, XLVI (September, 1964), 197-222.

Popenoe, David,   "On the Meaning of 'Urban' in Urban Studies," *Urban Affairs Quarterly*, I (September, 1965), 17-33.

Schaffer, A.,   "The Rural Church in a Metropolitan Area," *Rural Sociology*, XXIV (1959), 236-245.

Schlesinger, Arthur M., "A Critical Period in American Religion, 1875-1900," Massachusetts Historical Society, *Proceedings*, LXIV (June, 1932), 523-547.

Schroeder, W. W., "Conceptualization of Urbanization," *Review of Religious Research*, V (September, 1964), 74-79.

Shiner, Larry, "The Concept of Secularization in Empirical Research," *Journal for the Scientific Study of Religion*, VI (Fall, 1967), 207-220.

Shochat, Fern Dawson, "The Voluntary Cooperation Association of Los Angeles, 1913-1922," HSSCQ, XLV (June, 1962), 169-180.

Smith, Huston, "Secularization and the Sacred: The Contemporary Scene," in *The Religious Situation—1968.*   Boston: 1968.

Splitter, Henry Winfred, "Music in Los Angeles," HSSCQ, XXXVIII (December, 1956), 307.

Smylie, John, "National Ethos and the Church," *Theology Today*, XIX (October, 1963), 313-318.

Thernstrom, Stephan, "The Growth of Los Angeles in Historical Perspective: Myth and Reality," (Mimeograph report: Institute of Government and Public Affairs, University of California, Los Angeles, 1970.

Thernstrom, Stephan, and Peter R. Knights, "Men in Motion: Some Data and Speculations on Urban Population Mobility in Nineteenth-Century America," *Journal of Interdisciplinary History*, I (Fall, 1970), 23-41.

Throne, Mildred, "A Population Study of an Iowa County in 1850," *Iowa Journal of History*, LVII (1959), 305-330.

"A Tribute to Joseph M. Irvine," *Southern California Presbyterian* (December, 1957), 348.

Vernon, Glen M., "Measuring Religion: Two Methods Compared," *Review of Religious Research*, III (Spring, 1962), 159-165.

"Violence Indicators for Los Angeles in the 1960's," (Mimeograph report of the University of Southern California School of Social Welfare, 1969).

Wells, Carl D., "Adapting the Church to the City," *Social Research*, XV (1931), 317-322.

Wells, Carl D., "Urban Experience and Religious Loyalty," *Social Research*, XVI (1931), 157-163.

Williamson, M. Burton, "The Civic Association as a Factor in Greater Los Angeles," HSSCQ, VIII (1911), 180-187.

Wirth, Louis, "Urbanism as a Way of Life," *American Journal of Sociology*, XLIV (July, 1938), 1-24.

Wyatt-Brown, Bertram, "Prelude to Abolitionism: Sabbatarian Politics and the Rise of Second Party System," *Journal of American History*, LVIII (September, 1971), 316-341.

Yinger J. Milton, "Pluralism, Religion, and Secularism" *Journal for the Scientific Study of Religion*, VI (1967), 17-28.

Theses and Dissertations

Bloomgren, William "Aimee Semple McPherson and the Four-Square Gospel, 1921-1944," (Unpublished Master's Thesis, Standord University, Palo Alto, California, 1952.

Bond, J. Max, "The Negro in Los Angeles," (Unpublished Doctoral Dissertation, University of Southern California, 1936).

Bunney, A. F., "A Study of the Social Work Program of the Disciples of Christ in Los Angeles County," (Unpublished Master's Thesis, University of Southern California, 1933).

Callendar, Ruth, "A Study of Special Day Americanization and Citizenship Classes in the Los Angeles City Schools," (Unpublished Master's Thesis, University of Southern California, 1949).

Codius, Albert, "The Quest for Good Government in Los Angeles, 1890-1910," (Unpublished Doctoral Dissertation, Claremont Graduate School, 1953).

Cook, Francis Emmett, "Problems of Authority in Contemporary Preaching with Specific Reference to the Pulpits of Los Angeles," (Unpublished Master's Thesis, University of Southern California, 1928).

De Graff, Lawrence B., "Negro Migration to Los Angeles, 1930-1950," (Unpublished Doctoral Dissertation, University of California, Los Angeles, 1962).

Dorney, Richard T., "The Oneida Experiment and Social Change" (Unpublished Doctoral Dissertation, Union Theological Seminary, New York, 1953).

Eitzen, D. D., "A Quantitative Approach to Parish Problems," (Unpublished Doctoral Dissertation, University of Southern California, 1939).

Findley, James, "The Economic Boom of the Twenties in Los Angeles," (Unpublished Doctoral Dissertation, Claremont Graduate School, 1958.)

Fish, M. E., "The Adjustment of Large Downtown and Boulevard Churches to Socio-Cultural Factors in the Community," (Unpublished Doctoral Dissertation, University of Southern California, 1959).

Fish, M. E., "A Study of the Christian Youth Fellowship of the Wilshire Christian Church," (Unpublished Master's Thesis, University of Southern California, 1942).

Griffen, Clyde C., "An Urban Church in Ferment: The Episcopal Church in New York City, (Unpublished Doctoral Dissertation, Columbia University, New York, 1960).

Hamilton, Frederick R., "The Los Angeles *Times* Emergence From Parochialism," (Unpublished Master's thesis, University of California, Berkeley, 1958).

Hamilton, Robert, "The History and Influence of the Baptist Church in California, 1848-1899," (Unpublished Doctoral Dissertation, University of Southern California, Los Angeles, 1953).

Harkness, Elizabeth, "A History of the Presbytery of Los Angeles, 1850-1928," (Unpublished Master's Thesis, University of Southern California, Los Angeles, 1929).

Haskell, G. W., "Formative Factors in Life and Faith: Southern California Congregationalism, 1850-1908," (Unpublished Doctoral Dissertation, University of Southern California, Los Angeles, 1947).

Kassell, Lola, "A History of the Government of Los Angeles, 1781-1925," (Unpublished Master's Thesis, Occidental College, 1929).

Kinzer, Donald Louis, "The American Protective Association: A Study in Anti-Catholicism," (Unpublished Doctoral Dissertation, University of Washington, 1954).

Lacour, Lawrence Leland, "A Study of the Revival Method in America, 1920-1955: With Special Reference to Billy Sunday, Aimee Semple McPherson and Billy Graham," (Unpublished Doctoral Dissertation, Northwestern University, Evanston, Illinois, 1956).

May, William, "A Study of the Factors Influencing the Geographical Movement of Churches in a Metropolitian Area," (Unpublished Doctoral Dissertation, University of Pittsburgh, 1956).

Osamann, Ronald Eugene, "Some Aspects of the American Contribution to the Ecumenical Movement," (Unpublished Doctoral Dissertation, Princeton Theological Seminary, 1955).

Ridout, Lionel, "Foundations of the Episcopal Church in the Diocese of California, 1849-1893," (Unpublished Doctoral Dissertation, University of Southern California, 1953).

Riegler, Gordon, "The Attitudes of the People of Los Angeles Toward Prohibition from the Recommendation of the Eighteenth Amendment to the Time of Its Adoption," (Unpublished Master's Thesis, University of Southern California, 1924).

Ritter, Elizabeth, "The History of the Protestant Episcopal Church in Southern California," (Unpublished Master's Thesis, University of Southern California, Los Angeles, 1936).

Schoner, James R., "Institutional Flux in American Protestantism," (Unpublished Doctoral Dissertation, Union Theological Seminary, New York, 1957).

Warburton, Geoffrey W., "The World Church and Sectarian Typologies," (Unpublished Doctoral Dissertation, University of Southern California, 1927).

Wells, Carl Douglass, "A Changing Institution in an Urban Environment: A Study of the Changing Behavior Patterns of the Disciples of Christ in Los Angeles," (Unpublished Doctoral Dissertation, University of Southern California, 1931).

Wiclus, Isabel, "*La Fiesta de Los Angeles:* A Survey of the Yearly Celebrations, 1894-1898," (Unpublished Master's Thesis, University of California, Los Angeles, 1946.

Woods, Betty, "An Historical Survey of the Women's Christian Temperance Union of Southern California," (Unpublished Master's Thesis, Occidental College, Los Angeles, 1950).

INDEX